CUSTOMER RELATIONSHIP MANAGEMENT

Customer Relationship Management
A Global Perspective

GERHARD RAAB
Ludwigshafen University of Applied Sciences, Germany

RIAD A. AJAMI
Wright State University, USA

VIDYARANYA B. GARGEYA
The University of North Carolina at Greensboro, USA

G. JASON GODDARD
Wachovia Corporation, USA

Cover art, graphics and illustrations by Susan Resko

Routledge
Taylor & Francis Group

LONDON AND NEW YORK

First published in paperback 2024

First published 2008 by Gower Publishing

Published 2016 by Routledge
4 Park Square, Milton Park, Abingdon, Oxon OX14 4RN

and by Routledge
605 Third Avenue, New York, NY 10158

Routledge is an imprint of the Taylor & Francis Group, an informa business

Gower Applied Business Research
Our programme provides leaders, practitioners, scholars and researchers with thought provoking, cutting edge books that combine conceptual insights, interdisciplinary rigour and practical relevance in key areas of business and management.

British Library Cataloguing in Publication Data
Customer relationship management : a global perspective
1. Customer relations - Management
I. Raab, Gerhard
658.8'12

Library of Congress Cataloging-in-Publication Data
Customer relationship management : a global perspective / by Gerhard Raab ... [et al.].
p. cm.
Includes bibliographical references and index.
ISBN 978-0-7546-7156-5
1. Customer relations--Management. I. Raab, Gerhard. II. Title.

HF5415.5.C83625 2008
658.8'12--dc22

2007046694

ISBN 13: 978-0-7546-7156-5 (hbk)
ISBN 13: 978-1-03-283802-1 (pbk)
ISBN 13: 978-1-315-57563-6 (ebk)

DOI: 10.4324/9781315575636

Contents

List of Figures

Chapter 1

Customer Relationship Management: Global and Local Dimensions

Chapter Objectives:

- *Understand the global significance of Customer Relationship Management (CRM).*
- *Identify the primary sustainable competitive advantages.*
- *Discuss the pros and cons of international strategic theories.*
- *Elaborate on the primary components of international strategy.*
- *Discuss the three pillars of Customer Relationship Management (CRM).*
- *Elaborate on the advantages and objectives of Customer Relationship Management (CRM).*

Global Perspective on Customer Relationship Management

As global markets become increasingly integrated, all firms from the largest multinational to the smallest entrepreneur must be able to find a market niche which enables the firm to survive in highly competitive markets, and to prosper by finding the best ways to meet the needs and desires of the target consumers. This introductory section of the book will discuss current international strategies for success, and the tradeoffs that companies face with each strategic alternative selected.

History is littered with examples of situations where an appropriate strategy was not selected, to the downfall of the decision-makers or firms who failed to plan appropriately. An example of strategic error happened long ago during the reign of Genghis Khan. His empire was one of the largest in the history of the world, and spread from Mongolia through modern day Russia, and into Poland. The dynasty was short lived primarily due to the lack of adequate feedback between the leadership, which was centralized at the top, and the common villagers, who were spread over the vast terrain. Without a strong communication mechanism, the empire was doomed to a short lifespan. The same could be said for the modern corporation. Effective feedback is required for any entity or business, and in today's global economy the successful corporation will be the one that formulates a management structure conducive to timely feedback as it regards the wants and desires of the customers.

A comprehensive framework for achieving success is today a fundamental requirement, and this is where Customer Relationship Management (CRM) figures into the global economic landscape. In order for a firm to create and sustain international competitive advantages, there must be strong competency in understanding which customers provide the best long-term opportunities for profitable relationships. In the pages that follow, we will discuss how CRM can be utilized in order to increase the level of customer orientation, product quality, customer satisfaction, and customer retention in a global context. Successful CRM programs allow firms large and small to achieve efficiencies which would not be possible in an environment that does not include an accurate, timely, and sustained feedback mechanism necessary to anticipate the future needs and desires of the customer. At the multinational level, global efficiencies can be achieved via economies of scale and scope, and by catering to the specific desires of a firm's most profitable customers. As Genghis Khan found out long ago, you cannot be everything to everyone. His example proves that knowing your customer, and knowing what you represent as an organization, are key components to the success of any modern corporation. This is also essential for a successful CRM implementation.

Sustainable Competitive Advantages in a Global Economy

International businesses have the ability to exploit three sources of competitive advantage. All three of these advantages are enhanced or made possible via the implementation of CRM practices.

The first competitive advantage is **global efficiency**. By expanding internationally rather than remaining in its country of origin, a firm can lower its costs and improve the bottom line performance via location advantages. CRM is very important in this context, as a firm must fully understand the customer profile that is most likely to provide them with a profitable, long-term relationship.

A second competitive advantage is **multi-market flexibility**. Large multinational firms must respond to changes in numerous markets that are all inter-related. Successfully understanding the differences in markets worldwide will provide for a competitive advantage over the long-term. Small business enterprises are now realizing that the failure to understand market differences could make them vulnerable to foreign competition. Since at the core of CRM is the need to understand the customer, this strength can be utilized in achieving first-mover advantages against the competition.

A third competitive advantage is achieving **worldwide learning** in the modern corporation. The need for understanding the customer in various markets is essential, but so is the need for listening to the internal customer as well. As W. Edwards Deming, one of the doyens of the Total Quality Management movement has stated, if something cannot be measured then it cannot be improved. Thus, having measurable goals of determining best practices in numerous operating environments is of paramount importance. As many executives in today's business world can attest, a company with too much centralized control loses its ability to innovate as well as to adapt and respond locally to the needs of its customers. In the United States, there is a movement in the banking industry toward decentralizing the loan approval authority at the local level, rather than utilizing centralized lending departments. The goal is local responsiveness as well as collecting as much market knowledge as possible throughout the entire geographic region where the firm conducts its business. As will be discussed in later chapters, data collection strategies as achieved via CRM can aid a firm in retaining customers in a profitable fashion.

Overview of International Strategic Theory

Before we discuss the CRM perspective in detail, it will be helpful to briefly discuss the commonly accepted international strategic directions from which most corporations have to choose. At the heart of all of these strategies is the trade-off between the pressures for responsiveness to local tastes and preferences on the one hand, and the pressures for efficiency in an effort to reduce total cost on the other hand. As will be made evident throughout the course of this book, CRM is an example of a managerial philosophy that helps firms find the appropriate level of balance between these two pressure points via elucidating which customers are the most important for a given firm, and what is the most efficient way to satisfy the needs of this customer base.

One common strategy for internationally active firms is an attempt to replicate how business is conducted in the domestic market in all international markets where a firm competes. **Home replication strategy** is typically the default international strategy for firms that believe that their customers' tastes and preferences are consistent throughout the world. Firms engaging in this strategic alternative believe that the core competencies exhibited in their home markets should be reproduced in other markets. In some cases, markets can be highly similar, and home replication strategy can be a successful strategy for firms that compete in international markets that are very similar to the home market. More often than not, however, taking what you do exceptionally well at home and attempting to duplicate it in a foreign market may require at least some alterations, or a competitor would probably have already penetrated the market! In terms of the balancing act of local responsiveness and corporate efficiency, this strategy is short on the former, but long on the latter.

Another of the commonly accepted forms of international strategy is called **multi-domestic or multinational strategy**. Executives at firms that opt for this strategic alternative often view themselves as a collection of relatively independent operating subsidiaries, each of which focuses on a specific domestic market. The strategy is akin to a decentralized atmosphere, with the advantage of being highly customized to the markets in which the firm competes. As is often the case in a decentralized management framework, best practices from the alternative sites may not be communicated, and the firm loses valuable data collection ability from the lack of communication. Thus, this strategy is strong on local responsiveness, but is more than likely lacking in terms of corporate efficiency.

A third international strategic alternative is a **global strategy**. Under this scenario, the corporate leaders view the world as a single marketplace, with the primary goal of creating standardized goods and services that will meet the needs of customers worldwide. Coca-Cola is typically held up as an example of a corporation that is conducting its business via this alternative. Global strategy is the direct opposite of multi-domestic strategy, as the 'one size fits all' mentality is in opposition to the desire for customization for each market. The difference between this strategy and that of home replication is the need for determining an overall company focus that would best suit all of the markets where a firm competes, rather than simply replicating the home strategy in all markets. This strategic option requires diffusion of market-specific knowledge in order for the overarching strategy to be realized. This strategy attempts to capitalize on economies of scale and scope, and is thus typically strong in terms of corporate efficiency. The success of this strategy in terms of local responsiveness is directly related to the success of data collection in terms of understanding the tastes and preferences of the target customer, as well as the effectiveness of communicating these differences when deciding upon the global strategy.

A final selection available to corporate managers is **transnational strategy**. This strategic alternative is considered to be the 'Holy Grail' of corporate strategies at the international level. The firm attempts to combine the benefits of global scale efficiencies with the benefits of local responsiveness. This strategic alternative involves compromising with complexity, and trying to balance multinational and global concerns. This is typically done via assigning tasks and responsibilities to areas best able to achieve the desired balance between efficiency and flexibility. As we have seen over the last decade globally, firms have chosen to outsource many tasks offshore rather than simply opting for a centralized or a decentralized management platform. More often than not, CRM as a management alternative has been brought into practice via companies that are attempting to conduct business under this strategic direction than in any of the other alternatives. In today's global economy, those firms that can reduce cost while at the same time realizing and anticipating the needs and desires of their target customers will be most successful.

Components of Synergy and Strategy for Cross-border Operations

Now that we have discussed the most common forms of international strategy, another important topic deals with the components of a successful strategy. These components are a series of questions that a firm's leadership team should resolve in order to determine the strategic vision of the company over the long term.

One component of international strategy is determining the **distinctive competence**. This deals with an area, or areas, where a firm excels in relation to its competition. This could be due to a cutting-edge technological application, an efficient distribution network, a well-respected brand name, or other such advantages. In terms of CRM, answering this question is not an exercise conducted simply by a firm's leadership team. The customers must also be consulted in this process, as will be discussed in subsequent chapters of the book.

Another component of international strategy is the **scale or scope of operations**. This is certainly related to CRM, as the focus of this component concerns where a firm plans on conducting its business, as well as with whom. Scope may be defined in terms of geography, or it may be concerned with deciding on the appropriate product or service niche in which to compete. Strategic goals in this area must be measurable, feasible, and time-limited in order to be successful. Strategic goals that are not measurable, or have an excessively long gestation period, may prove to be unattainable.

A third component of international strategy deals with **resource deployment**. Once the determination has been made concerning what makes a firm successful, as well as where and how it desires to compete, the next phase in the strategic process is to decide on how resources can be allocated. Depending on which of the four international strategic alternatives have been chosen, resource deployment can be determined from a centralized platform with the intent on global efficiency, or in a more decentralized environment.

A last component of international strategy that we will cover is **synergy**. Firms that are engaged in a CRM environment often ask probing questions concerning how best to maximize profitability via cross-selling to its existing customer base. This is the essence of synergy. If a firm is able to identify which customers are of paramount importance, as well as how best to meet and exceed their expectations, the firm will benefit via increased profitability. As will be discussed in subsequent chapters, it is more expensive to attract new customers, than it is to sell complementary products and services to those customers who already are within the existing customer base of the firm.

The McNeely Principle

To conclude with this introductory section on international strategy, it is important to understand that strategic alternatives are not made in a vacuum. When deciding on how to compete in a given market, firms must be careful in understanding what distinctive competencies are at play by their competitors, so as to not get caught competing with a bigger, stronger firm in the same way. Even a perfectly envisioned strategy can wind up as a disaster if a firm decides to compete for the same business, in the same form or fashion, as a larger, more financially secure competitor. This may remind readers of the case of the professional boxer 'Hurricane' Peter McNeely. During the middle 1990s, Mr. McNeely was a young contending heavyweight boxer from Massachusetts, who received the chance of a lifetime. He was the first opponent of Mike Tyson, during his comeback campaign after serving time in prison. Since even the most casual boxing fan was aware of Tyson's strengths (raw power and speed), McNeely shocked the fans by announcing that he was going to match Tyson in both categories, in effect competing directly with an opponent who was more talented, and was planning on using the same strategy when they met in the ring. The result was a first round knockout loss for Mr. McNeely, along with relegation back to the world of obscurity. Managers may find this analogy useful when considering strategic alternatives, and when remembering the importance of selecting a *distinctive* competence that will produce a long-run success, rather than a short-run disaster of the 'hurricane' variety.

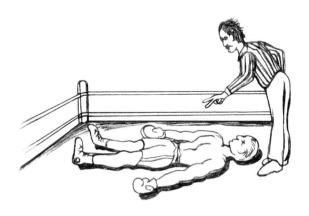

The Concept and Relevance of Customer Relationship Management

The rise and appeal of CRM has come from a heightening of competition, which has been felt by companies in all fields and of all sizes. Add to that an increasingly sated market, replaceable products with ever shorter product cycles, constantly changing and ever higher customer standards and expectations as to quality, price, reliable service, as well as expectations regarding market transparence via improved access to relevant information, and CRM has come to the forefront of today's successful companies.

To keep the lead ahead of the competition, and in order to secure competitive advantages for the future, customer expectations are more and more becoming the center of attention in entrepreneurial activities. The insight that having regular clientele is one of the most important factors of success, and that botched customer relationships are an enormous cost factor, has led to CRM being placed right at the top of the agenda in the boardroom. It is not a new insight, but one that has nevertheless often been unrecognized in the past years. Meanwhile, from an economic point of view, the consideration of customer relationship has for many managers become a decisive target.

'Know your customer and you know what they buy', could be the motto of CRM. CRM characterizes a management philosophy that is a complete orientation of the company toward existing and potential customer relationships. The customer is at the center of all company considerations. The goal is the *management of durable and profitable customer relationships.*

- **Durable** means building up customer trust, aiming at high customer regularity, and cultivating life-long relationships.
- **Relationship** indicates that the company should orient itself more around the customer.
- **Profitable** means during the course of the customer relationship, each customer's contribution to the company profit will be maximized.
- **Management** describes the capacity to coordinate and further develop, across all organizational borders, all interactions with current and potential customers.

In this day and age, companies should be in the position to fulfill the wants of the customer with the right offer at the right time. They are forced to develop a high degree of flexibility, in order to react to customer wishes with considerable speed, and to offer people ever more individualistic products and services. The whole chain of contact is important; from the first contact with the customer to the establishment of the next contact. A company that knows that a customer served today, can tomorrow become a regular, trusted customer, bears the first fruit of CRM philosophy. The supplier that wants to claim its market position for tomorrow needs to be ready to efficiently and effectively organize its business relationships.

The Three Pillars of Integral Customer Relationship Management

Many activities of companies have the objective of steering the sales markets through exact knowledge of customer potential, sales channels, and sales motives, and to guide the expectations and wants of customers via diverse features and motives. These measures have technical support through the employment of modern information technologies and company-spanning software systems, which offer the opportunity to coordinate the worldwide activities of a company in a customer-oriented manner.

However, having efficient dealings with the customer, which is crucial to a firm's survival, requires more than just a technical infrastructure. The introduction of integrated data banks which save collected customer information, and make this available to all levels of the company, are, without additional measures, only a basic element which does not promise success. A study by Accenture, formally Andersen Consulting, reports that less than half of the intended effect of a CRM project depends on the technology: In the study, technology's share was 40 percent (Göbbel, 2001, p. 27).

Only an integral assessment seems meaningful, one that combines the technical and human perspectives, which carries out an expansion to include the central aspects of the organizational structure. Only when CRM is internalized by the top management, is understood by the employees, and is anchored into the structure of the company can this venture be of use. The best technology would be useless without the people who work with it. Often the sale of the product or service is decided right at the point of sale. This underlines the saying of Hilmar Kopper, Chairman of the supervisory board of Deutsche Bank, 'We could improve sales by

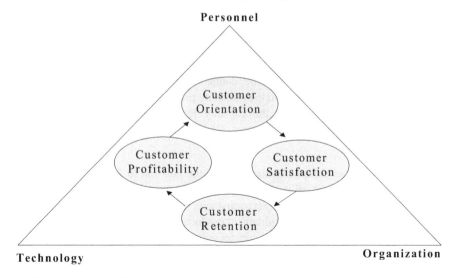

Figure 1.1: The pillars and process of Customer Relationship Management

25 percent if the employees would get used to greeting every customer they see in a friendly way.'

As an integrated, overall concept, CRM is therefore a deciding factor with regard to bolstering a company's success. As Figure 1.1 implies, the three pillars of CRM are a company's personnel, a firm's technology, as well as the structure of the organization itself. Each of the phases of the process of CRM, which will be discussed in later chapters, is part of an integrated whole. Better knowledge of people's wishes yields the possibility of a long-term, sustained increasing of the level of their satisfaction, and of strengthening the customer's loyalty, or rather their willingness to commit, to the company. This has, direct consequences on the costs and profits of the firm. Rising cost awareness increasingly requires that companies plan their marketing activities with great precision in order to engage the target group, without wasteful spending to achieve a good cost to benefit ratio. In the end the concept of CRM—like all other company activities—has the economic goal of raising profit.

Advantages and Objective of Customer Relationship Management

Many considerations justify investment in the setting up and realizing of CRM (Ederer, Seiwert & Küstenmacher, 2000, p. 84).

- Every satisfied customer brings in at least three more customers.
- An unhappy customer communicates his negative experience to ten more potential customers.
- The rate of repeat sales climbs with increased reliance and satisfaction with the performance of their suppliers.
- Regular customers exhibit less price sensitivity than new customers.

- Customer-oriented companies can even charge higher prices than the competition.
- Marketing and sales costs for maintaining customer relationships drop.
- Reducing the level of customers leaving the firm by five percent can raise profit by as much as 85 percent (Töpfer, 1996, p. 92).

It is becoming clear what an immense increase in effectiveness the implementation of CRM can provide. A large number of leading companies have already recognized the success potential of CRM and are using it to their long-term competitive advantage.

For example, airlines, through engaging frequent flyer programs, established the first steps of CRM years ago. Indeed, SAS, British Airways and Lufthansa have determinedly established almost identical bonus programs and are thus able to achieve a competitive advantage (www.bbdo.de). German BA (British Airways) analyzed just how important the 'miles and more' program and customer cards are for the various airlines: 12 percent of frequent flyers buy their tickets because of a customer commitment program. For the German charter airline Condor, this is true for 20 percent of their sales (Kowalski and Kroker, 2000, p. 338).

Business enterprises are also strongly dedicating themselves to customer commitment. The British retailer Tesco achieved a 'first mover advantage' through the introduction of customer cards. In just a few years, the company became one of the leading and most profitable companies in its industry.

In the automobile industry, there are also many examples. General Motors has powerfully strengthened CRM to secure prices. Renault is utilizing integrated loyalty programs to find out which brands will have a positive image. Daimler Chrysler ran an integrated CRM project via a European call center, which involved a unified sales canvassing and loyalty program. In the automobile industry alone it can be seen that CRM is the decisive instrument in the battle against the competition. Failure to provide an automobile that caters to the needs and desires of the customer can lead to

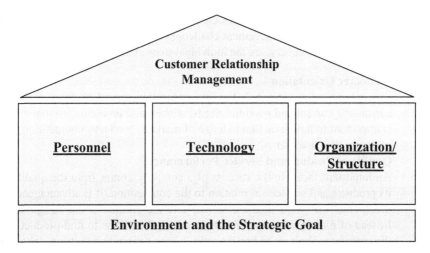

Figure 1.2: The design of integrated Customer Relationship Management

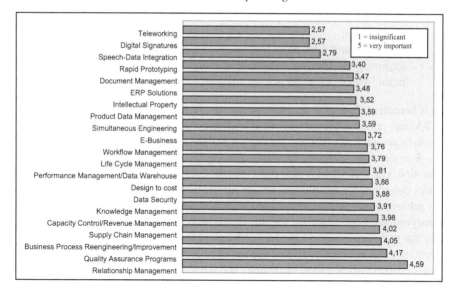

Figure 1.3: Significance of Customer Relationship Management (Kroker, 2000, pp. 18–21)

the production of vehicles that the customers do not want. This has become obvious to a few large automobile producers over the last 20 years.

In recent times, companies have increased investment in CRM solutions. American Express was able to improve its customer profitability. Barclays Bank is a similar case. A study concerning credit cards showed that a five percent rise in customer loyalty results in a 25 to 30 percent rise in profit (www.bbdo.de).

These examples are impressive demonstrations of CRM's success. The following survey from CSC Ploenzke AG makes clear what significance qualified customer management will have for management challenges to come.

Below, by way of summary, are the individual steps in the CRM chain of effects:

- **Customer Orientation**
  The entirety of a company's thought and action should be focused on the customer's current and potential needs, wishes, and problems. To that end, it is important to have exact knowledge of markets, products, competition, and of course the customer.
- **Quality of Product and Service Performance**
  An important factor in the success of a company comes from the quality of its products and services in relation to the competition. It is advantageous to incorporate the wants of the customer into the product in the design stage. Instead of finding customers for the product, the idea is to find products for the customer. The cost to benefit ratio is here definitely a factor to take into consideration.

- **Customer Satisfaction**
  After the consuming or use of a product, the customers will ask themselves if they were happy with the product. If the answer is yes they will tend to choose the product when they shop again, to recommend it to others, and to perhaps become a regular customer.
- **Customer Retention**
  The key to building up a regular clientele is obtaining satisfied customers. Companies that succeed in precisely adapting their spectrum of performance to the ideas and expectations of their customers, or who even manage to surpass them, generate satisfaction and thus create a basis for future business.
- **Customer Value and Company Success**
  There is a close relationship between customer commitment and profit level. The profit per customer increases with the growing duration of a customer's relationship to a company.

In the following chapters, the individual stages of CRM will be explained in greater detail and by way of examples. The goal is to give the reader an integrated view, as well as to provide help in delivering customer-oriented management. Readers should note the benefits and complications of pursuing a global CRM strategy in the pages that follow. In this chapter, we have set the stage for the consideration of a new, dynamic, distinctive competence, that of global CRM.

A table follows which summarizes the differences of strategic focus and resource capabilities for three of the most viable international strategies discussed in this chapter.

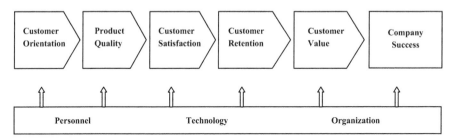

Figure 1.4: Process and stages of Customer Relationship Management

	Multi-domestic Strategy	**Global Strategy**	**Transnational Strategy**
Strategic Focus & Perspectives	Adapting to regional/ national differences and accommodating customer preferences	Aggregated and centralized to global scale	Compromising with complexity to balance local variations with worldwide innovations and learning
Deployment of Firm Specific Resources & Capabilities	Resources/capabilities are partitioned/ decentralized, effectively at the local level	Efficient centralization/ standardization to global scale/ cost, scope, and critical mass	Resources and capabilities are recombined to capture competence and process advantages interdependently for CRM

Questions for Discussion

1. Discuss the four primary international strategic theories and how each of them compares with respect to achieving local responsiveness and corporate efficiency.

2. Consider a multinational firm that you believe is following each of the international strategic theories discussed in the chapter. Then discuss the benefits that might be achieved by implementing CRM at each company.

3. How might the implementation of CRM help to achieve each of the components of international strategy?

4. Elaborate as to why the three pillars of CRM must be integrated, and why the process is a continuing journey of improvement.

5. Briefly discuss the four steps in the CRM chain of effects. Then relate these concepts to your organization or university.

Chapter 2

Customer Orientation

Chapter Objectives:

- *Elaborate on the various factors that influence customer orientation.*
- *Discuss the link between employee and customer orientation.*
- *Explain the features of a customer-oriented renumeration system.*
- *Understand the best practices of selecting customer-oriented personnel.*
- *Compare and contrast the different technological methods of achieving customer orientation.*
- *Understand the importance of data mining in a successful customer orientation program.*
- *Discuss how decision trees are utilized in the data mining process.*
- *Identify the form of organizational structure which is most conducive with customer orientation.*

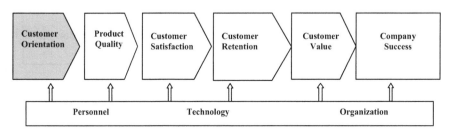

Figure 2.1: The concept and relevance of customer orientation

The Concept and Relevance of Customer Orientation

Customer orientation is one of the most important factors of success needed to survive in an environment characterized by enormous competition. Customer-oriented companies manage to arrive relatively quickly in a situation where they can rapidly and effectively react to new market opportunities, so that they can, via customer-focused concepts, adjust to newly-developed customer wants. Although customer orientation has been supported for years now, and is the guiding principle

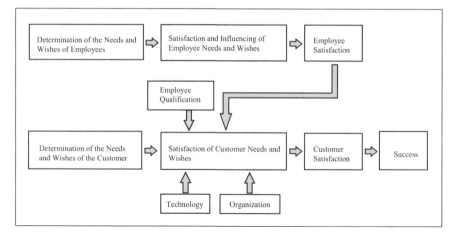

**Figure 2.2: Interaction of factors that influence customer
orientation and customer satisfaction**

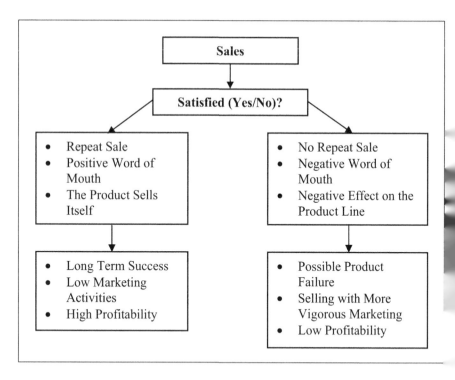

**Figure 2.3: Customer orientation and long-term business
success (based on Simon & Homburg, 1989, p. 20)**

of many companies, just as before the offered product is more often than not the center of attention.

However, customer orientation entails focusing the sum of all company thoughts and actions on the customer's needs, wishes, and problems. The achieving of maximum customer orientation is based on suitable structures, and on the employment of modern technological solutions, management, and employees, all acting and thinking with the point of view of the customer in mind.

The goal of customer orientation is always customer satisfaction. Satisfied customers are more likely to choose the product again, to passively or actively recommend it, and to react with less price sensitivity. They might even become loyal customers, who no longer take competing offers into consideration. This simplifies their decision, in the sense that their choice of the product or service has become a matter of habit (Simon & Homburg, 1998, p. 20).

According to the American management strategists, Haines and McCoy, a company that wants to create a sound basis for customer-oriented action needs to fulfill the following ten demands. These criteria can be seen as a catalog of measures for companies, who are still far from optimal customer orientation (Haines & McCoy, 1995, S. 27–28).

The Ten Requirements for a Customer-Oriented Company

1. **Cultivate a close contact with your customer.** This goes especially for employees with management roles (This requirement includes: seeing, touching, feeling, i.e., meeting at regular intervals — outside of the business context — to have face–to–face talks with the customer).
2. **Strive to be in a position of trust, in relation to the customers needs, expectations and wishes.** It should be the goal of your whole organization to exceed the expectations of your customer.
3. **Check the satisfaction of your customer with your products and services on a regular basis.** A constant flow of information between you and your customer is very important — be it positive, neutral, or negative. Do not block it out, be open to it!
4. **Concentrate on all areas of performance, with which you can add value for the customer.** For example quality and service, eco-friendliness, economy of action, acceptance of customer wishes and needs, fast delivery and performance, good security, etc.
5. **Consider your customer in your decision making, in theme groups, meetings, planning and even in internal business considerations.** Don't block them out.
6. **Require from every person in your organization that they meet and serve your customers personally at least one or more days a year;** There is no substitute for staying with the pulse of your customers.
7. **Adapt to, and if necessary structure your business processes around, the needs and perceptions of your customers.** Go from the top to the bottom, and adapt all functional areas of your organization accordingly.
8. **Structure your organization according to the market.** Orient your organization such that it fits your market (i.e., 1 customer = 1 supplier).
9. **Develop a customer recovery strategy (CRS) and use it.** Reward CRS behavior especially within function spanning teams with customer contact. Both Marriott and Nordstrom take that old saying very seriously, "When a customer is satisfied, he tells three other people, but when he isn't satisfied, he tells his story to eleven other people". Both organizations are very quick to react to every complaint.
10. **You should only hire and encourage customer friendly employees.** Although from a healthy, human point of view, this appears to be self evident, the truth is that most organizations are so concerned with their own affairs, that they lose track of their very reason for being — the customer.

Figure 2.4: Ten criteria for a customer-oriented company (Haines & McCoy, 1995, pp. 27–28)

Personnel and Customer Orientation

Satisfied Employees as the Basis for Customer Orientation

Countless studies verify that only universal internal employee orientation within the company can lead to lasting external customer orientation, and thus to a competitive advantage. The basis is the implementation of a customer-oriented company structure in the minds of the employees. However, this is not achieved merely by anchoring customer orientation in the goals and in the guiding principles of the company. This is of course a good first step. Still, experience shows that this remains ineffective when the employees are not really convinced, and do not really 'live' customer orientation. (Homburg & Werner, 1998, p. 174). To what extent this is the case can be measured by how many employees can generate interest in the wishes of the customers—in other words: How friendly are the employees to the customers? In businesses with personal customer contact like the financial services industry or the supermarket industry, successful customer orientation is only possible as a result of the permanent performance efficiency and commitment of the employees.

Between employee orientation on the one hand and customer orientation on the other, the following connection can be derived:

- Employees who are satisfied with the quality of internal cooperation, and who are satisfactorily supported in their customer-oriented tasks, are more likely to be able to generate interest in the external quality being presented to the customer. Successful internal cooperation can be recognized by answering in the affirmative to the following questions:
  - How well do different departments cooperate?
  - Is customer orientation on the part of the management encouraged and supported?
  - In what way are the employees given the opportunity to include themselves and their readiness to serve in the company?
- Employees who are rewarded for high-quality work with incentives (praise from customers and management, bonus pay due to customer satisfaction, customer-oriented remuneration, etc.) are more motivated. This recognition affords the employees with an experience of success, which in turn enhances employee satisfaction and the willingness to commit.

The following results of a year 2000 study by the German Customer Monitor, contains information concerning which aspects of customer-oriented action are important, and how members of organizations have rated the level of employee orientation in their own companies. 2000 representative employees were chosen for the survey, from all branches of industry and from companies of all different sizes. While many aspects of customer orientation were identified, it is apparent from the table below that maintaining a commitment to the customer, as well as including them in the product or service design process, is of paramount importance. It is also apparent that there have been differing levels of success in terms of management providing a good model for customer orientation, as well as for all employees being prepared to deal with customer complaints. The results in these categories were mixed.

Topic	Total 2000	Total 2000	Production	Commerce	Traffic/ News	Private Service Provider	Civil Service
Basis	2.036	2.036	687	182	62	631	257
Maintenance of and commitment to customers has a high status in company	1,50	92,3	95,3	97,6	93,4	92,3	79,1
Customer expectations are worked with and considered in the decision-making process	1,67	88,5	93,1	91,2	88,8	88,5	77,6
Correspondence and brochures are easily understood by the customers	1,70	90,0	92,4	98,7	83,6	90,0	81,6
Customer enquiries and complaints are actively encouraged and are used to improve quality	1,70	86,0	89,2	84,1	90,4	87,0	78,2
Known quality deficits are quickly eliminated	1,72	86,7	91,2	92,1	78,2	88,1	71,2
Customer satisfaction and customer care are values treasured by everyone in the company	1,74	89,6	90,7	96,2	79,5	92,3	79,7
Development and introduction of innovations have a high value	1,76	82,4	87,1	84,4	85,6	84,2	66,4
The outer image of the company is up-to-date and appealing	1,76	85,4	87,8	86,9	88,2	87,7	72,5
Fast and flexible acceptance of customer wishes is supported via EDP	1,85	80,0	85,5	77,4	81,2	81,4	66,8
Management provides a good model of customer orientation	1,95	78,0	81,3	81,7	62,0	80,5	69,0
All employees are prepared to deal with customer complaints	2,06	71,2	65,8	77,0	68,2	80,9	64,6
Continuous, timely information concerning current advertising statements	2,13	67,3	62,0	77,6	78,4	73,7	63,1
Regular reception of information about the satisfaction of the customer	2,14	66,9	63,8	67,1	52,8	74,1	62,1
Support of employees with regard to customer contact from all departments	2,17	69,1	75,1	70,4	63,9	68,8	57,8
Sufficient competence in decisions relevant to fulfilling customer wishes	2,24	62,4	60,1	66,1	48,8	67,2	53,2
Training of employees on a regular basis for customer contact	2,29	58,6	61,0	49,3	80,5	61,2	51,6
Regularly recurring department-spanning discussions on customer orientation	2,33	55,7	52,1	50,6	54,6	60,8	57,4
Estimate of customer satisfaction with the performance of employee's own organization[1]	2,51	47,9	53,4	48,2	22,4	53,8	26,2

[1]The estimate of customer satisfaction with the performance of employee's own company is measured on the following scale: (1) Completely satisfied, (2) Very satisfied, (3) Satisfied, (4) A little dissatisfied, (5) Dissatisfied
All other topics are measured on the scale: (1) Totally, (2) To a large extent, (3) Not really, (4) Absolutely not

Figure 2.5: Customer orientation from the point of view of employees, in companies sorted by industry branch. (Average value; rate of agreement – referring to the first two values, given in percent) (www.servicebarometer/mitarbeiterorientierung)

Topic	Total 2000	Total 2000	Production	Commerce	Traffic/ News	Private Service Provider	Civil Service
Basis	2.036	2.036	687	182	62	631	257
Global satisfaction of employees with employer[1]	2,70	41,8	42,0	40,9	33,2	48,3	33,4
If they would choose the employer again[2]	1,88	77,0	76,4	71,7	68,8	79,1	82,6
Recommendation of employer within circle of friends and collegues[2]	2,15	67,5	69,4	55,7	58,4	67,4	74,2
Recommendation of products/services of their own organization[3]	1,65	84,0	85,7	88,8	80,6	83,9	78,9
Team orientation within their department[3]	1,50	90,5	90,9	90,2	93,9	91,0	89,7
Knowledge and explanation of quality targets when there are new employees[3]	1,61	91,0	93,4	90,4	82,2	91,2	87,4
High ability to compete in their own organization[3]	1,63	87,7	91,8	93,4	77,7	88,8	70,7
High willingness to commit and engage on behalf of the organization[3]	1,65	90,8	92,6	93,7	87,5	92,4	83,9
Criticism regarding shoddy work[3]	1,66	85,0	90,2	89,9	73,8	79,9	80,9
Mutual agreement with one's superior, regarding clear goals	1,78	81,9	83,9	77,1	84,0	82,5	81,1
Proud to be working at the company[3]	1,86	83,8	85,8	77,6	72,3	86,4	78,6
Good information about matters that concern the employees[3]	1,95	78,0	78,1	75,7	74,1	79,6	76,9
Feedback from the superior regarding reaching of goals[3]	2,14	66,3	69,6	61,2	64,6	68,3	57,7
Encouragement and reward via suggestions for improvement[3]	2,14	64,0	65,9	53,5	84,7	63,3	66,9
Recognition of good work from superior[3]	2,17	65,6	66,6	64,1	57,2	67,3	63,6
Employees have a say in important decisions[3]	2,27	62,2	61,5	60,2	46,1	67,3	58,5

[1] Measured on a scale of: (1) Completely satisfied, (2) Very satisfied, (3) Satisfied, (4) A little dissatisfied, (5) Dissatisfied
[2] Measured on the scale of: (1) Definitely true , (2) Seems true, (3) Perhaps, (4) Seems not true, (5) Definitely not true
[3] Measured on the scale: (1) Totally, (2) To a large extent, (3) Not really, (4) Absolutely not

Figure 2.6: Employee orientation in companies sorted by industry branch (Average value; rate of agreement (Referring to the first two values, given in percent) (www.servicebarometer.de/kundenmonitor/mit-arbeiterorientierung)

Customer-oriented Remuneration System

The realization that employees can be guided toward certain behavior, in that their purchasing power is made dependent on such behavior, is also playing an increasingly important role in the area of customer orientation. Traditional systems of remuneration are in this case only applicable in a limited way. They are often based on 'tougher' criteria like sales or profit, and can, for example, lead to serious consequences for employees with strong customer orientation (Homburg & Werner, 1998, S. 172):

- The employees concentrate on the attractive, star or big profit customers. Customers with a lot of potential but with less promise of immediate profit are given less attention.
- In striving to make as many sales as quickly as possible, less consideration is given to the nature of the customer relationship and to the long-term profitability of the customer. The employee only reserves a small amount of time for the customer. Also customers who, upon more careful inspection, would be seen to be uninteresting for the company, are courted.

On the other hand, what is more potentially successful in the area of customer orientation is remuneration, which brings in more qualitative aspects of customer orientation. This has the motivating effect of making it once again clear to the employees that in the end it is the customer who pays them. A suitable measure of these qualitative aspects hinges on customer satisfaction. Customer satisfaction is here an indicator of the level of striving toward customer orientation, and also is a measure of the performance of individual employees.

The demands that such a customer-oriented remuneration system has to fulfill are listed below (Homburg & Werner, 1998, S. 201):

- **Influence:** Within the pay cycle the employee has to have had measurable influence on customer satisfaction.
- **Accountability:** There needs to be a correspondence between the system of reference of the calculated customer satisfaction value, and the organizational unit to be assessed. For example, the sales force should be judged on the overall customer satisfaction and relationship profitability rather than on a volume basis.
- **Motivational Effect:** The remuneration system must be designed such that it succeeds in providing additional incentives for desirable behavior, and especially in assuring a balanced incentive structure.
- **Flexibility:** The remuneration system must be able to adapt to changing organizational goals and employee behavior stemming from prevailing circumstances.
- **Transparence:** The remuneration system needs to be transparent and comprehensible.
- **Acceptance:** The elements of the remuneration system have to be accepted and thought of as fair and reliable by all participants.

In addition, there is the decisive condition that this remuneration system, based on the measuring of customer satisfaction (see Chapter 4), be carried out systematically, regularly, and with discrimination.

The implementing of a customer-oriented remuneration system is a sensitive and critical undertaking, even despite observing the above-mentioned requirements, which such a system needs to fulfill. Many employees are skeptical at first, because they fear that they will end up worse off in a system of compensation that rests in part or to a large extent on the satisfaction of customers. It is therefore important to involve the employee. It is also very important that superiors take on the task of motivating and encouraging the employees by providing them with non-monetary incentives like praise, recognition, or through giving them additional responsibility (Homburg & Werner, 1998, S. 172).

Moreover, the utilization of customer-oriented remuneration systems should by no means be limited to organizational areas with direct customer contact. Since customer orientation embraces both interactive behavior as well as product quality, all organizational areas along the chain of value creation have an indirect or direct influence on customer satisfaction (Homburg & Jensen, 2000, pp. 55–74).

In the context of increasing customer orientation, Opel Bank/Opel Leasing carries out a remuneration system that awards across a broad range of salary levels. It is oriented on the principles of internal and external fairness of reward, as well as on the performance and readiness to change of employees. The goal is, among other things, to encourage the employee in his motivation for personal development. Figure 2.7 illustrates this.

For the different fields of the chart, the typical remunerations of comparable positions are collected, in which each time the 1st and 3rd quartile of the market worth are determined as corner points of the salary margins. From this information, results in the different salary levels can be seen when looking at the chart vertically. When horizontally observed, the chart displays the possibilities for development of the employee within a given organizational area, in which the individual establishment of remuneration within applicable salary levels (1st to 3rd quartile of the market worth) determines the assessment of individual behaviors, for example in connection with customer orientation or readiness to change.

This remuneration system, described in its basic form, is enhanced via a performance bonus, which is assessed according to the success level relative to desired results. In this way, there is the assurance that exceptional performance will be honored (Gresch, 1997, p. 10).

	Specialist	Assistant	Specialist/Advisor	Manager
Sales				
Credit Management				
Customer Service				
Etc.	Salary Level 1	Salary Level 2	Salary Level 3	Salary Level 4

**Figure 2.7: The Opel Bank/Opel Leasing
remuneration system (Gresch, 1997, p. 10)**

Customer-oriented Selection of Personnel, Assessment, and Development

While the professional knowledge and abilities of applicants can be thoroughly checked during the course of the selection process by reviewing the résumé, to come up with statements about behavior of future employees, structured interviews and assessment centers are good methods. It is of central importance in a customer-oriented organization to analyze aspects like team orientation, customer orientation, quality awareness and communicative qualities of potential employees. In order to check these factors when preparing for a job interview, specific questions should be developed which seek to reveal what kind of behavior the person would display in different situations (Customer orientation: How did you handle the last customer complaint you received? Team orientation: Describe some positive and negative experiences you had during the course of your last team project.). The goal should be to get the applicants to make statements that shed light on real situations or tasks, and which clearly reveal their behavior. The so described behavior can then be assessed together with the professional knowledge and skills of the applicant (Gresch, 1997, S. 10).

Computer-aided procedures are increasingly supporting the task of personnel selection. Over time they have been adopted by many big companies—from Siemens to Deutsche Bank. On the basis of research, it has been found to be advantageous that arbitrary subjectivity in the selection of personnel be avoided. Moreover, computer-aided procedures enable the meaningful selection of which applicants should be invited in for a personal interview. Computer-aided procedures can reveal information regarding important requirements, like intelligence, concentration, work behavior, language skills, capacity for abstraction, customer orientation, ability to endure strain, leadership qualities, motivation, work attitude, and other test questions that vary from company to company. In order to determine specific qualities, the applicant is presented with tasks relevant to different every day work situations, like for example: '*The boss enters the room, just as the telephone rings and a coworker calls out to you from the neighboring room. What priority do you have here?*' In this way it is possible to complete a file containing information on the appropriate requirements for each job. Leading suppliers in this area are the Bochumer Company, Eligo, and the Düsseldorf Software Company, and H.R. Management Software (Brommer, 2001, pp. 84–85).

After hiring, there appears an integral, total assessment concept, which, as an instrument that promises success and is sensitive to staff politics, follows the development of the employee. It is important that the correspondence of given goals and the 'striving behavior' of the employees are used as measures of performance. The targets determine what should be achieved, and the behavior characteristics determine how it will be achieved. Targets have to always be objectively measurable, according to content and scope, and they should be chronologically definable. Both quantitative and qualitative aspects should be assessed, as well as individual modes of behavior.

The assessment of personality and behavior of employees should not, however, only be carried out by superiors, as this often gives rise to the impression of subjectivity or arbitrarity, which frequently carries with it a counterproductive effect.

It is more meaningful to bring many people into the assessment who can offer a realistic judgment of the person, like for instance, superiors, coworkers on the same level, team members, internal and external customers, and also the assessed person. This way, feedback from as many perspectives as possible is obtained. Eight to ten assessments are enough, on the one hand, to obtain definitive results, and, on the other hand, to keep administrative expenditure at a tenable level. Here management staff serve as coaches, who give feedback in open communication concerning strengths and weaknesses, as well as providing training and encouragement to team members. It is expected that the employee, on the basis of the assessment results, take an active roll in his own personal development, because the employee is meant to orient his performance behavior on the assessment system criteria. In many cases, employees are able to compare their self-evaluations with how others view them, in an effort to more thoroughly assess individual strengths and weaknesses.

In order to use the results of this integral, multifaceted assessment concept for further analyses, and in order to take appropriate, coordinated personnel management measures, a standardized questionnaire can be of help in staff meetings. The questionnaire is made up of four parts:

In the first part, the measure of the past years' goal achievement in relation to the employees is assessed. On the basis of the measurable goal description the level of goal achievement can be determined. It may be relevant to list the influence factors that may have decisively affected achievement of the goal. This part of the assessment is relevant when the influence factors were beyond the employee's power to affect them.

In the second part, the goals of the coming year are agreed upon. The goal description should be easily measurable, to objectify the determination of goal achievement level. When more subjective goals are included, it is advisable that there be sufficient discussion as to how such goals will be measured early in the process, as opposed to later.

In the third part, the performance behavior of the employee is assessed. In the example above, work behavior, teamwork, company thinking and action, as well as knowledge and ability, are differentiated. Other categories would also be possible. Again, comparing the responses from the actual employee, their coworkers, external customers, and management can be very useful in terms of finding perception differences.

In the fourth part, the assessment of the management and working situation by the employee is included. In the example, the areas of satisfaction with the work situation, support of management, and teamwork are differentiated. Companies that reward and value honest communication can expect to receive better feedback in this category than those firms that are not as receptive to constructive criticism.

A fifth part can be added to the questionnaire, and can be designed according to position and company, which assesses the employee's potential for development. An example is shown in Figure 2.9.

In this context, the significance attached by companies to the personal and professional development of employees is revealed. Opel Bank/Opel Leasing has for example, initiated a program for supporting training outside of work, with the goal of getting employees to take part in furthering their education outside of the

1. Assessment of Goal Achievement/Task Fulfillment

Task/Goal	Measurable Goal Description	Level of Goal Achievement	List of Influencing Factors
1.			
2.			
etc.			

2. Future Goals/Tasks

Goal/Task	Measurable Goal Description	Deadline
1.		
2.		
etc.		

3. Assessment of Performance Behavior

a) Work Behavior

		Comments
Customer Orientation	+ + + 0 – – –	
Goal-Oriented Work Modes (Planning, Organization, Priorities)	+ + + 0 – – –	
Work Behavior (Stress Level, Endurance)	+ + + 0 – – –	
Learning Ability	+ + + 0 – – –	
Personal Motivation, Independence	+ + + 0 – – –	
_____	+ + + 0 – – –	

b) Teamwork

Ability to Communicate	+ + + 0 – – –	
Ability to Work in a Team	+ + + 0 – – –	
Openness	+ + + 0 – – –	
Empathy	+ + + 0 – – –	
_____	+ + + 0 – – –	

c) Company Thinking and Action

Innovation Capacity	+ + + 0 – – –	
Adaptiveness	+ + + 0 – – –	
Integral Thinking	+ + + 0 – – –	
Negotiation Skills	+ + + 0 – – –	
_____	+ + + 0 – – –	

d) Knowledge and Ability

Professional Know How	+ + + 0 – – –	
General Knowledge	+ + + 0 – – –	
Leadership Competence	+ + + 0 – – –	
_____	+ + + 0 – – –	

4. Assessment of Work and Management Situation (As Assessed by Employees)

1. How satisfied are you with the ...		Improvement Suggestions/Measures
- content and demands of your tasks?	+ + + 0 – – –	
- amount of room for personal decisions and action?	+ + + 0 – – –	
- recognition for your performance?	+ + + 0 – – –	
_____	+ + + 0 – – –	

2. What is your assessment of the management with regard to...		Improvement Suggestions/Measures
- information?	+ + + 0 – – –	
- planning, organization, work routine?	+ + + 0 – – –	
- training?	+ + + 0 – – –	
- work equipment and organization?	+ + + 0 – – –	
_____	+ + + 0 – – –	

3. What is your assessment of teamwork ...		Improvement Suggestions/Measures
- between yourself and the management?	+ + + 0 – – –	
- within the unit?	+ + + 0 – – –	
- within the department?	+ + + 0 – – –	
- with other departments?	+ + + 0 – – –	
_____	+ + + 0 – – –	

Figure 2.8: Personnel assessment questionnaire of the Bayrischen Vereinsbank for an executive (Wunderer & Jaritz, 1999, pp. 132–133)

Support and Training
Ideas/goals concerning career development from the perspective of the employee
Ideas/goals concerning career development from the perspective of the manager
Friendly support measures in the organizational unit
Seminars/special measures (suggestions)

Figure 2.9: Example of a questionnaire concerning employee support (Wunderer & Jaritz, 1999, pp. 132–133)

workday. Employees are supported with a generous training budget, thus offering the possibility of acquiring knowledge that can have significance for their present or future professional activity (Gresch, 1997, p. 11). Many companies have begun to reimburse their employees for educational offerings that may not necessarily improve the employee's day-to-day knowledge of their jobs, but will impact the employee's level of satisfaction via quality of life measures. In the end, a happy employee is a loyal employee.

Flexibility of Employees in Dealings with Customers

In order for employees to behave appropriately and be able to react to individual customer wishes, a certain measure of independent, responsible action is a prerequisite. The goal here is for employees to be capable of making decisions right on the spot. This way, customer problems are solved quickly, and as much as possible, customer satisfaction is achieved. These thoughts form the basis of the following considerations (Homburg & Werner, 1998, pp. 208–209):

- Between the company, the superiors, and employees, a basis of trust needs to be achieved, which encourages readiness to make efforts and to take responsibility. This includes a certain amount of tolerance for error.
- The employees must be given the opportunity for independent and responsible action. A too all-embracing control should, where possible, be avoided.
- Companies and superiors should help enable employees to independently and responsibly fulfill their tasks. To that end, focused employee training needs to be carried out.
- Employees need to be prepared to accept responsibility, and superiors need to learn to let go of responsibility.

The goal-oriented introduction and realization of responsible action in a company is explained below according to a four-part procedure.

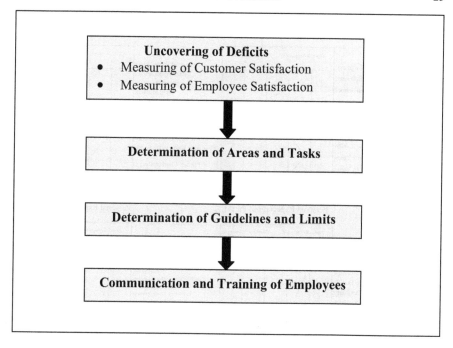

Uncovering of Deficits
- Measuring of Customer Satisfaction
- Measuring of Employee Satisfaction

Determination of Areas and Tasks

Determination of Guidelines and Limits

Communication and Training of Employees

Figure 2.10: Process of employee development of responsible action (based on Homburg & Werner, 1998, p. 210)

The next task involves a systematic uncovering of deficits within the company. In which areas would it make sense, on the basis of their competence, to transfer responsibility to employees? Helpful hints for solutions to these dilemmas can be derived by the measuring of customer satisfaction. This is where clearly formulated suggestions for improvement can frequently be found. A measuring of employee satisfaction, which explicitly points to improvement of competencies, as well as an evaluation of the results of the assessment concept presented above, can also be of help.

In the banking industry for example, due to pronounced changes in the area of transactions involving corporate customers of banks, a study was carried out with the theme, 'Cultivation and forms of realizing personnel development in credit institutions.' The goal of the study was to place the corporate customers' essential quality demands, as revealed by the study, on relationship managers. To this end professional and personal demands were differentiated. The personal demands were subdivided into three areas: intellectual potential, behavior in relation to customers, and behavior in relation to employees and superiors.

Figure 2.11 presents the results of the study on average. These concentrate on the 440 biggest credit institutions in western Germany (Oehler, 1995, p. 141).

In summary, it can be concluded that any criteria which belongs to the area of personal concerns, typically enjoys a higher priority than features which commonly

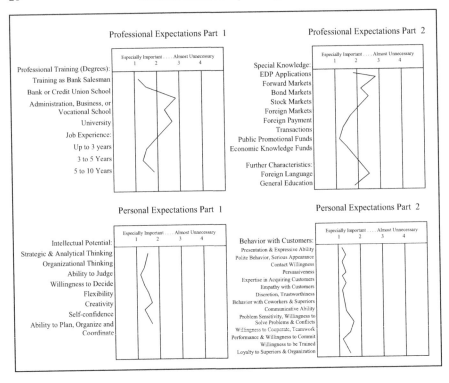

Figure 2.11: Study of personal and professional expectations by a corporate customer consultant in the banking field (Oehler, 1995, p. 141)

would be considered part of the professional and method competencies of corporate customer relationship management.

If the deficits are systematically uncovered within a company, areas and tasks based on them can be discovered, which to a large extent may be cases where allowance for more freedom of action is at issue. Often these are departments that have a close relationship to customers.

After the determination of tasks and departments, then a company must decide upon guidelines and limits should be decided upon. In Ritz Carlton Hotels, for example, employees have access to a maximum sum of US$2,000.00 to clear up customer complaints at their own discretion.

A last important step is to communicate these decided upon guidelines to the affected staff members, perhaps during their training time. Employees have to learn to do their tasks independently and responsibly, as well as to correctly assess their own performance. Often there is distortion between what a company or an employee believes constitutes service and quality, and what the customer believes should constitute these items. The following figure illustrates how a company self-assessment can differ from a customer assessment on eight different dimensions of quality.

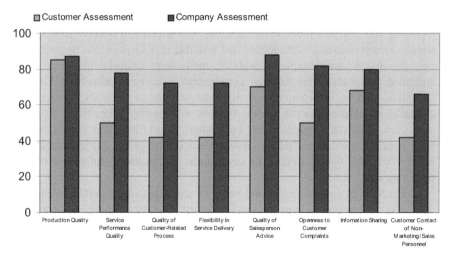

Figure 2.12: Distorted perceptions—how companies see their performance and how customers see it (ideal value = 100) (Homburg, 1996, p. 147)

As you can see from Figure 2.12, there were large perception gaps for many of the categories, and for each quality dimension, the company assessment was higher than that of the customer. Improvement of the entire organization in terms of the quality of its products and services can be achieved if an honest and open feedback mechanism exists between the leadership of a company and its employees.

Technology and Customer Orientation

For effective and efficient orientation toward the customer, thorough market and customer knowledge is a prerequisite. Only then is it organizationally possible to realize an individualized offering model and effective customer care. If this information is collected and analyzed in appropriate ways, a potential of enormous worth arises. Often the information that already exists in the company simply needs to be evaluated. 'When diverse information about the customers exist in various departments, there's nothing better to do than to evaluate it from various perspectives', says Johannes Wechsler, Managing Director of the software provider Applix. A similar point of view is held by Arthur Parker, Vice President of Global Business Intelligence Solutions EMEA at IBM, 'Customer relationships should be systematically developed, rather than arising out of a chain of coincidences. From analyzing the information on hand, future sales are more readily foreseeable' (Göbbel, 2001, p. 27).

With the engagement of key technologies like data warehousing and data mining this information can be evaluated and administrated in a focused manner.

A **Data Warehouse** is a data bank especially designed for decision making with regard to the customer information it contains. The data is made up of historical as well as current data, which is collected from diverse, company-wide data sources, filtered, and transformed. Augmented, a data warehouse can be compared to reporting and analyses tools. Information is well sorted and quickly accessible in storage (www.bbdo.de). Connections and possible relationships can be established very rapidly. As an example in practice, many large financial institutions have compiled data warehouses for their commercial customer relationships. Financial statements can be incorporated into the data warehouse when they are received annually, which provides the lending officers with quality information in order to assess future borrowing needs for their customers. This information, when combined with demographic data and deposit information, can serve as a useful sourcing tool for new business opportunities. The key is to be able to successfully mine the data for future use.

Data Mining can be understood to be an analysis tool for collected customer data. It is used primarily in two cases. In the first case, data mining can be used via intelligent statistical procedures where adequate segmentations can be identified, which enable the output of a targeted item of information. In the second case, data mining can be used for the calculation of purchase probabilities. By means of statistical procedures and neural networks it is possible, for example, on the basis of specific parameters, to show the repeat purchase probability of customers or potential customers (www.bbdo.de).

The three most important procedures of data mining for the forecasting and describing of data are segmentation, classifying, and associating (Schinzer, Bange & Mertens, 1999, p. 104–107). Each of these procedures in turn makes use of various techniques. The method used is determined by the searched for pattern, and heavily exhibits therefore a problem orientation that is situationally conditioned. The more detailed description of methods that follows, therefore, limits itself to the most commonly used techniques. These are neural networks, cluster analyses, and decision tree procedures for finding sequence patterns and association rules.

Segmentation—also called Clustering—involves dividing a data bank into groups of matching or similar data records. In other words: the data records, which have been combined into units, share a certain number of interesting characteristics.

As far as applications in business are concerned, segmentation has notable advantages. From out of huge data stocks a company can filter out a potential customer. In the context of a target group, marketing a product offer can be specialized and the precision of demand predictions can be enhanced, which are necessary for production planning and the calculation of stock capacity for new products. For segmentation, statistical cluster analyses procedures and a special form of neural networks, so called kohonen nets, are mainly used.

Classification and regression The task of classification procedures is to assign elements, whose characteristics are unknown, to existing classes, or to make predictions concerning unknown values of an existing data stock. On the basis of shared attributes of the elements in each class, a model to describe the classes is developed, which during the course of the classification ends up being portrayed in structures or rules. Classification procedures are used in database marketing for example, to increase efficiency of direct advertising, to improve product range design, and to prevent loss of customers. The discovery of credit card fraud and the evaluation of default risk are further areas in which data mining is useful.

A classification-related procedure of regression is often used for the creation of prediction models. An object is here classified on the basis of its attribute, though not its class, rather a relevant index like sales turnover or profitability, for example, demand functions for a product in supermarkets, which involve many variables (like location in the business, the amount of shelving space, price, marketing measures, customer structure of the business, time of year, and time of day).

Associating With the help of associating, dependencies between different data records can be filtered out. Correlations between concurrently occurring items are described. A typical use of association is via shopping basket analysis. By viewing a great number of transactions, purchasing trends should be apparent, which will reveal the purchasing behavior of customers. Firms that successfully use the associating technique will be in a better position to determine the stage of the life cycle of their customers. Product offers, product positioning, or targeted marketing, can all be improved using this method. It should be mentioned here that this is a primary mechanism for improving the net profit margin of a firm. There are countless examples of poor marketing segmentation efforts leading to the wasteful production of marketing material that is sent to uninterested potential customers. The better a firm is at identifying potential customers for a marketing campaign, the better the company will do in terms of achieved revenue gains as well as the avoidance of unnecessary costs. Companies as varied as the grocery chain Tesco and the online retailer Amazon.com have used the associating technique successfully over the last few years.

Data Mining Analyses Techniques

While there are many implementable techniques used in data mining, in this chapter only the ones that are used most often will be presented. Cluster analyses, decision trees, neural networks, as well as association procedures and sequence patterns are all commonly utilized data mining techniques. Each technique is suitable in different degrees for the data mining procedures of classification, segmentation, and associating. In the marketplace, most suppliers offer whole toolboxes of varying methods that can be used. Judgment of the database and the related suitability of the techniques are, in the end, up to the user.

Standard products, like for example, those from the Siebel Family, are currently rising in popularity. These products allow the integrated conducting of marketing, sales, and service processes, based on a data stock of units with product and customer information. If, for example, a customer complains, the appropriate information will be there, for the use of the customer advisor, in the next discussion with the customer (Schmid, Bach & Österle, 2000, p. 17).

Cluster Analysis

Cluster analysis is an explanatory segmentation procedure. The goal is to summarize representative quantities of data according to their grouped (clustered) characteristics. In the process, the data quantities should be reduced to fewer, more easily manageable and interpretable classes, whereby the data stocks within clusters should be as

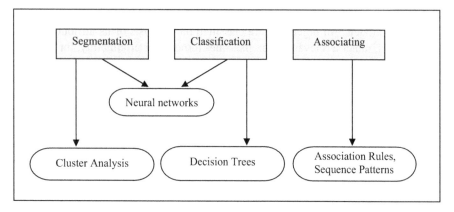

Figure 2.13: Application of data mining techniques for various tasks

homogenous as possible, and those between the individual clusters as heterogeneous as possible. The similarity of data stocks is measured via a comparison of matching variables, which have to display the same scale level. As a measure of similarity, correlation coefficients (similarity increases with increasing values) can be used, as can distance measures (similarity decreases with increasing values). To group data stocks, i.e., to identify the cluster, distance measures are commonly used. These can quantify a similarity of data stocks via their distance from each other, whereby, depending on the cluster algorithm, there are varying procedures for calculating distances (Kurz, 1998, p. 269).

Depending on whether individual clusters are exactly assigned to a cluster, or whether individual clusters are packets in themselves, one speaks of either partitions or hierarchies. The partitioning procedures operate on the basis of a given grouping of objects, and arrange the individual elements with the help of an exchange algorithm between the groups, until a given target function reaches an optimum (Backhaus, 1996, p. 281). The approach with hierarchical procedures, on the other hand, is to summarize or subdivide individual classes. It is a dividing procedure that begins with an individual cluster, which is then broken down into further clusters. The other alternative is the agglomerative method. Here, each object is considered to be a group, and then the objects are, during the course of the process, summarized pair-wise by means of approximation. The following figure is a dendrogram, which is especially practical for illustrating the results of hierarchical procedures (Berson, Smith & Thearling, 1999, S. 148–154).

Cluster analysis is often used as the first step in studying large, complex data stocks. The clusters obtained in this way can be utilized by other data mining techniques as a basis for achieving even better results.

As an example, a large commercial bank may want to determine which of its customers might be eligible for preapproval for a credit card. By using cluster analysis, the marketing research department may be able to quantify a list of current bank customers, who would appear to be best suited for a credit card based on a

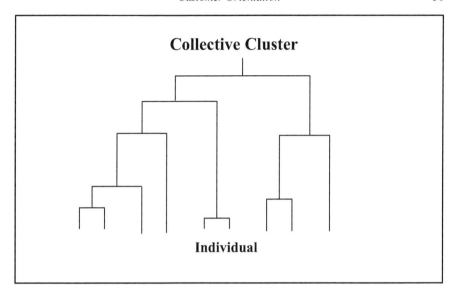

Figure 2.14: Construction principle in heirarchical procedures (dendrogram) (Berson, Smith & Thearling, 1999, p. 150)

predetermined list of customer qualities (such as repayment on other credit products, deposit balance histories, current levels of indebtedness, etc.).

Decision Trees

Decision trees are used for classifying the data organized via data mining. With their help, classification and prognoses models can be constructed, which are then used to classify a quantity of data records in a tree-like structure. Decision trees are generated according to a top-down rule, meaning the data records are placed in branches of the decision tree. In each branch the variables are determined using a splitting criterion, according to which the data records are divided. This process is repeated until the data records reach a leaf. A leaf is a branch beyond which no further branching out will take place. The higher a variable's information content with regard to the target size, the higher up the decision tree the variable is found.

On the basis of the leaves, the classification of the decision maker can be read. This is why in this context one also speaks of classification trees. The kind of statistical procedure, which is determined by the variable according to which the data records are divided, is crucial in the generation of a decision tree (Krahl, Windheuser & Zick, 1998, p. 70).

The following decision tree presents the leaving behavior of customers in a telecommunications company (Berson & Smith, 1997, p. 351).

In total, the decision tree generated four classes, whose members are the leaves that can be derived from them. An example for a possible decision tree can be described using the following 'if then' rule:

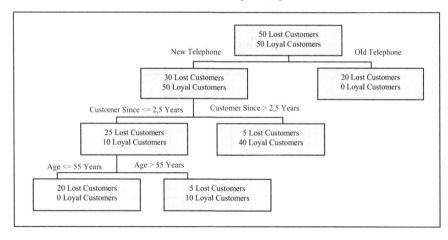

Figure 2.15: Decision tree (Berson & Smith, 1997, p. 351)

'If telephone = new and customer since > 2.5 years, then number of customers gone = 5.'

With the help of this rule unclassified data records can be unambiguously classified as leaves, i.e., as classes of the decision tree, which the value of the target variables can prognosticate. As you can see from Figure 2.15, and the discussion here, classifying customers in this manner can help the firm identify possible areas of improvement, so that in the future less customers will be likely to conduct their business with a competitor.

Neural Networks

Neural networks constitute one of the most important data mining techniques and are used in the classification and segmentation of very large data stocks. With the help of neural networks, precise prognosis models can be developed, which can be utilized to solve many different kinds of problems (Berson & Smith, 1997, p. 375).

Neural networks are seen as a special form of nonlinear statistical models. With neural networks, the aim is to learn the human brain's abilities, and to simulate them in a computation model. Neural processes learn from historical data and try to carry a targeted learning effect over to new data. The situation resembles that of a biological nervous system (Nakhaeizadeh, 1996, pp. 149–159). A neuron is the smallest element of a neural network and corresponds with a biological nerve cell. A neuron processes a progression of input sizes to reach an output. The inputs are connected to the neuron according to a particular intensity (Krahl, Windheuser & Zick, 1998, p. 64). Figure 2.16 shows an example of a neural network with two hidden layers.

The neurons are organized in layers, where each layer is connected with a neuron of the neighboring layer. Every branch contains various inputs and summarizes these inputs. At the same time each branch produces a reaction dependent on the input that each branch contains. When the sum of inputs is high, the branch will display a

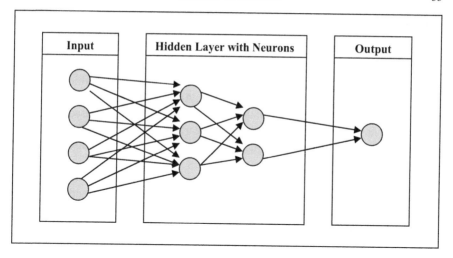

Figure 2.16: Neural network with two hidden layers

strong reaction. If the sum of inputs is weak, the branch will react weakly (from the Lühe, 1998, p. 293). Neural network procedure is important when creating regression models and also in time series modeling. The key for a customer-oriented firm is the ability to predict, with some level of accuracy, the future purchasing probability of its customer base.

There are many practical examples of the use of neural networks today. In the medical field, neural networks can be utilized to help in the prognises of patient care, especially as it relates to the internal medicine field. Neural networks are also utilized in the banking industry. Neural networks are utilized in small business loan scoring models, as the purpose of these models is to come to the same conclusion as an experienced commercial lender. These expert systems utilize prior data on loan repayment in order to determine which future loan requests should be accepted or rejected. Unlike consumer lending, the commercial segment has numerous other variables that must be considered when considering the extension of credit by a financial institution. Beyond the consumer lending variables such as the personal credit score, personal income, and personal net worth, small business loan scoring models must consider additional factors. These factors include the age of the business (given the high failure rates for entrepreneurial ventures within the first five years), the standard industry classification code of the business (given the different repayment histories depending on the industry in question), the net income and net worth of the company, and relationship profitability considerations such as the level of deposits and other products. These examples of neural networks aid firms in better predicting future behaviors based on data collected in the past.

Associating

Association rules search data mining tools for significant independencies between fields of analysis objects. They describe correlations between simultaneously occurring variables, whereby these could, for example, be articles which customers buy all together in one trip to the supermarket. An association rule could be written like the following, 'In 45 percent of the cases where salmon is purchased, white wine is also purchased, and these two products appear in two percent of all transactions.' The concept of associating is similar to the concept of complementary products in economics instruction.

Sequence analysis, with regard to sequential patterns, also falls within the area of associations. Sequence analysis assumes data histories, and then within a certain timeframe seeks relationships between the probabilities of occurrence of various events (Krahl, Windheuser & Zick, 1998, p. 80).

Organizational Structure and Customer Orientation

The fundamental difficulty of an insufficiently customer-oriented start-up company often has to do with widespread specialization. In this situation intermediaries arise, which results in a considerable increase in the inefficiency of communication and coordination. This leads to decision-making problems. Processes take longer. Furthermore, only very few employees have a total overview of the organization's activities. It becomes more and more difficult to supply the customers with optimal, relevant information. Although it is true that a certain measure of specialization is unavoidable, forms of organization need to be found which allow for a certain level of specialization, while at the same time supporting customer orientation (Homburg & Werner, 1998, pp. 190–191).

Against this background, in recent years an increasing number of organizational forms have been established which firmly evaluate company structures from the perspective of an integrated process orientation. Here the form of the organization operates according to the goal of reaching as high a level of efficient coordination of company units as possible, and especially to avoid the classic intermediary problems. As much as possible functional barriers, formalisms, and multiple checks within a process are avoided. This is achieved on the one hand via traditional, linear oriented, and hierarchical control mechanisms which are replaced by group related responsibility (i.e., team structures), and on the other hand by the introduction of modern communication and information technologies, which accelerate, and enable better coordination of business processes (Meffert, 2000, p. 1087).

In order to assure the success of the process-oriented organization, the following rules should be observed (Sommerlatte & Wedekind, 1990, p. 25):

- For every strategically significant performance process there should be a party who is responsible for that process, such that it is supervised and controlled in a function and department-spanning manner.

- For processes that involve several functional areas, the form of the project organization will be chosen. At the same time, project teams will be comprised of members of all functional areas of the company.
- The number of intermediaries between functional areas should be kept to a minimum. Unavoidable intermediaries will be marked by unambiguous descriptions of the coordinated course of action.

In addition to these rules, at any time all necessary information about products, prices, and customers, independent from each other, should be obtainable and processable by the responsible employee. For a traveling sales representative, for example, it makes sense for them to have a portable computer, from which at any time can be obtained current customer and capacity information. In this way, the salesperson is granted the possibility of independently conducting orders directly and at the customer's location. Additionally, it could be crucial for employees with direct customer contact to know in which services the customer was especially interested, what product or service they purchased most recently, if there were any problems, what the customer may have found unsatisfactory, and what services they especially liked. In this way, a targeted orientation of organizational activities toward the wishes and needs of the customer can take place.

Any organizational structure oriented toward customer needs requires the integration of all units involved in the value creation process, from the first level of value creation to the fulfillment of the contract. This is illustrated in Figure 2.17.

There is no link in this chain where customer-oriented behavior would not be possible. The conveyance of customer standards—customer wishes—must be attended to at all organizational levels. As you can see from Figure 2.18, some organizations have feedback that travels from the customer contact personnel to top management, while other organizations allow for two-way communication up and down the organization, and this form of feedback includes input directly from the customer as well.

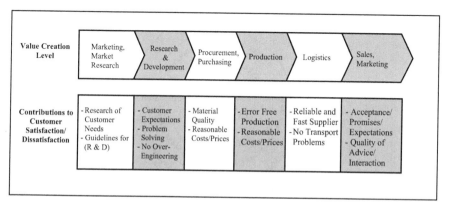

Figure 2.17: Possible contributions of value creation to customer satisfaction (Simon & Homburg, 1998, p. 21)

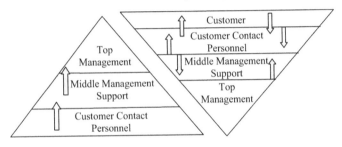

**Figure 2.18: Hierarchy pyramid in focused customer
orientation (Gronroos, 2000, p. 305)**

Organizational plans, which management is normally fixated on, determine the mindset with which traditional company structures are lived and planned. All organizational units and processes are subsumed under the management. The customer is not a constituent of the organization plan. It is here seemingly forgotten that, in terms of a company's justification for existing, the customer is the decisive criterion, and therefore should, in organization planning, take priority above all other internal company units. On the second level below the customer should be placed the employees who come in immediate contact with the customer (customer contact personnel). In the traditional hierarchy, these can be seen as supposedly insignificant employees. Studies have shown that a positive initial approach to personnel has a very significant effect on later turnover. This fact serves to underline, that precisely these employees require intensive development in order to fulfill customer expectations (Erlbeck, 1999, p. 75).

The bakery chain Der Beck from Erlangen, Germany, exemplifies this concept. In this organization, the customer is very clearly, as is shown in the figure below, placed in the center of attention. This organizational plan (Figure 2.19)is hung up in a conspicuous place in all the different branches.

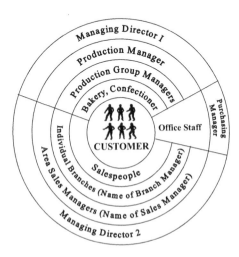

Figure 2.19: The customer at the center of attention (Erlbeck, 1999, p. 76)

The management personnel are listed by name around the customer (branch manager, internal management). The managing directors are listed around the outer rim. Among their tasks is customer care. With the help of customer analysis data, useful pointers can be obtained as to how organizational units can operate in a more customer-oriented manner. In the third level, support personnel can be found (e.g., order processing, marketing department), who only have indirect customer contact, and who support the customer contact personnel (Erlbeck, 1999, p. 77).

From the customer perspective, higher customer orientation is often connected with the question of whether there are services available, such as a hotline, a central repair center, or an answering service for complaints. Although the customer and their needs are not divisible, it can be possible that they have more than one contact person. This raises the fear that the customer may not know who should be contacted when problems arise. Furthermore, the various departments are prone to pass the buck onto the next department each time a problem comes up. The consequence of this is an angry customer, who in the worse case will find another company with which to conduct their business. To remedy this, in recent years there has been a sharp rise in the establishment of call centers. Of particular importance are their size and the number of employees who are available for high and low frequency calling times. Depending on the company, it can make sense to create teams within the call centers which specialize in different customer needs, like for example, complaints, technical consultation, ordering, or general customer help (Homburg & Werner, 1998, p. 195).

Figure 2.20 presents the central aspects to be kept in mind in organizing a call center.

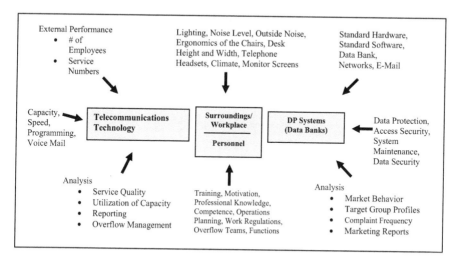

Figure 2.20: Central aspects in the establishment of call centers (Homburg & Werner, 1998, p. 194)

Questions for Discussion

1. Discuss how having satisfied and engaged employees contributes to the overall success of a company. Consider your organization or university when compiling your answer.

2. Assume that you are in charge of hiring at your firm or university. What specific questions would you consider including in your interview process in order to obtain the most customer-oriented personnel?

3. Considering the international strategies discussed in Chapter 1, discuss the benefits and shortcomings of each strategic alternative when considering creating an environmental of customer orientation.

4. Compare and contrast the different technological methods of achieving customer orientation. Which of these methods could be used to enhance customer orientation at your firm or university?

5. From both a cost and quality of service standpoint, what are the strengths and weaknesses of establishing a call center for handling direct customer inquiries?

6. How might a customer-oriented renumeration system be implemented at your firm? What changes to your current incentives would be necessary for this to occur?

Chapter 3

Product Quality

Chapter Objectives:

- *Define the multiple dimensions of quality.*
- *Elaborate on the components of the Kano model.*
- *Understand how the results of the Kano model are interpreted.*
- *Discuss the importance of Quality Function Deployment (QFD) in improving the quality of a product or service.*
- *Elaborate on the four planning phases of the Quality Function Deployment (QFD).*
- *Briefly outline the ten areas of the House of Quality.*

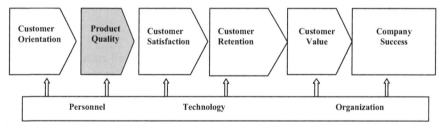

Figure 3.1: The concept of quality

The Concept of Quality

The starting point of a customer-oriented company strategy consists of the needs and expectations of the customer. In order to truly fulfill or even exceed these, an appropriate level of product quality needs to be guaranteed. In this case the concept of product, in addition to meaning something in the form of a tangible good, also means services, or service performance. Companies that can competently offer what their customers actually want, gain many advantages over the competition, at the same time as achieving a high level of customer satisfaction.

In the meantime, many companies have understood that quality of performance has to hit the mark. To maintain and increase company success, managers need to pay the utmost attention to product and service performance quality.

In recent years, both in the literature and in practice, many assessments have been put forward to interpret the concept of quality. Among these are the manufacturer-

oriented, the customer-oriented, and the competition-oriented concepts of quality (Garvin, 1984a, pp. 25–43; Garvin, 1984b, pp. 40–43). The illustration above exhibits that there are many dimensions of quality from which an organization must choose.

- **The Manufacturer-oriented Quality Concept**
  The manufacturer-oriented quality concept integrates within itself a product- and process-related understanding of quality. In a product-related understanding of quality, variations in quality are reflected in the different features which are characteristic of a given product. Quality is here objectively measurable. The process-related assessment hinges on the observance of specifications, and on the attainment of a 'no errors' situation. Any divergence from specifications signifies a dilution of quality.
- **The Customer-oriented Quality Concept**
  This definition involves both a user-oriented, as well as a value-oriented understanding of quality. According to the user-oriented assessment of quality, quality arises exclusively from the customer's perspective. This is founded on the idea that it is the person requesting the service who in the end decides if the quality of the performance is good or bad; the user benefit is subjectively evaluated.
- **The Competition-oriented Quality Concept**
  The competitive relationship always plays a roll when the company strategy is to become 'quality leader', e.g., when it wants to present its performance as 'qualitatively' superior. In this way the company places its performance quality in a comparative relationship with that of other companies.

Really, if one were forced to choose from these, the customer-oriented understanding of quality makes the most sense. This assumption is founded on the fact that in today's prevailing buyer's market, a customer will desert a company which does not deliver the quality of product or service they desire. As a consequence, sale turnover and profit suffer. Furthermore, a customer-oriented understanding of quality automatically implies an attitude which focuses determinedly on customer satisfaction (Scharnbacher & Kiefer, 1998, pp. 28–29).

The increasing significance of quality, and of its consequences for a company, is also supported by the so-called PIMS study (Profit Impact of Marketing Strategies). This project, initiated in 1972 by the Strategic Planning Institute, analyzed the connection between company strategy and company success. As a result of the study, it could be established that quality was an important influencing factor, wherein the increase of service performance and product quality had a positive effect on market share and profitability (Buzell, Gale & Greif, 1989, p. 91). Figure 3.2 illustrates this concept.

It was also established that when quality is perceived as superior, it can exercise an influence on company success in two ways (Buzzell, Gale & Greif, 1989, p. 92):

1. In the short term, superior quality leads to an increase in profit with regard to so-called premium prices, which customers react less sensitively to if the quality is outstanding.
2. Viewed in the long term, high quality leads to market expansion and to market share gain. The short-term costs of improving quality are offset by an increased level of learning and due to the degression effect. Focusing on high quality will reduce the overall costs of a firm over time due to the lack of costs associated with correcting errors in production.

In the first case, the higher price directly adds to profit, and in the second case the increase in market share has a positive effect on sales and consequently leads to better utilization of capacity, and perhaps to an increase of capacity.

Just how drastic an effect quality problems can have is born out by this study of new car buyers, carried out by the car industry. Many of the German as well as US car manufacturers were relegated to the lower ranks due to numerous recall actions, poor service, and inadequate quality assurance. Successful market leaders such as Toyota, which is leading the way in terms of profitability (and soon in terms of volume) in the auto industry, scored very well in this survey of perceived quality.

ROI

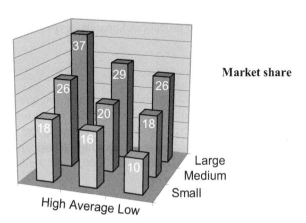

Quality

Figure 3.2: Connection between quality, market share, and ROI (Buzzell, Gale & Greif, 1989, p. 94)

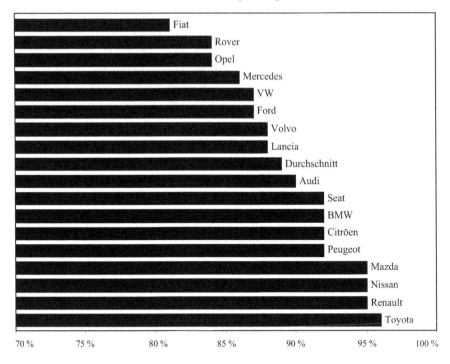

**Figure 3.3 Customer dissatisfaction, proportionate to very and
completely satisfied customers (Scharrer, 2000, p. 32)**

Two methods, the 'Kano model' and 'quality function deployment (QFD)',
will be presented below, which in recent years have successfully contributed to the
systematic customer orientation of product and process development.

The Kano Model

The Kano model provides a useful method of answering the question of whether
measures for increasing product quality have an effect on customer satisfaction.
The model, named after Noriaki Kano of Japan, is based on the idea of dividing
customer standards of company performance according to basic, performance, and
thrill standards (Herrmann, Huber & Braunstein, 2000, p. 47; Bailom, Hinterhuber,
Matzler & Sauerwein, 1996, pp. 117–125).

Basic Standards (Must Be)

Basic standards embody criteria which a product absolutely must fulfill. If the offered
service does not satisfy these criteria, the customer will be dissatisfied. If the person
receiving the service sees these expectations as having been fulfilled, he does not
express satisfaction, but is merely not dissatisfied with the product.

The providing of a vehicle registration document, as part of the purchasing of a new vehicle via a dealer, can serve as a typical example of a basic standard. If the purchaser of an s-class car from Daimler Chrysler had to go all the way to the place of registration, in order to register the car there, the dealer and manufacturer could hardly be surprised if this were experienced by the customer as a dip in his level of satisfaction. Another example of a basic standard is the airbag. Car purchasers now take for granted that a new car will have an airbag. However, its presence does not promote satisfaction, only avoids dissatisfaction. If a car manufacturer leaves this feature out, it will have to deal with annoyed customers, or the loss of business.

Performance Standards (One-dimensional)

With the performance standard, satisfaction is proportionate to the level of fulfillment. The higher the level of fulfillment, the more satisfied, and vice versa. Performance standards are generally explicitly expected by the customer.

With cars this could mean the ability to accelerate, and with personal computers, this would entail memory capacity. Performance standards are features that the customers will always want to constantly improve.

Thrill Standards (Attractive)

Thrill standards are those product criteria which have the highest influence on customer satisfaction with a product. They are not explicitly formulated by the customer and are also not expected. Fulfilling these standards leads to an overflowing of customer satisfaction. If these standards are not fulfilled there is no feeling of dissatisfaction.

A purchaser of a personal computer, for example, would react with surprise if a dealer proceeded to install the software as part of the purchase, without charging extra. A customer might also be thrilled by the prospect of arriving at her car loaded down with shopping bags, and not having to put these bags down onto a possibly wet ground, to search for her car key, because the doors of the car have already opened via a remote signal.

What customers experience as basic, performance, and thrill standards depend on their prevailing preferences, and therefore they often differ from customer to customer. Moreover the classification changes with time. What thrills customers today, will be explicitly expected tomorrow, and the day after tomorrow the same performance feature will be seen as basic, and taken for granted.

Advantages of the Kano Model

The advantages of the classification of customer standards according to the Kano model are as follows (Berger, Blauth & Boger, 1993):

- Better understanding of product standards: those criteria can be identified which have the greatest influence on customer satisfaction.
- From the classification of product standards in basic, performance, and thrill standards, priorities for product development can be derived. For example, it is far less meaningful to invest in the further development of basic standards, when these have already been satisfactorily fulfilled, than it is to invest in the improvement of performance or thrill standards, which have a bigger influence on the perception of product quality, and therefore also on customer satisfaction.
- The Kano method delivers a helping hand with trade-offs in product development. If two product features cannot be simultaneously fulfilled for technical or financial reasons, those criteria which have greater effect on customer satisfaction can be identified.

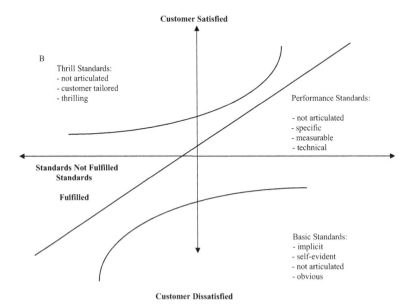

**Figure 3.4: The Kano model of customer satisfaction
(Berger, Blauth & Boger, 1993, pp. 3–35)**

- In general, basic, performance, and thrill standards differ according to the expectations of benefits for varying segments of the customer population. On this basis, custom-made performance packages can be developed for focused problem solving, which guarantee an optimal level of satisfaction for the various segments.
- The discovery and fulfillment of thrill standards offers many possibilities for differentiation. A product which merely fulfills the basic and performance standards, is perceived as average and therefore exchangeable (Hinterhuber, Aichner & Lobenwein, 1994).
- The Kano model of customer satisfaction can be combined with QFD, which will be more precisely defined later. A prerequisite here is the identification of customer needs, of their ranking and priority. (Handlbauer, 1995, pp. 263–284). In particular, the importance of individual product characteristics for customer satisfaction is discovered through the utilization of the Kano model, and thereby an optimized precondition for product development activity is attained.

The Course of a Kano Project

Before designing the actual Kano questionnaire it is necessary to find out the relevant standards from the perspective of the customer. To that end there are various methods, like for example, the analysis of complaints, discussions with the customer, or focus group interviews. Studies of Griffin & Hauser have here shown that 20–30 qualitative customer interviews in homogenous segments are enough, in order to find out over 90 percent of all desired product standards (Griffin & Hauser, 1993, pp. 1–27).

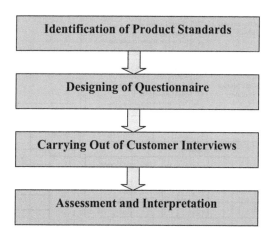

Figure 3.5: The course of a 'Kano Project' (Bailom, Hinterhuber, Matzler & Sauerwein, 1996, p. 199)

After the product and performance features relevant to the customer have been ascertained, the Kano questionnaire can be designed. Kano devised two special question types with five possible answers, in order to filter out the relevant basic, performance, and thrill product features.

The first question refers to the reaction, if the relevant product feature (functional form of the question) is present; the second refers to the reaction, if the relevant product feature is not present (dysfunctional form of the question). Via the combination of the answers to both questions, the product standards can be classified, by means of specific evaluation procedures (see Figure 3.6).

The following reports refer to a study concerning a large airline, in the area of airfreight.

From out of the combination of questions in the rows and columns of the assessment table, there appears in the table of results in the above example, an entry in the category P. This product feature is a performance standard for the customer. If the combination of answers falls into the category I, 'indifferent', then it follows that this product characteristic is not important to the customer. He would not be prepared to pay extra for it. The category U stands for a dubious, 'unusable result'. This combination result generally only arises when the person questioned misunderstands or erroneously answers the question. If the result from the assessment table is O, 'opposed' or 'opposite', then it can be inferred that this product characteristic is not desired or that even the opposite is expected.

A hierarchy of product or service standards is clearly observable: basic standards come before performance standards, which come before thrill standards. If a company lacks necessary competencies with regard to basic standards, it needs to be determined how fast these can be developed, or if they can be purchased.

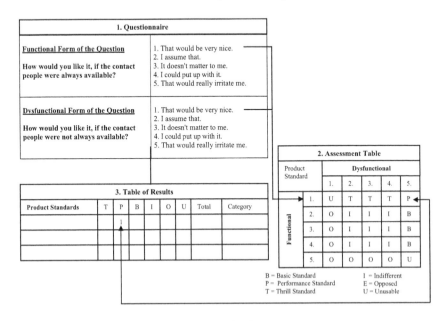

Figure 3.6: The Kano method assessment process

In addition to the Kano questions, it is advisable to get the customer to assess the different criteria of his current product, as well as to gather the relative significance of the individual criteria (on a scale of from 'very important' to 'totally unimportant').

In the evaluation of data, the Kano method falls back on the satisfaction inducing coefficient. This coefficient provides information about how securely the product feature is in the position to increase satisfaction, or conversely, how negatively satisfaction would be affected in the event that this product feature was not being fulfilled. In it, the number of classifications into basic, performance, and thrill standards, as well as product characteristics to which the customer is indifferent, are for a product feature combined into a mathematical relationship, as is shown in Figure 3.7.

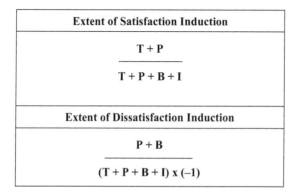

Figure 3.7: Extent of satisfaction and dissatisfaction induction

The measure of dissatisfaction is appended by a negative sign, which illustrates that the non-fulfillment of a promised or expected service induces dissatisfaction. The positive satisfaction coefficient ranges from 0 to 1. The closer the value is to 1, the more the influence on satisfaction is positive. If the value is close to -1, this means that very many of the people asked were unhappy with the service. A value near 0 signifies that if this feature is not fulfilled, it produces hardly any movement toward dissatisfaction.

Figure 3.8 presents the study results in the airfreight area of an airline. The results portfolio shows that the product standard, 'fulfill all special wishes', has a very pronounced influence on satisfaction when it is attained. If it is not fulfilled it produces negligible dissatisfaction.

The product standard 'personnel especially friendly' has a very big affect on satisfaction when fulfilled, and just as much affect in the direction of dissatisfaction if it is not fulfilled.

If the product standard 'regular visits' is fulfilled or not fulfilled, it has little influence in the direction of either satisfaction or dissatisfaction.

A failure to fulfill 'error free freight paperwork' produces a very pronounced level of dissatisfaction, while fulfilling it produces hardly any increase in satisfaction.

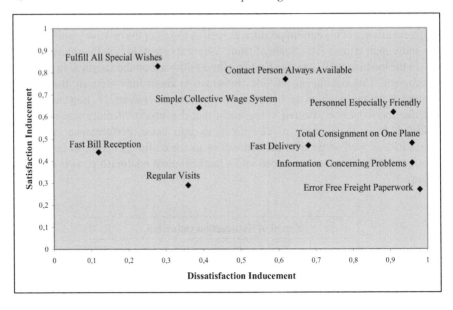

Figure 3.8: Portfolio of results

At this juncture, it can be advised that the evaluation of a Kano survey is possible, without further detailed statistical know-how, if it is limited to the formation of frequency and relationship figures. The program SPSS and the table calculation program EXCEL are here recommended as statistics software support.

Quality Function Deployment

QFD is a method of customer-oriented product development, or rather customer-oriented quality management. In a nutshell, it is about converting customer wishes into concrete product features. Customer wishes can be ascertained via the questioning of individual customers during personal interviews, through focus group discussions, and/or by using the Kano method. After finding out customer standards it is then necessary to engage in carrying these wishes over into concrete features. QFD furthers the attaining of this goal.

The origin of QFD can be traced back to Japan in the late sixties, where the Mitsubishi heavy industries shipyard in Kobe conceptually developed the procedure, and made it public for the first time (Akao, 1992, p. 13). Today, the method is successfully being used by companies like AT&T, Digital Equipment, Ford, General Motors, Hewlett-Packard, Mercedes-Benz, Siemens, and Volkswagen (Hauser & Clausing, 1998, p. 61; Klein, 1999, p. 10; Niemand, 1996, p. 43). The application of QFD is not limited to the investment and consumer goods sectors, as it can also be used in the service performance area (e.g., banks, commercial enterprises). The method of QFD consists of four planning phases:

1. Conversion of customer wishes into actual construction features: in this phase the idea is to take the customer wishes that have been discovered and transform them into product features.
2. Conversion of construction features into plans for assembly and components: decisions are made here as to how to assemble the product features discussed in the first phase.
3. Conversion of assemblies and components into process plans: The decided upon assemblies and components are assigned to the processes which will contribute to their realization.
4. Conversion of process plans to work plans: In the last phase of product planning the processes are converted to concrete work and checking instructions, which compliment and add detail to the process plans.

Each of these planning phases is supported and visualized via a so-called '**House of Quality**'. This endeavor assures the universal conversion of customer wishes all the way to actualized work instructions, where the benefit of each operational stage is made significant against a background of market standards This offers the advantage of encouraging the productive cooperation of various organizational areas (marketing, sales, production), and of obtaining the varying points of view and professional competencies involved.

In its structure, the House of Quality consists of ten areas. These areas will be described below, for the first phase of QFD, on the basis of an example taken from the automobile industry (Hauser & Clausing, 1998, pp. 59–79) (see Figure 3.9). The example limits itself to standards in relation to automobile doors. It will be noticed that the individual areas are not strictly stipulated. The House of Quality creates a methodological space, which, according to the situation-specific conditions, can and should be adapted. The areas of the House of Quality described here have proven themselves, and may be relevant for most practical questions.

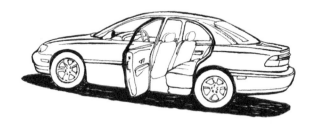

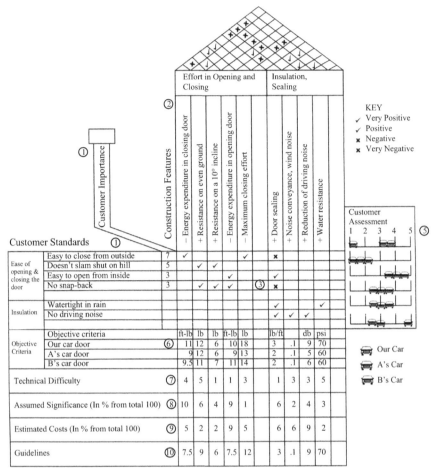

Figure 3.9: House of Quality

Areas of the House of Quality:

1. In the first area, the customer standards (customer wishes) are entered. Moreover, this area includes the importance of the standards from the point of view of the customer. The evaluations of each customer standard are normally presented in percentage values, whereby all evaluations add up to 100 percent.
2. The second area describes the technical construction features, which have an influence on the customer standards.
3. In the third area, it is established how much each technical construction feature influences the customer standards (relationship matrix). The assessment is based on experiences, customer reactions, and/or appropriate data, which come from statistical studies or from experiments.

4. The fourth area deals with the question, how much would the alteration of a construction feature influence the other construction features (roof matrix)? It should become clear which problems arise in realizing the customer standards, and where technical solutions mutually compliment or hinder each other. If it works, for example, to reduce the energy expenditure in closing the door (customer standard of easy to close from outside), then this hinders the improvement of resistance on a ten degree incline (customer standard of door not slamming closed on hill).

5. The fifth area is comparison with the competition, whereby the comparison is from the customer's perspective (Benchmarking). Ideally, this assessment will be based on well-founded customer surveys.

6. In the sixth area, criteria are established for the assessment of technical construction features, and for the comparison of the company's own product with the competition's products, on the basis of these criteria.

7. The seventh area is an assessment with regard to the technical difficulty of realizing an improvement to the feature in question. The assessment of the difficulty proceeds according to a numerical scale (e.g. from 1 = no problem, to 6 = not attainable). An exclusively internal assessment of technical attainability can lead to over hasty rejection of solutions, which from a market point of view would have been necessary. For this reason, in this area it is advisable to objectify, e.g., bring in external and independent experts.

8. The eighth area is concerned with the significance of individual construction features. The assumed significance proceeds according to a background of information with regard to customer standards, customer importance, customer assessment (benchmarking), and technical difficulty. A determination like this is not simple, but on the basis of the available information it is justifiable and comprehensible.

9. In the ninth area there is an assessment of the proportionate cost of the current construction features. It makes sense, in addition to the usual finding out of the proportionate cost, also to consider what the customer is prepared to pay for a particular construction feature. The relevant information can be gathered via well-founded surveys and/or via conjoint measurement. In such a course of action, there also arises a connection between QFD and target costing.

10. The tenth area documents the targets with regard to the individual construction features. On the basis of the assumed significance of the individual construction features, the prevailing proportionate cost, and customer assessment, specific and measurable guidelines are determined. If, for example, the product standard with regard to driving noise is observed, one can see that the supplier being studied has a lower value here than the competition. However, the customer experiences, or rather judges, the supplier to be better than the competition. The consequence is that as a guideline an objective quality criterion of '9 db' will be maintained, as is shown in Figure 3.9.

After creating a House of Quality for converting customer standards to construction features, the conversion of the next phase follows according to a new, appropriate House of Quality. (see Figure 3.10). For example, if the guideline indicates an adjustment of a compressor to a value of 3.6 (work instruction in Phase 4), this signifies a speed of 100 rotations per minute. In this connection, the press produces (process sealing press in phase 3) a weather proofing sealing bulge of even diameter (assembly sealing in phase 2). This sealing guarantees a good insulation and raises the door closing effort only by an inconsequential degree (construction feature in phase 1). These construction features fulfill the expectations of the customer regarding a dry and quiet car, with doors that are easy to close (Hauser & Clausing, 1998, S. 79).

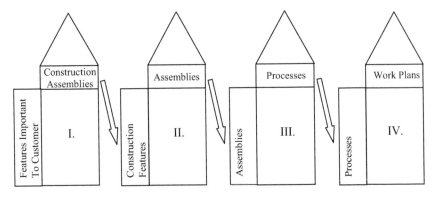

Figure 3.10: Phases of Quality Function Deployment (QFD) and House of Quality

Questions for Discussion

1. Discuss the strengths and weaknesses of quality-oriented definitions from the perspective of the manufacturer, the customer, and the competition.

2. Utilizing the Kano model, consider which of the features below would be considered basic, performance, and thrill standards for your automobile, your bank, and your grocery store:

Quality Aspect	Auto	Bank	Grocer
Friendliness of employee			
Speed of transaction processing			
Zero defects—billing process			
Zero defects—product performance			
Low cost relative to competition			
Wide array of product choices			
High level of safety/security of products			
Quick resolution of problems			

3. How would be the most reliable way to implement the Kano model in your firm or university? What improvements might result from its implementation?

4. How might QFD and the House of Quality be utilized to improve customer quality at your organization?

5. How can your organization's definition of quality most accurately be revealed? What are some common pitfalls associated with defining quality?

Appendix

Extension of the Kano Model and Quality Function Deployment
Asia World Bank Case Study

Congratulations! You have just been hired to work in Asia World Bank's marketing research department. Asia World Bank has recently completed a survey of select retail banking customers in your region in order to determine how to better meet the needs of its valued clients. As a new hire, your supervisor has asked for feedback pertaining to the results of the recent completion of a Kano survey as well as a recent construction of the House of Quality for the retail-banking segment for your region at Asia World Bank.

To aid you in your analysis of the findings, your supervisor has supplied a copy of the original Kano survey that was completed by approximately two hundred clients in a random selection process. You have also been provided a copy of the Kano analysis chart, showing which of the product and service features at Asia World Bank were considered 'attractive, one-dimensional, and must be' features. Your supervisor has also supplied you with a completed House of Quality diagram for the same study, which compares the relationship between customer attributes and service characteristics that were determined from the Kano survey and from discussions within the marketing research department. Your assignment is as follows:

1. Summarize the findings of both the Kano model survey and the QFD (House of Quality) survey. Does there appear to be an alignment with the customer attribute preferences and the service characteristics for both studies? Do the studies provide any conflicting information?

2. What important information can you learn from these studies in terms of areas of future strategic focus for Asia World Bank?

3. What are your recommendations as to the implementation of improvement initiatives based on the results of these studies?

4. What suggestions for improvement do you have for future studies of this sort at Asia World Bank?

Asia World Bank KANO Survey

Age: 18—25 ____ 26—39 ____ 40 —60 ____ Over 6C Gender: _____

The response scale for each question contains the following options (twice, for parts a and b):

I like it that way. / *It must be that way.* / *I am neutral.* / *I can live with it that way.* / *I dislike it that way.*

1.a. If your local branch was open on Saturday mornings, how would you feel?

   b. If your local branch was not open on Saturday mornings, how would you feel?

2.a. If you were able to communicate directly with your local banker by e-mail, how would you feel?

   b. If you were not able to communicate directly with your local banker by e-mail, how would you feel?

3.a. If Asia World Bank locates ATMs in safe locations rather than in numerous locations, how would you feel?

   b. If Asia World Bank does not locate ATMs in safe locations rather than in numerous locations, how would you feel?

4.a. If local branch hours are 8 am—5 pm Mon through Friday, and the bank focuses on ATMs and phone access, how would you feel?

   b. If local branch hours are not 8 am—5 pm Mon through Friday, and the bank focuses on ATMs and phone access, how would you feel?

5.a. If you have access to an ATM in your grocery store, how do you feel?

   b. If you do not have access to an ATM in your grocery store, how do you feel?

6.a. If you can complete your banking transactions online, how do you feel?

   b. If you cannot complete your banking transactions online, how do you feel?

Page 2   Asia World Bank KANO Survey

7.a. If your account problems are resolved within your local branch, how do you feel?

   b. If your account problems are not resolved within your local branch, how do you feel?

8.a. If you had an account problem and could have it resolved through online Internet communication, how would you feel?

   b. If you had an account problem and could not have it resolved through online Internet communication, how would you feel?

9.a. If Asia World Bank offers a wide choice of financial products, how do you feel?

   b. If Asia World Bank does not offer a wide choice of financial products, how do you feel?

10.a. If Asia World Bank offers a limited amount of choices for deposits, investments, and loan solutions, how do you feel?

   b. If Asia World Bank does not offer a limited amount of choices for deposits, investments, and loan solutions, how do you feel?

11.a. If you were able to view and lock-in Certificate of Deposit interest rates by accessing the bank's Internet website, how would you feel?

   b. If you were not able to view & lock-in Certificate of Deposit interest rates by accessing the bank's Internet website, how would you feel?

12.a. If Asia World Bank offers investment, deposit and credit advice in the local branch, how do you feel?

   b. If Asia World Bank does not offer investment, deposit and credit advice in the local branch, how would you feel?

Kano Model Survey *(continues overleaf)*

	I like it that way.	It must be that way.	I am neutral.	I can live with it that way.	I dislike it that way.	I like it that way.	It must be that way.	I am neutral.	I can live with it that way.	I dislike it that way.

13.a. If Asia World Bank offers a customized strategy for your banking needs created by a financial advisor, how do you feel?

   b. If Asia World Bank does not offer a customized strategy for your banking needs created by a financial advisor, how do you feel?

14.a. If Asia World Bank provides product introduction seminars for customers, how do you feel?

   b. If Asia World Bank does not provide product introduction seminars for customers, how do you feel?

15.a. If you could obtain investment advice by phoning a toll-free number, how would you feel?

   b. If you could not obtain investment advice by phoning a toll-free number, how would you feel?

16.a. If you chose to conduct the majority of your bank business using online technology, how would you feel about paying a monthly fee for the service?

   b. If you chose to conduct the majority of your bank business using online technology, how would you feel about not paying a monthly fee for the service?

How many different banks do you do business with? _____

Kano Model Survey *(concluded)*

Asia World Bank Kano Model Questionnaire Results

| # Banks | 1 | 2 | 1 | 2 | 1 | 1 | 2 | 2 |
| Age | 26—39 | 26—39 | 40—60 | 40—60 | 40—60 | 26—39 | 26—39 | Over 60 |
Gender	Female	Female	Female	Male	Male	Male	Male	Male
1. Saturday hours	P	P	I	I	I	T	I	I
2. Email to banker	P	I	P	I	T	T	T	I
3. Safe ATMs	P	P	P	I	P	T	E	B
4. 8—5, M—F	U	I	T	I	U	T	I	U
5. ATM in grocery	P	I	I	I	I	T	I	I
6. Online banking	B	P	P	I	T	P	B	I
7. Local solutions	B	P	P	P	B	P	I	P
8. Online solutions	B	P	P	I	E	I	P	I
9. Wide product choice	P	I	P	I	P	P	T	I
10. Limited product choice	E	I	E	I	E	E	I	I
11. CDs online	B	I	P	I	P	T	T	I
12. Branch investment advice	P	I	I	I	P	P	I	E
13. Customized financial advice	P	I	I	T	P	T	T	E
14. Seminars for customers	B	I	I	I	I	T	T	E
15. Phone advice	P	I	E	I	E	I	P	E
16. Fee for online access	E	I	E	E	E	E	E	E

Basic/Must Be	B
Performance/One-Dimensional	P
Thrill/Attractive	T
Indifferent	I
Opposed/Reverse	O
Unusable/Questionable	U

Kano Model Questionnaire Results

Asia World Bank House of Quality Diagram

Customer Attributes	Importance	Fast, Stable, & Secure Technology	ATM Technology	Online Technology	Empowered Employees	Employee Training	Product Knowledge	Empathy for Customers	Good Verbal Communication Skills	Streamlined Loan Approval	Custom Tailored Service	Extended Service Hours	Efficient Operations	Flexible Work Schedules	Good Morale	Low Turnover of Employees	Good Pay & Benefits
		Technology			Training					Operations				Human Resources			
Willingness & Ability to Solve Problems	1	0	0	+	+	+	+	+	+	+	+	+	+	+	+	+	+
Fast Service	2	+	+	+	+	+	+	0	+	+	-	+	+	+	+	+	0
Product Choice	3	0	+	+	0	+	+	0	0	-	+	0	-	0	0	0	0
Security	4	+	+	+	-	+	0	+	0	+	0	-	+	-	+	+	+
Convenience	5	+	+	+	0	0	+	0	+	+	+	+	+	+	0	+	0
Good Advice	6	0	0	0	+	+	+	+	+	0	+	0	0	0	+	+	0
Competitive Price	7	-	-	-	0	-	0	0	0	+	-	-	+	-	0	+	-
Friendly Service	8	0	0	0	+	+	0	+	+	0	+	0	0	+	+	+	+

House of Quality Diagram

Chapter 4

Customer Satisfaction

Chapter Objectives:

- *Understand the importance of customer satisfaction to company performance.*
- *Differentiate between the 'should' and 'is' factors of customer satisfaction.*
- *Discuss the different levels of customer satisfaction utilizing the Customer Satisfaction Development Model.*
- *Elaborate on the theory of Cognitive Dissonance.*
- *Discuss how Contrast Theory and Assimilation Contrast Theory relate to Cognitive Dissonance.*
- *Explain the advantages of a continuous customer satisfaction study for an organization.*
- *Discuss the eight phases of a customer satisfaction study.*
- *Distinguish between the two subjective forms of customer satisfaction measurement.*

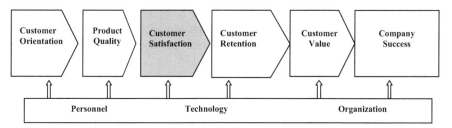

Figure 4.1: The concept and relevance of customer satisfaction

The Concept and Relevance of Customer Satisfaction

If one wants to elucidate the phenomenon of customer retention, it is first necessary to come up with a clear, conceptual definition of the notion of satisfaction. In order to be able to retain customers, companies must be able to satisfy the needs and desires of their customers. The English word 'satisfaction' stems from the Latin, from the words 'satis' (enough) and 'facere' (to make). In light of these early findings, one can say that customer satisfaction is all about 'doing enough for the customer' (Rust, Zahorik & Keinigham, 1996, p. 229). In its general use, the concept of satisfaction indicates psychological states such as well-being, happiness, and contentment.

To achieve a customer's satisfaction, it is necessary to be aware of his expectations, and to be knowledgeable of what he likes and does not like. It is not uncommon for companies to hold the satisfaction of a customer to be self-evident, or for them to believe that their long relationship with a customer allows them to exactly know their level of satisfaction. A low rate of complaint is very often rashly equated with customer satisfaction. However, this is frequently a misconception. Experience shows that only about four percent of all unsatisfied customers complain; the other 96 percent keep to themselves, deciding to switch companies (Wilson, 1991, p. 134).

Some impressive research results and empirical values, coming from various fields, concerning the economic affect of customer satisfaction, will be brought together in the following section. They show the importance, meaning and benefit of customer satisfaction for a company (Töpfer & Mann, 1999, p. 60).

Examples from various fields:

- It is about 600 percent more expensive to get new customers than to keep the existing ones.
- With satisfied customers the chance is about 300 percent higher that they will stay, than it is in the case of unsatisfied customers.
- The chance that very satisfied customers will become the best form of advertising for a company is almost as high as 100 percent.
- 95 percent of annoyed customers will stay loyal, if the problem can be solved within five days.
- 75 percent of customers who switch to the competition do so because of being disturbed by poor service quality.
- 25 percent of customers who switch to the competition do so because of being bothered by inadequate goods or too high of a price.
- Over 30 percent of American service provider expenses originate in improvement expenditure.
- Over 30 percent of annual sales revenue is forgone due to the correction of errors by the average American company.
- Every percentage point of sustained customer satisfaction amounts to a 7.25 percent climb in the return on investment (ROI).
- If the customer rejection rate is reduced by five percent, thereby enhancing customer commitment, this amounts to a 28–85 percent increase in profit.

Customer Satisfaction Viewed According to a Theoretical Model

In its classical definition, customer satisfaction is the degree of correspondence between the expectations that a potential customer has for a product or service, and the perceived service that is in fact provided. If the perceived service fulfills or exceeds the standard of comparison it is based on, customer satisfaction arises.

A service that falls short in comparison to expectations leads to dissatisfaction. In the prior chapter, we discussed how the Kano method can be used in order to determine which product and service features are expected as part of the basic offering, and which features help to pleasantly surprise the customer, which increases customer satisfaction.

Objectively measurable customer satisfaction results therefore, from an inner process of comparison between:

- The personal needs, wishes, and expectations of customers on the one hand (the 'should' factor) and;
- The perceived quality of products and services on the other hand (the 'is' factor).

From that the following relationship can be derived:

Should < Is	=>	**Convinced Customer**
Should = Is	=>	**Ostensibly Satisfied Customer**
Should > Is	=>	**Disappointed Customer**

Figure 4.2: Origination of customer satisfaction

The 'Should' Factor (Level of Standard)

The 'should' factor (also known as 'should service') is understood to be the sum of ideas and expectations with regard to a product or company service, (like for example, friendly and helpful salespeople, informed advice, reasonable price, high quality, a long guarantee period, etc.). The 'should' factor is influenced by the following factors (Rapp, 1995, pp. 31–32):

- **Personal Needs**
  The expectations regarding a company's service are strongly influenced by the individual standards of varying customers (a customer who uses his PC for working at home has different standards than a customer who uses his PC for multimedia purposes).
- **Extent of Experience**
  All of a customer's prior experiences create an important basis for their expectations concerning a company's service (a customer who has worked a lot with different PCs has different expectations than a non-professional).
- **Direct Communication Regarding the Company's Service**
  Direct communication by the company via public media or private communication is a decisive factor with regard to the customer's expectations (a customer expects definite service features which have been promised in advertisements and by salespeople).

- **Indirect Communication Regarding the Company's Service**
  Indirect communication includes word of mouth between friends and acquaintances, communication concerning a spectrum of service via independent media (for example, consumer organizations which provide an independent product/service rating service, like the German consumer safety group known as Stiftung Warentest, or like Consumer Reports in the United States), or communication stemming from the competition regarding the same or a comparable company service.

In the end, the actual experience of a product is evaluated on the basis of expectations. The 'should' factor represents the standard of comparison for evaluating a product. The standard of comparison that a customer's expectations are based on is not always the same. One can differentiate the following standards:

- **Expected Performance**
  That which the customer can expect based on prior experience. This standard of comparison is made up of experiences with the same or similar products (also with other brands).
- **Desired Performance**
  What the customer ideally imagines. The optimum standard of comparison is being used here.
- **Minimum Tolerable Performance**
  This is the minimum that a customer can expect.
- **Adequate Performance**
  What the customer sees as being reasonable, and which can be achieved according to reasonable means.
- **Product Type Norms**
  Normally present level of standard. According to this standard of comparison the normal or the typical is expected.
- **Best Brand Norms**
  The level of standards that are present with the best choices currently being offered.
- **Comparison Level**
  Experience with similar products, or knowledge of those that other consumers have received. Here the relationship between costs and benefits is decisive.

There is no general answer as to which standard of comparison a customer will apply. The complex structure and dynamic quality of people's expectations make generalizations impossible. As legendary economist John Kenneth Galbraith has said, 'There is certainly no absolute standard of beauty. That precisely is what makes its pursuit so interesting.' (Galbraith, 1967, p. 221). For this reason, the standard of comparison can take on various forms, according to each individual and according to each situation.

The 'Is' Factor (Perception)

The 'is' factor (also known as 'is service') characterizes the actual, perceived experience of the customers in their use or consumption of the product. It is only with the help of this factor that the customers can establish whether their expectations have been fulfilled.

For the customer, the perceived service is of paramount importance. Here it is crucial to establish that the reality of the good or service which is being sold is not the only consideration; all services, features, and warranties which are bound up with it should also be encompassed. As is shown in Figure 4.3, in order to assess the firm's ability to meet the 'is factor' for its customers, there is a need to view the entire product and service experience through the eyes of the customer.

Homburg and Rudolph (1998, p. 41) differentiate between the objective and subjective service. The objective service is the actually received service. This is the same for all customers. The subjectively perceived offer is revealed by the level of standards, and by the expectations of various customers being placed in relationship to the service. Therefore, as a result of a varying level of standards, an individually perceived product-service results. Only by appropriately orienting the business toward the satisfaction of the needs of the customers will a firm be able to understand what the majority of its customers' desire.

A 'Should' and 'Is' Comparison of Customer Satisfaction

The 'should' and 'is' comparison leads to a fulfillment or non-fulfillment of expectations. The feeling of satisfaction or dissatisfaction originates from the individual evaluation of their feelings concerning the shopping or purchasing experience. Depending on whether the customer is satisfied or dissatisfied, different behavior reactions can be derived:

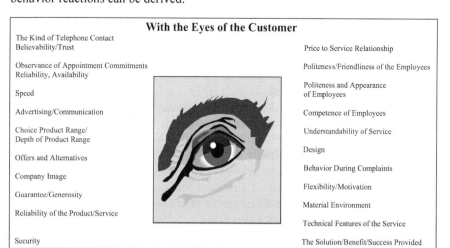

With the Eyes of the Customer

The Kind of Telephone Contact
Believability/Trust

Observance of Appointment Commitments
Reliability, Availability

Speed

Advertising/Communication

Choice Product Range/
Depth of Product Range

Offers and Alternatives

Company Image

Guarantee/Generosity

Reliability of the Product/Service

Security

Price to Service Relationship

Politeness/Friendliness of the Employees

Politeness and Appearance
of Employees

Competence of Employees

Understandability of Service

Design

Behavior During Complaints

Flexibility/Motivation

Material Environment

Technical Features of the Service

The Solution/Benefit/Success Provided

Figure 4.3: The customer's perception of quality
(Meyer, Dornach & Muller, 1998, p. 30)

From dissatisfaction there arises, for the customer, the following possibilities for action:

- **Rejection**
  In the case of a rejection (also known as a defection), the customer has the option of either a change of business, brand, or product, or he may opt to entirely relinquish the product. In the case of a change of business, the customers stay with the same product, but they get that product from another provider. An unhappy Mercedes driver, for example, may stay with their brand, but the customer will get a new car from a different car dealer. In the case of a brand change, dissatisfied consumers decide to give their business to a competing brand. This would be in the case where the above-mentioned Mercedes driver would opt to buy an Audi instead. In a product change, the customers decide in favor of a different product category. The customer remains true to their service provider, but they opt for another product. The last possibility open to a customer is to relinquish the current product altogether.
- **Negative Word of Mouth Advertising**
  Negative word of mouth advertising entails dissatisfied customers disclosing negative opinions concerning the product or company. According to a well-established marketing literature rule of thumb—that negative word of mouth propaganda is ten times as effective as positive customer feedback—the ramifications of this form of negative advertising are considerable. Bad news travels faster than good news.
- **Complaints**
  This is the individual form of rejection. The consumer encounters the company directly and complains about a defective product or faulty service.

Satisfied customers have the following possibilities for action:

- **Cross-Selling**
  Cross-selling means that satisfied customers will be prepared to buy other products from a provider. Why should a customer who is happy with the quality of a company's product and service opt for another provider?
- **Customer Commitment**
  Customer commitment describes the constancy of a customer's contact with a company, which is understood as a special bond, and which is based on voluntary choice and satisfaction (Fest, 1999, p. 106).
- **Decreasing Price Sensitivity**
  The introduction of higher prices is easier with satisfied customers than it is with unsatisfied customers. Consumers who can trust in a company's quality and service are as a rule also prepared to pay more.
- **Positive Word of Mouth Advertising**
  Positive word of mouth advertising entails satisfied consumers telling other people positive things about the company or product. The customer will actively recommend the product or service.

The preceding discussion helps to further expand upon the ideas expressed by the economist Albert O. Hirschman in his classic book, 'Exit, Voice, & Loyalty' (Hirschman, 1972). Hirschman's view was that customers and employees had the three primary options, which were referenced in the book's title, for dealing with an organizational decline. It will become apparent to the reader that these three options of exiting the firm, voicing concern for the organizational decline, or remaining loyal to the firm are in the main determined by whether a customer is satisfied with the overall performance of the firm. In Hirschman's view, the more disenchanted an individual was with the organization, the more likely they were to exit. Hirschman's work set the stage for subsequent studies on customer satisfaction as have been discussed in this chapter. In the following section, the topic of variety seeking (see Figure 4.4), which has attracted increasing scientific interest in recent years, will be dealt with in detail.

Variety seeking is the phenomenon whereby consumers display an inclination for change that can be traced back to a need for variety (Haseborg & Mäßen, 1997, p. 164). This inclination has led to variety seeking being identified as an important factor in the description, prognosis, and control of consumer behavior.

The tendency of variety seeking is understood as a personality trait of consumers that display a 'desire for a new and novel stimulus' (Hoyer & Ridgway, 1983, p. 115) (individual specific definition). People strive according to behavior aimed at an inner level of stimulus that is experienced as satisfying or comfortable. In this context a fundamental need for stimulus is being assumed. The necessary stimulus offers new, diverse, and intense impressions. In the area of consumer behavior, stimulation, with the satisfaction it brings in relation to the consumer's need for variety, is evoked through the use of various products. The consumer who is endeavoring to achieve his optimal level of stimulus will examine his environment for those stimuli that serve to satisfy and maintain this level of stimulus. The various products that characterize his

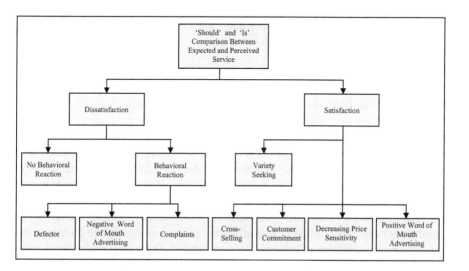

Figure 4.4: The reaction of customers when dissatisfied or satisfied

environment enable the maintenance, alteration, and satisfaction of his inner level of stimulus. For example, through variety seeking a consumer can return to balance motives like curiosity, boredom (satiety), or the need for uniqueness or exclusivity (McAlister & Pessemier, 1982, p. 312).

The behavior of variety seekers reveals itself through an individual specific assessment, and likewise through a product-oriented assessment (product specific definition). It is of note that generally the tendency for variety seeking becomes more marked when the number of product alternatives increases, when there is a lower perceived difference between the products, when the brand trust is low, and when the perceived product risk is low (Hoyer & Ridgway, 1983, pp. 116–117).

Additionally, there arises the possibility of a study that is product feature specific (product feature specific definition). 'For an individual consumer, particular product features will come under more consideration than others, in terms of satisfying the need for variety. For example, a consumer may, in the choice and consumption of soft drinks, on one occasion opt for a fruity drink, and another time for a less fruity drink, which in both cases must be caffeine free' (Haseborg & Mäßen, 1997, p. 165).

The assessment of variety seeking offers an explanation for the often-observed fact that customers will also change a provider or product, even when they are satisfied with this provider or product. It can be shown, in the context of an empirical study concerning a well-known German automobile manufacturer, that variety seeking exercises a considerable negative influence on the factor of customer commitment (Peter, 1998, pp. 77–79). Clearly, a significant development of the personality feature of variety seeking leads to customers abandoning products or providers, even in the case of high customer satisfaction. For the organization therefore, it is of decisive importance how many of its customers are variety seekers and/or to what extent the current product encourages variety seeking. A lasting relationship to the customer is not, in this case, attained via the optimization of customer satisfaction, but instead is more likely achieved through measures that technically, economically, psychologically, or emotionally persuade the customer to commit, so that the commitment supersedes the wish for change.

Customer Satisfaction Development

The 'should' and 'is' comparison explained above provides a starting point for securing the present satisfaction of the customer. From this status quo model measures can be derived which raise customer satisfaction on the basis of present standards. As necessary as this information is for raising customer satisfaction, it is limited to present customer standards and does not live up to the demands of proactive management. Proactive management anticipates future customer or market standards and develops corresponding strategies.

The following Customer Satisfaction Development (CSD) model is an assessment that not only takes into effect the present wishes of the customer; but also the future standards of customers are considered. The model's foundation relies on Bruggemann's (1974, pp. 281–284) process-oriented notion for attaining work satisfaction. This model is illustrated in Figure 4.5.

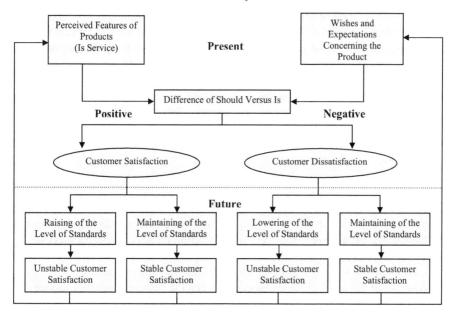

Figure 4.5: Model assessment toward the analysis of customer satisfaction

The present satisfaction or dissatisfaction of a customer results from the 'should' and 'is' comparison. When viewed in the long term, this leads to maintenance, lowering, or raising of the individual level of standards. If the product or service adds up to expectations, then maintenance of the level of standards is achieved. However, if the actual product and the expectations concerning it drift apart from each other, then either a raising or lowering of individual level of standards occurs.

Raising of the level of standards: unstable customer satisfaction
The rising of the level of standards represents each situation where the perceived product service highly exceeds the personal expectations of the customer. Thus, the customer is pleased to the highest extent with the product or with the services accompanying the product.

This phenomenon is none more apparent than in the personal computer industry. In this business, every innovation results in customer expectations being raised. While not long ago customers were satisfied with simple functions and application possibilities, today a very impressively outfitted computer is standard equipment. It is becoming apparent here that customer satisfaction is not a goal that is attainable once and for all. Instead it is a continuously developing, dynamic target.

Maintenance of the level of standards: stable customer satisfaction
If perceptions more or less positively correspond with expectations, then one can speak of stabilized customer satisfaction. The customer is satisfied and constantly maintains their level of standards. Marketing research however, is unanimous in finding that the exact fulfillment of expectations is neither simple, nor reflective

of the optimal state of affairs. This kind of customer satisfaction is effective from a short-term perspective, but in the long term it threatens the loss of customers. If a competitor reacts first to raised customer needs and wishes, and loss of market share to the competition ensues, then clearly the firm should have erected barriers to change earlier, which could have hindered or made impossible a customer's turning to a competitor's product. But this does not take into account the appropriate long-term strategy for a customer-centric company. Erecting barriers after the fact is a reactionary way of doing business, and it is advisable that a company be more proactive in order to successfully anticipate the future needs and desires of its customers.

The goal of a company should therefore be to continuously exceed the consumer's expectations, in that the company again and again enriches with additional benefits, qualitatively improves, and technologically develops what it has to offer. In other words, the objective should be to keep in focus the goal of steadily raising the level of standards, because only this form of satisfaction furthers long-term success.

Lowering of the level of standards: unstable customer satisfaction
Lowering of the level of standards occurs when the perceived product service does not correspond with expectations. The customer is not satisfied. There may be a few reasons for this. Either the customer's expectations are too high, or the service is, in fact, unsatisfactory (or both). In this situation, it is necessary for the company to know how its customers behave when dissatisfied, because only then can they understand how and where they can apply the appropriate marketing techniques, so that the customer can be brought back into a state of satisfaction.

Maintenance of the level of standards: stable customer satisfaction
Stable customer satisfaction exists when perceptions more or less negatively correspond with the customer's expectations. This case may manifest itself according to circumstances in oligarchic states or in monopolies. Even if a customer is not happy with the provider or the product, they do not have the possibility of choosing from alternative offers. Either there are no similar providers around, like the way it was in Germany and in the United States during the telephone monopolies, or a change to another company involves enormously high costs for the customer. An example of this is private health insurance in Germany. The decision for a private health insurance company is usually a lifetime decision, because to change back later to public health insurance is only possible in exceptional cases. Switching later to another private health insurance company is also rarely worthwhile, in that the insured in most cases loses the already accumulated payments. In this way, the customer is persuaded to remain with his current provider in spite of dissatisfaction.

Another example would be the liberalization of the electricity market in Germany. Recently, state utility companies have become openly critical of the private companies they have agreed to allow to use their power grid infrastructure. The state utility companies have continuously been coming up with new strategies in order to keep customers, like for example, in the high fees for changing companies, and/or the extra fees for using their grid infrastructure. Since 1998, 2.1 percent of households have managed to leave their former (state) company. Competition in the utility market exists, therefore, only on paper, despite warnings from the antitrust commission and quite a few legal actions (Delhaes, 2001, p. 136).

On the basis of the CSD model assessment, a portfolio can be derived, which, in connection with information having to do with individual customer segments, can reveal which measures and strategic decisions a company must initiate and realize in order to achieve a higher level of customer satisfaction in the future.

Faultfinders are customers whose level of standards sink or remain constant, and who are not satisfied with the present service. The focus of strategic measures lies here in the area of price management. This group of malcontents are typically very price conscious, and are apt to consider other competing products if the price is right.

Travelers are customers whose level of standards increase, and who are not satisfied with the present service. The focus of strategic measures here lies in the area of improving the company's quality of service. In an environment that is not customer oriented, the ability to understand the nature of the lack of satisfaction may be lost, as would be the business for the firm. By seeking feedback from the customers, there remains the possibility of keeping them with the firm once their needs are met.

Convenients are customers whose level of standards remain constant and who are satisfied with the present service. The focus of strategic measures here lies in the area of quality assurance. These are customers who are most likely to remain loyal, unless there is a perceived drop in the quality of the product service provided.

Pushers are customers whose level of standards increase, and who are satisfied with the present service. The focus of strategic measures here lies in the area of the company's capacity for innovation. These are the customers who in effect push the firm to continuously improve their level of product service.

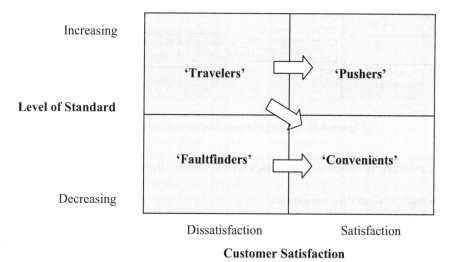

Figure 4.6: Relationship between level of standards and customer satisfaction

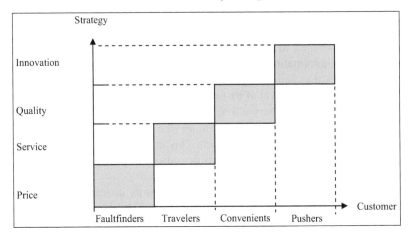

Figure 4.7: Strategic focus with regard to different customer types

In the area of CSD experience, it has been shown that the raising of customer satisfaction often has less to do with so-called hard factors like organization and technology, but instead is something that is dependent on the capacities of management and employees. In order to successfully put to use the knowledge gleaned from the portfolio analysis, it is necessary to draw the appropriate consequences at the level of management, and to activate the potential of managers and employees toward the optimal realization of strategic goals. Toward this end, in the area of CSD, the management screening method is used for potential analysis and potential development.

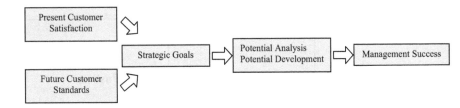

Figure 4.8: Strategic goals and potential development

Customer Satisfaction from a Behavioral Science Perspective

Theory of Cognitive Dissonance

The theory of cognitive dissonance developed by Festinger (1957) operates under the assumption that individuals strive to maintain or to regain the freedom to object to thought processes. Engaging cognitions like opinions, values, items of knowledge, and also feelings, for an individual in an *imbalance* (this is labeled as cognitive dissonance), manifest as uncomfortable psychic tension.

Festinger's basic assumption is that every individual is seeking cognitive consonance (harmony), and so when disturbed by dissonance, the person seeks to eliminate this state by reducing the dissonance. This takes place according to the following possibilities (Wottawa & Gluminstri, 1995, p. 164):

• The addition of new cognitions that may encourage consonance or reduce dissonance.
• Rejection or suppression of the dissonant cognition (subtraction).
• Exchange of the dissonant cognition with consonant cognition (substitution).

Dissonance can also arise in various phases of the purchasing process (Nieschlag, Dichtl & Hörschgen, 1994, p. 558):

• After the acquisition of information that contradicts earlier experience or which alters information and decision behavior.
• After the decision to purchase (post decisional dissonance), in cases where the customer has relinquished positive aspects of the rejected option, and has accepted negative aspects of the chosen option. This shows itself in various ways: for one, in the reevaluation of the chosen option to the credit of the rejected option; another way is via the weakening of assurance that a correct decision has been made; and thirdly via selective seeking for consonant information (confirmation).
• During use of the product, if the product does not correspond with expectations.

In order to satisfy the customers, it is important to guarantee the presence of consonance-inducing information during the course of the entire purchasing process. Although consonance-inducing measures are important, the task is not to allow cognitive dissonance to arise in the first place.

The customer is especially receptive to consonant information in the post purchase phase. This is substantiated by a study done concerning the rate of cancellation of purchase contracts in the automobile sector.

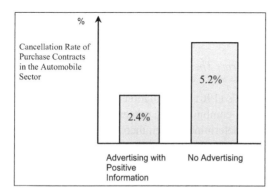

Figure 4.9: Cancellation rate of purchase contracts in the automobile sector after consonant information (Donnelly & Ivancevich, 1970, pp. 339–400)

As you can see from Figure 4.9, the study concluded that positive advertising did help to reduce the level of purchase contract cancellations in the automobile sector. In connection with the theme of 'customer satisfaction', it is often concluded on the basis of the theory of cognitive dissonance that reducing dissonance may be all that is required, owing to the tendency of experiences adapting to expectations. It is important to meet high product standards, which results in higher levels of customer satisfaction. However, this assumption leaves out of consideration at what level of dissonance the above process no longer applies, and where other behavior patterns (e.g., switching products) arise. This will be explained in more detail below.

The Contrast Theory

The contrast theory is based on Helson's 'adaption level theory' (1964), and states that a person corrects their perceptions when expectations and performance do not correspond. In this case, however, in contrast to the theory of cognitive dissonance, the difference is exaggerated. This can arise in two ways (Homburg & Rudolph, 1998, pp. 34–35):

- If the performance is worse than expectations, the person corrects his perceptions such that the product or service appears worse than it actually is.
- If the performance is better than expectations, the person will separate their perceptions from their expectations and overvalue the product or service.

A sports analogy might make this concept easier to understand. Assume that an individual is a recreational tennis player, and has had much success in defeating other players in the neighborhood. Due to this success, the individual decides to join the city tennis league, where the majority of the players have played competitive tennis at the high school or university level in the past. Since the recreational player is used to winning, a stunning loss or a streak of losses may make the recreational player question his ability. It may not have been that the recreational player performed any worse than previously, only the level of the competition had improved. The recreational player must adjust their perception of their own ability in order to deal with the situation. This same scenario can appear in the marketplace, where there is a tendency of perceiving the quality of service to be much worse than it actually was, just because the service was beneath the customer's level of expectations.

The Assimilation Contrast Theory

In Sherif and Hovland's (1961) assimilation contrast theory, the propositions of the preceding theories are combined. The perceived discrepancy between the '*should*' and '*is*' performance determines which theory will come into play. If the perceived service departs only negligibly from expectations, then it still falls in the area of the customer's assumptions. The customer tends to align their perceptions with their expectations, in order to assimilate them. If the discrepancy passes the level of tolerance, then the contrast effect sets in.

Revisiting our recreational tennis-playing friend, the key to a successful improvement in the city league will be in how they deal with the increased level of competition. If the recreational player expected some setbacks in the city league in an effort to improve their game, then it is less likely that the contrast effect would set in. Having realistic performance expectations goes a long way to eliminating the discrepancies between '*should*' and '*is*' performance.

Measuring Customer Satisfaction

The Goal of Measuring Customer Satisfaction

Like all company activities, striving for customer satisfaction is subject to the economical imperative. This means that the results of a customer satisfaction analysis must bring in more than it costs. The satisfaction of a customer is accordingly a means to increase profit (Simon & Homburg, 1998, p. 30).

Customer satisfaction can only be implemented as a strategic venture. Therefore, the goal of customer satisfaction research should be to present the customer situation as much as possible objectively and all-inclusively. To that end, some basic standards of measurement can be employed. These standards should be employed:

- systematically
- regularly
- objectively
- pervasively – in a way that is differentiated according to market segments (e.g. regions, states, customer groups, branches).

The advantages of a continuous study of customer satisfaction are obvious:

- **Customer-oriented Management**
  During the course of a customer satisfaction analysis, a customer shares their goals, needs, and wishes. The company is thereby given the opportunity to adjust what it has to offer to the expectations and perceptions of the customer. Because of reliable feedback received from the customer's side, it is possible for the company to guide its actions toward establishing and assuring a long-term relationship with the customer.
- **Comparison with the Competition**
  A customer will only maintain a relationship with a company if the products and services being offered lead to satisfaction and are better than alternative offers. Therefore, it is of fundamental importance that a company compares its service with that of competitors.
- **Comparison over Time**
  It is important for a company to not only use satisfaction studies to ascertain possible sources of satisfaction or dissatisfaction, but to also use them for analyzing and deriving possible strategies for action. Via regular studies, comparisons can be derived with regard to product and service quality over a given time period.

• **Profit from Specific Insights**
Through innovation and strategic changes, the rapid and early attainment of customer satisfaction can be an advantage. By goal-oriented teamwork, products and services can be developed or directly adjusted to the expectations of potential customers.

The Eight Phases of a Customer Satisfaction Study

A measurement of customer satisfaction can be divided into eight phases

Phase 1: establishment of the study's subject matter and goals
In this phase, it must be clarified who should be surveyed. In the study, existing customers, former customers, and the competition's customers should be included. For the different groups there are naturally different research goals.

Phase 2: exploratory phase
In general, the exploratory phase consists of extensive discussions with customers, during which it should be discovered what customer standards and expectations are being applied to the product or service. Out of that analysis will come insights helpful for the choice and design of appropriate study methods.

Phase 3: choice and design of study methods
In this phase, decisions are made concerning the type of survey (complete survey or sample survey), the survey method (telephone survey, written survey, or personal interview), and the format of the questions (open or closed questions). The type of survey will typically be decided based on the size of the total population being surveyed (if large, then a sample is appropriate). The survey method is also dictated based on the size of the customer base, as well as based on the sensitivity of the questions being asked. Generally, it is preferable to offer some open-ended questions if you are unsure how the survey respondents will respond.

Phase 4: pretest
In the pretest phase the chosen study method should be tested on a small number of customers (about 20 people). If flaws show themselves in this phase, then the method needs to be reworked. A company can save time and money by including a test phase.

Phase 5: implementation of the study
In this phase, the study is carried out. Before the actual survey, the customer should be given notice via a letter of what is to come. In this way, the distance between the questioner and the questioned is reduced and the motivation to cooperate is increased. After the study, it is advisable, via an additional mailing, to allow the customer an opportunity to provide feedback.

Phase 6: analysis of study data

After the implementation phase comes the analysis of the collected data. Here three alternatives can be differentiated:

- Descriptive analysis, which processes data graphically (average value, modal value, median).
- Univariate and bivariate procedures, which reveal correlations or differences between one or two variables, for example relationships between price and sales volume.
- Multivariate procedures that serve the purpose of studying several variables, like for example, regression or cluster analysis. The objective of regression analysis consists of an examination of relationships between one dependent (metrically scaled) variable and, as a rule, several independent (metrically scaled) variables. The dividing up of variables into dependent and independent variables is done in advance due to a logical relationship. Regression analysis is subject to a definite direction of the relationship, which is not reversible (dependence analysis). Cluster analysis has as its goal to bring a number of objects (people, products, companies), according to their similarity, into a natural order of groups or classes that are differentiated from each other. The groups, formed in this way, should differ from each other as much as possible in that the objects contained in them, with regard to the studied properties or distinctive characteristics, display a marked homogeneity not shared with contrasting groups (Meffert, 2000, pp. 165–169). Thus, in cluster analysis, measurement of a correlation, and additionally a rectifying development between variables, is in the foreground (interdependence analysis).

The overriding goal in the interpretation of data is the identifying of weak points, in order to proceed with eliminating them via focused improvement efforts.

Phase 7: formulation of plans of action

On the basis of evaluated data, corresponding approaches to action can now be formulated toward the enhancement of satisfaction. Since not all of the surveyed criterion influence satisfaction to an equal extent, improvement of measures should be initiated, which presumably will have the greatest influence on customer satisfaction.

Phase 8: implementation of plans of action

The implemented plans of action for the enhancement of customer satisfaction should be regularly reviewed and analyzed with regard to their success or lack thereof. In this way emerging weak points can be identified early on, reengineered and debugged.

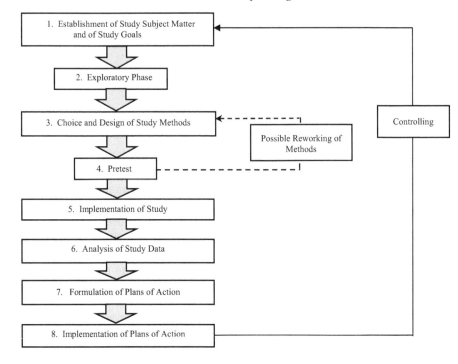

Figure 4.10: The eight phases of a customer satisfaction study

Procedures for Measuring Customer Satisfaction

In the literature, the following classification of procedures for measuring customer satisfaction has prevailed. Accordingly, the procedures are broken down with regard to measuring satisfaction within subjective or objective procedures.

Objective procedures for measuring customer satisfaction
Objective procedures rest on the observation of verifiable and definitely measurable criteria, like, for example:

- sales
- profit
- market share
- rate of repurchase
- rate of customer loss

The conclusiveness of these economic figures is, to be sure, often rather limited. Other factors of influence, like, for example the competitive situation, market growth, new innovations, etcetera, also qualify these indicators. Rising profit cannot necessarily be traced back to rising customer satisfaction. In practice, the employment of subjective procedures is more advisable.

Subjective procedures for measuring customer satisfaction
These procedures do not involve any directly observable quantities, but rather determine values indicating the customer's subjectively perceived level of satisfaction. Feature-oriented and event-oriented procedures can here be differentiated:

- **Feature-oriented Procedures**
  Feature-oriented procedures are based on the assumption that all of a customer's experience of satisfaction can be traced back to an assessment of the individual features of the product. In feature-oriented procedures, there is a differentiation between implicit and explicit measurement.
  Implicit measurement is shown via the systematic recording and study of complaint behavior, for example. In this context, active complaint behavior is assumed. In reality, however, this is often not a given. According to various empirical studies, high time expenditure, poor prospects of success, or anger connected with the problem, are all reasons why customers take no measures to make a complaint. Accordingly, companies who take a low rate of complaint to be an index of customer satisfaction are typically in error.
  Explicit methods of satisfaction are measured on the basis of one-dimensional or multidimensional satisfaction scales.
  One-dimensional procedures measure customer satisfaction on the basis of one of several indicators (e.g. overall satisfaction). However, this leads to problems if conclusions are to be drawn as to which factors in particular are responsible for the dissatisfaction of customers. One-dimensional procedures make it very hard to stack rank the indicators of customer satisfaction.
  Multidimensional procedures lead to convincing judgments, because several different services are assessed. This is conducive to finding out the state of overall satisfaction. Basically, they are quite practical, and gather the positive as well as the negative judgments of customers. On the other hand, even these procedures exhibit disadvantages; as a rule they do not gather all relevant data, and are not in the position to portray individual psychological processes or consumer experiences completely, concretely, and with the necessary urgency.

- **Event-oriented Procedures**
  Event-oriented measuring procedures disclose customer satisfaction on the basis of actual events during the consuming process. Of the most important variations, the critical incident technique and the sequential incident technique are here of note. These measuring methods are for finding out about experiences relevant to satisfaction, for identifying experienced customer problems, and for the determination of minimum and value increasing qualities. There are disadvantages with regard to standardization and comparability. Their suitability as guiding information is consequently not as highly valued as that of feature-oriented procedures.

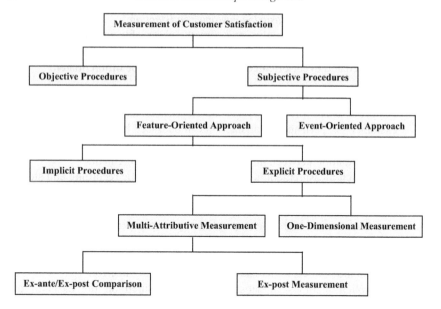

Figure 4.11: Procedures for measuring customer satisfaction (Homburg & Werner, 1998, p. 133; Topfer & Mann, 1999, pp. 59–110)

Questions for Discussion

1. How is customer satisfaction defined at your company or university? Describe how customer satisfaction can be best measured at your organization.

2. Provide some examples when the level of service that you received was less than your expectations. What led to the level of experience being less than what you desired? What was the result of your experience? Make sure to use the 'should' and 'is' terminology in your answers.

3. What are some suggested strategies for a firm to best alleviate customer losses due to the variety-seeking phenomenon?

4. Using the CSD model, discuss how the four different customer types (faultfinders, travelers, convenients, and pushers) are influencing the standards of service in the banking, automotive, and information technology industries.

5. How has the understanding of customer satisfaction expanded since Albert O. Hirschman's famous book, *Exit, Voice, & Loyalty* first appeared in the 1970s?

6. Using the eight phases of a customer satisfaction study, discuss how such a study could be implemented successfully in your company or university.

Chapter 5

Customer Retention

Chapter Objectives:

- *Understand the difference between being constrained and being loyal.*
- *Describe the five categories of the causes of commitment.*
- *Elaborate on the advantages of customer retention.*
- *Discuss methodologies for achieving customer retention.*
- *Describe the benefits of creating customer clubs and customer cards.*
- *Elaborate on the importance of an effective complaint management system.*
- *Describe the process and the benefits of CHAID for improving customer retention.*

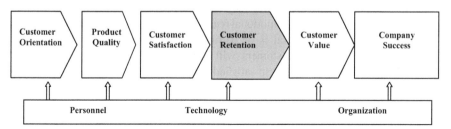

Figure 5.1: Concept and relevance of customer retention

The Concept and Relevance of Customer Retention

Customer retention, with regard to customer satisfaction, is becoming increasingly significant, because customers today have the opportunity to choose from such a large range of products and services, and because the competition within various markets is becoming ever fiercer. Following the adage that one has to invest six times as much in a new customer as in an already existing one, companies are discovering new potential in the building up and maintenance of a stable customer base. This is the source of commercial success and long-term growth. In the area of mobile phones in Germany, for example, the future race for who is accumulating customers the fastest will have to take place without the market leader, D2. This strengthens the declaration of Jürgen von Kucklowski, Chairman of the executive board at Mannesman Mobilfunk, 'If in two years we're only number two in the German market in terms of the number of customers, but we're on the top in terms of service and maintenance of value, I'll be able to live with that.' (Berke, 2004). The mobile service provider of the future will bolster itself through nurturing current client relationships, and by concentrating on more developed customer loyalty programs, rather than on acquiring new customers. If a company can manage to lower its customer loss rate by about five percent, they can, depending on the industry increase their profit by as much as 85 percent, according to empirical studies (Töpfer, 1996, p. 92).

Bliemel and Eggert (1998, p. 38) understand customer retention to be a, 'System of activities for enhancing the transaction process, on the basis of the positive positioning of the customer, and the resultant readiness for successive purchasing.' Homburg and Bruhn's definition puts more emphasis on the guiding of customer retention. They speak of customer commitment management. This, 'Comprises all of a company's measures which are targeted at the positive shaping of the customer's current behavior patterns, as well as the future intentions of the customer with regard to the provider, or its services, in order to stabilize or expand the future relationship with the customer' (Homburg & Bruhn, 2000, p. 8).

From the point of view of the customer, two possibilities need to be differentiated with regard to customer satisfaction. These possibilities are on the one hand being constrained, and on the other hand being loyal. Both alternatives are briefly presented in Figure 5.2.

Loyalty is present in voluntary commitment. This is the case when customers remain with a company even when they have the opportunity to change at anytime. Here rational, economic, and emotional reasons can be cited. In the area of emotional reasons, customer satisfaction is of particular significance. It must be given the highest priority, because customers will only remain loyal under a company's existing conditions, if they are so satisfied with the company that they do not want to change.

A **constrained** situation is where customers have no factual or legal possibility to change their provider, or if this can only be done with great difficulty or at great

	Loyal	Constrained
Provider's Customer Retention Activity	Management of Customer Satisfaction and Customer Trust	Creation of Barriers to Change
Resulting Commitment	Do Not Want to Change	Cannot Change
Customer Freedom	Not Restricted	Restricted
Interest in Commitment	Comes from Customer	Comes from Provider

Figure 5.2: Comparison of being loyal and being constrained (Bliemel & Eggert, 1998, p. 44)

expense. They are involuntarily bound to a company. This is the case, for example, in oligarchical political situations or in monopolies, but can also come about through contracts or via compatibility standards (in the computer or hi-fi arena). Citizens of many countries in the world can relate to the concept of not having much choice in the way of political representation or in industries monopolized by one major player. The ability to change is thus constrained due to the lack of available alternatives.

Causes of Customer Retention/Commitment

'Customer retention is the result of the more or less pronounced dependence of customers with regard to the provider' (Plinke & Söllner, 2000, p. 57). However, the customer gives himself over to this dependence, only under the condition that the benefit of the customer commitment exceeds the benefit of a subsequent, non-binding single purchase. (Backhaus & Baumeister, 2000, p. 204). Five categories of causes of commitment can be differentiated (Homburg & Bruhn, 2000, pp. 10–11):

* Situational causes of commitment.
* Contractual causes of commitment.
* Economic causes of commitment.
* Technical/functional causes of commitment.
* Psychological causes of commitment.

Situational causes of commitment belong above all to external factors, like the convenient location of a provider. The benefit for the customer lies here in a short journey or in easy accessibility. We can all relate to the convenience of a neighborhood grocery store or fuelling station as an example of loyalty based on location. Real estate developers fully understand this concept, which is why retail locations are often located very close to residential communities.

Contractual causes of commitment rest on the legal arrangement between the customer and the provider. Here security is accomplished via a longer delivery period or through monetary incentives benefiting the customer. There may be a situation where a customer has reasons to remain loyal until such time as a performance contract or lease agreement ends.

Economic causes of commitment describe situations in which it is financially disadvantageous for one party to end the business relationship. In this case, the customer either objectively or subjectively experiences the occurrence of costs involved in switching companies as too high. The costs of switching are not to be understood as directly coming about, but rather as opportunity costs, arising as a result of a comparison of the benefit between the existing customer-provider relationship and the new one being entered (Backhaus & Baumeister, 2000, p. 204). Because the customer here values the existing commitment more highly, economic customer commitment can be construed to be a form of loyalty.

The customer's technical dependence on the provider creates a basis for **technical/ functional causes of commitment**. At the beginning of the commitment, the customer has to decide on a certain standard or for a particular technical condition. Switching to another provider will bring with it compatibility and procurement problems (e.g.

Microsoft). Therefore, this form of customer commitment is more properly viewed as constrained rather than as loyal.

Psychological causes of commitment do not represent any direct material advantage for an individual, but instead take the form of positive discoveries with regard to the provider. A customer, who during the course of numerous contacts and transactions has positive experiences with a manufacturer, will develop trust. Since customers will always strive to come to a purchasing decision containing the least risk, they will choose the provider who subjectively appears the least risky.

In addition to appearing as the development of trust, however, psychological causes of commitment also appear as shared values, which arise during the course of a business relationship; they involve examples of communication and behavior, mutual ideas and memories, or a mutual moral commitment. The tradition, cultivated by the consumers, of buying from a given company, like identification with the image of the company or with the product, also forms psychological barriers to change (Herrmann & Johnson, 1999, p. 586).

The goal of psychological customer commitment is to establish an emotional relationship, in which at any time it is possible for the customer to change, but where this possibility is excluded because of personal preferences.

Advantages of Customer Retention

The advantages of customer retention have already been indicated in a few places. In tough, tooth and nail competition, the companies that have managed in the past to closely bind their customers to themselves, thereby immunizing customers against competitor attempts to lure them away, always have the advantage. Several factors come into play here (Herrmann, Huber & Braunstein, 2000, p. 51):

- As the duration of the business relationship grows, independent from the type of commitment, mutual tolerance also grows. This shows itself, for example, in that relationships with regular customers do not deteriorate in the same way when they are in arrears with a payment. Conversely, customers will continue to trust their regular supplier if that supplier on occasion displays unsatisfactory service. This greater reciprocal trust depends especially on the large number of interactions which long-time relationships between business partners entails.
- This intensive situation of working together leads among other things to a strong mutual readiness to share information and make complaints. Companies like Lufthansa and Deutsche Bahn use the cooperative behavior of their regular customers systematically, in that they organize customer forums. Here the customers reveal their observations concerning product quality, and share ideas and annoyances, as to what could be done better, all of which serves as a basis for an innovative form of service.
- A further effect of customer retention, which strengthens the security of the manufacturer, lies in the reduction of various risks, like for example, the fear of insolvency. When the company knows the needs of its customers well.

production risks are also diminished. Closely connected with this is the lowering of investment risk, once management has more vigorously concentrated its politics of innovation on the requirements of the sales market.

- Firm customer relationships, as a rule, also bring with them increased advantages in the area of expenditures. There can be various reasons for the savings, like for example, the lowering of customer processing costs, more efficient ordering procedures, and less price elasticity (Diller, 1996, p. 82).
- Finally, with increasing customer trust there is also growing readiness to refer the company, and the tendency to recommend it. As is generally known, word of mouth advertising is experienced as more believable when it is not seen as being influenced by the company.

From the described advantages, it can be concluded that there exists a positive relationship between customer retention and the commercial success of a company. Numerous commercial studies on this topic support this assumption. It could be established, for example, that in 100 companies in various service industries, the degree of customer retention and the level of profit are closely correlated (Herrmann, Huber & Braunstein, 2000, p. 51). Profit per consumer increases with the increasing duration of the relationship, although it depends on the industry, to varying degrees. Hence, *customer satisfaction first pays off when it leads to the next step, the loyalty of the customer.*

The following figures show the relationship between customer commitment and company success, according to the example of a credit card company and a garage. In both accounts the profitability grows with the increase of the business relationship's duration.

This should make intuitive sense to the reader. As the duration of a customer relationship increases, the firm experiences less costs associated with finding replacement customers. The higher the percentage of long-term relationships at a given firm, the higher the bottom-line profit potential.

Tools of Customer Retention

Customer retention can be achieved in various ways. First and foremost is via the quality of the product itself, followed by the price of the product, the communication between the company and the customer, and the modes of distribution.

Product

Customer commitment via the product quality itself can come about, for example, through a product development process shared by the customer and the provider. The requisite satisfaction is thereby achieved in that that jointly developed product fulfills the customer's expectations. Furthermore, the customer is strongly integrated via the development process, getting to personally know the company contact, and therefore also develops an emotional connection. Over and above that, quality

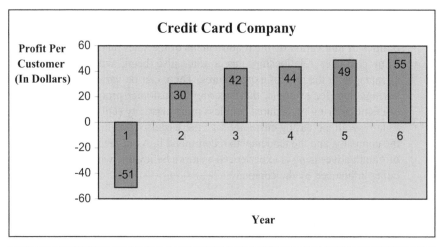

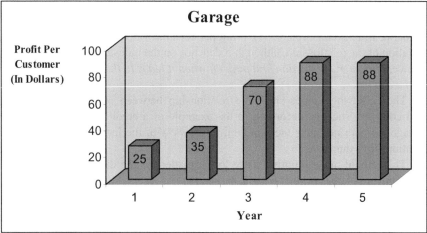

Figure 5.3: The increase of profit with the growth of a customer relationship's duration (Hermann, Huber & Braunstein, 2000, p. 49)

standards, designs, or additional product services, can also contribute to customer commitment.

With regard to commitment in the form of barriers to changing companies, there is the possibility of binding the customer to the company via special technical standards. In many cases, for commercial consumers, investment in particular technologies involves organizational changes. For example, a special training program for the employees will accompany the implementation of a new computer system. Apart from that, under these circumstances, stored data needs to be adapted to the new system, and a restructuring of work procedures needs to be undertaken. The costs connected with all of this represent an enormous barrier to change (Herrmann & Johnson, 1999, p. 586).

Price

Discount and bonus systems are among the most well-known tools in this category. Using these tools, the customer can be persuaded to purchase again from the same supplier, in order to earn discounts and bonuses as rewards for loyalty. Customers can also be made loyal via satisfaction-dependent pricing systems and money back guarantees in the case of dissatisfaction. For example, in the power supply business, an attempt to secure customer commitment is made using sharp differences in pricing. In this case, special contracts and standard customers pay different prices, which are graded according to purchase quantity. A potential customer who is a granted better conditions with the growing length of the business relationship or with increased purchase quantity, will carefully consider whether they will choose another supplier, thereby forfeiting this benefit. Another possibility consists of contracts that vary in the level of basic amounts, and in price per unit.

Communication

Continuous communication with the customer should lead to an increase in the customer's loyalty to the company. Classic elements here include personal contacts with the customer in the form of customer forums, field service, direct mailing efforts, telephone contact, and of course, an efficient complaint management system. In the future, companies will ever more actively use communication over the Internet, e-mail, and Voice Over IP technology. For example, the Internet-based company, Amazon.com, has recently had success in achieving repeat purchases by tracking not only what an individual customer purchases, but what other customers who also purchased the same item have purchased in the past. Via e-mail communication, customers of Amazon.com can view similar items based on purchases made by other customers. If a customer has an interest in a certain topic, certain form of music, or certain hobby, reviewing items of interest as determined by Amazon.com can be very helpful. In the absence of such communication efforts, these customers may satisfy their purchasing requirements elsewhere.

Distribution

Included in the standard modes of distribution are commerce, catalogue sales, direct delivery, and subscriptions. Also, the sale of products over the Internet (e-commerce) will in the future become increasingly more important. The Amazon.com example discussed in the previous section is also relevant here as the e-mails sent to customers detailing similar items of interest often act as customized sales catalogues for the firm.

Figure 5.4 presents the various tools of customer commitment in an overview format.

Which tools should be implemented depends on the individual goals of a company. A company has to decide for itself whether it wants to concentrate on interaction with the customers, the satisfaction of customers, or on barriers to change. Perhaps

Tool Category \ Primary Effect	Focus Interaction	Focus Satisfaction	Focus Barriers to Change
Product Policy	• Joint Product Development • Internalization/ Externalization	• Individual Offers • Quality Standards • Service Standards • Additional Services • Special Product Design	• Individual Technical Standards • Value Added Service
Price Policy	• Customer Cards (Raising Level of Information)	• Price Guarantees • Satisfaction-Dependent Pricing Systems	• Discount and Bonus Systems • Price Differentiation • Price Bundling • Financial Incentives • Customer Cards (Granting Discounts)
Communication Policy	• Direct Mail • Event Marketing • Online Marketing • Proactive Customer Contacts • Service Numbers • Customer Forums/Advisors	• Customer Clubs • Customer Magazines • Telemarketing • Complaint Management • Personal Communication	• Individualized Mailings (High Value for the Customer) • Establishment of Customer Specific Channels of Communication
Distribution Policy	• Internet/Lotteries • Product Sampling • Visits to the Workshop	• Online Ordering • Catalogue Sales • Direct Delivery	• Subscriptions • Customer-Oriented Choice of Location

Figure 5.4: Tools of customer commitment (Homburg & Bruhn, 2000, p. 21)

a combination of all of the above measures would also make sense. Just try not to focus on too many factors all at once.

Below, the three tools of customer commitment that have been gaining steadily in significance recently, will be more clearly explained—customer cards, customer clubs, and professional complaint management.

Customer Clubs

A customer club is an organization of customers, who are offered special services as a result of their membership. Those interested can join these clubs on a voluntary basis. Special services can include up-to-date information, privileges of a financial sort, the entitlement to special services, attractive offers, and also private events. These services are available exclusively to club members. In this way, the company attempts to instill membership with extra emotional value, to suggest exclusivity or additional benefit.

Customer clubs can be divided into closed and open clubs. While open clubs are freely accessible to everyone or to all customers, in closed clubs there are limitations. An example of this is membership or admission fees. Not every customer can afford or wants to pay these fees. Consequently, it is possible to specifically evaluate members and target groups.

The goals of customer groups are to (Belz & Tomczak, 1996, p. 23):

- maintain the loyalty of regular customers;
- acquire new customers;
- increase market share;
- support market research;
- develop and optimize a customer data bank.

As a rule, joining a customer club brings along with it an increased identification of the customer with the company and their services rendered. As a result of stronger commitment to and trust in the company, the rate of purchase of the company's core services, along with the cross-buying activity of customers, can be increased, and the level of price sensitivity can be lowered. Furthermore, club members generally recommend the club by word of mouth to friends and acquaintances.

There are various advertising media where a club can reach and communicate with its members. One possibility is the use of customer magazines. These are usually sent to the members of the clubs at regular intervals. Direct mailings are another possibility. They consist of 2–4 pages and contain information concerning the activities of the clubs, events, and current news. Customer clubs also should not rule out the use of a telephone hotline. In this way, the club achieves a situation where it is available at all times to members in case problems arise. An example of a customer club is the VW Club.

Customer trust has, strangely enough, declined in the last few years, simultaneous with an increase in automobile quality. In the face of this, to increase the customer loyalty of VW drivers, Volkswagen founded the VW Club. 'With the Volkswagen Club the goal of increasing loyalty is primarily achieved through more fun, pleasure and greater mobility, whereby loyalty relates back to the dealer as well as to the brand itself' (Holland & Heeg, 1998, p. 100).

In 1998, the VW Club had about 260,000 members and yearly its membership increases by around 60,000. Membership in the club is free. Club members are offered services like traffic telephone, guide service, route planning, emergency and breakdown services, as well as leisure time-oriented offers like tickets and travel support. Additionally the VW Club guarantees an extensive assistance package in the case of breakdowns, accidents, or sickness while abroad. Members receive a club card. This can be equipped with a payment function, or can serve simply as a club identification card, according to the wishes of each member. Another service is the free *VW Magazine*, which is sent to all members. In this magazine, information about current events, club services, and cooperation partners can be found.

Customers are awarded with trust points for the loyalty they display toward the company. These club member points can be cashed in at Volkswagen Club Partnerships worldwide to obtain original components and accessories. The customers can use the collected points to make outstanding payments, or can opt to use them to purchase a product (www.vw-club.de).

The Club Service Center is the hotline of the club. This hotline caters to the needs of the customers, and at the same time maintains the customer databank.

Customer Cards

Customer cards have over time evolved from their original function as a means of payment into a marketing tool. At the moment there are about 20 million customer cards in circulation (www.agv.de). The success of customer cards depends on the functions and services offered, in that these should amount to a genuine benefit for the customer. Companies attempt to bind the customer to them with ingenious service offers and systems of discount. Whether it is department stores, supermarkets, or gas stations—many companies are currently attempting to entice with varying forms of customer cards. Whoever owns one, can obtain for example, special price advantages, trust and bonus points, as well as credit.

Through offering special services, companies validate the feeling of being a regular customer, thus encouraging the customer to take the companies more seriously. The consumer is personally addressed, receives offers only for cardholders, and can see themselves as being a valued company patron. Through the use of customer cards, the frequency of visits is increased, and on average a rise in the quantity of purchases is observed.

There are various kinds of customer cards (www.experian.de/karten):

- customer cards without a payment function;
- customer cards with a payment function;
- customer cards with revolving credit;
- customer cards with a bonus function;
- customer cards with a discount function.

Customer cards without a payment function have the advantage that they can be used as bonus or discount cards. Discount and bonus cards are primarily provided by customer clubs, although some restaurant franchises have begun issuing discount cards for repeat purchases.

With a card that has a payment function, the issuer of the card has the possibility of finding out how high of a turnover they have attained with a customer. The company receives up-to-date data, i.e., information concerning the purchasing behavior of the customer. This means that companies can bring together anonymous information obtained through the EC cash card, with customer-oriented data. By granting credit therefore, the activities of the card are amassed.

In the case of a customer card with revolving credit, the customer is awarded credit. However, this generally comes to pass in cooperation with a bank, as the revolving credit facility is underwritten and approved by the bank.

Through the issuing of a customer card with a bonus function, the company achieves an intensive customer commitment. Here points are credited to an account for the customer with every purchase, which they can cash in at a later time against money or goods. The incentive of collecting points should not be underestimated.

With the customer discount card, the customers are awarded discounts that they can immediately collect with the card. Discounts collected can then be redeemed by the customers against bonus points. In the case of exchangeable or necessary products serving daily needs, the discount represents an incentive to shop at the place where the discount is being offered.

Five customer cards and their functions are compared below:

Issuer	Function
Karstadt/Hertie	3% Discount, also possible without payment function (Coupon, as a bonus or paid out in cash).
Payback	No payment function. With a purchase a discount of between 1 and 3% is received. Starting at a certain point, credit accrued in this way can be transferred to the customer's account. He can choose from various deals in the Payback Shop.
Douglas	Card with payment function, Douglas Magazine five times per year, small surprises and coupons for test sample (an annual fee applies).
Ikea	Cashless shopping, financed purchasing, assurance of transportation while shopping, the customer magazine "room".
Quelle	Cashless shopping, payment in installments.

Figure 5.5: Comparison of customer cards (www.agv.de)

Complaint Management

Even when the customer management motto 'do it right the first time' enjoys a privileged place, the complete satisfaction of all customer wishes is not always assured, and possible mistakes in the rendering of services may not be excluded. In the area of customer commitment, extensive and effective complaint management should therefore be seen as an important tool. As a rule, customers invariably complain when they are not satisfied with the service received, or with individual elements of the service. The motive at the basis of all complaints is accordingly the disappointment of expectations that have been experienced with regard to a product or service. The service received does not add up to the customer's subjective wishes. For this reason, the customers look to the company, complaining with the hope of solving the problem that has arisen (Christianus, 1999, p. 71).

Yet many companies tackle complaints as if they were merely a nagging disturbance of their daily work. Customer complaints are either brushed off or only dealt with reluctantly. Employees experience complaints as personal attacks and build up corresponding defensive positions against them. This leads to some superiors using complaints as a means of pressuring employees. This leads to the loss of customers. When used correctly, complaints can certainly become an excellent source of information. Through an analysis of complaints Homburg & Werner (1998, p. 44) have determined the following:

- Complaint-ridden elements of service can be identified and improved.
- Weaknesses in the service offer can be identified and improved.
- The level of complaint can be identified.

Furthermore, it is often overlooked that dissatisfied customers give the company a chance, via customer-friendly handling of complaints, to win them back by persuading them of the company's readiness and ability to serve. As discussed in the prior chapter, Albert O. Hirschman's famous book, *Exit, Voice, and Loyalty*, theorized that a customer (or indeed an employee) of a firm had three options when faced with dissatisfaction. These options were to either exit the firm, voice their concerns about their dissatisfaction, or to remain loyal in spite of their dissatisfaction. Unfortunately, most customers prefer the exit scenario rather than voicing their concerns, and as we have seen, the problem of customer loyalty can best be improved via a customer relationship management system. Any firm that does not conduct an evaluation of why customers are choosing to exit runs the risk of the trend continuing if the problem is not corrected in a timely manner.

Based on prior research, grievances or outright complaints are above all caused by the occurrence of defective products (56.9 percent of the total sample). Unsatisfactory service behavior on behalf of employees is in second place at 15.9 percent. The botching of delivery or assembly is at 15.3 percent. Grievances regarding the price or bill are in 8.7 percent of the cases the reason for complaint (Niebisch & Betz, 1998, p. 30).

The way of dealing with complaints in many companies reveals itself to be incomplete. The average satisfaction of customers with the reaction to their complaints is only 14.1 percent, and those completely satisfied made up only 3.9 percent of those asked. About half (49 percent) showed themselves to be disappointed either with the reaction of the company, or the employees, to their complaint. The study showed that these customers stated that they were either not at all or only slightly satisfied. Only 36.9 percent of the respondents were more or less satisfied (Niebisch & Betz, 1998, p. 30).

An active complaint management system should truly benefit the company, by reestablishing customer satisfaction, through a handling of the complaint that is as persuasive as possible. In order to assure a professional way of dealing with complaints, the following four aspects should be considered (Christianus, 1999, pp. 72–73):

- **The Input Procedure**
  At first, the dissatisfaction of the individual customers has to be known by the company. Then the task of complaint management is to direct the flow of complaints. The company can only help the customers who actively complain. Therefore the 'silent majority' needs to be encouraged to speak up. One requirement to ensure participation by the 'silent majority' is the lack of repercussions or hassles associated with the filing of a complaint. Another requirement is that any suggestion boxes or other methods of collecting complaints be checked frequently, so that the dissatisfaction can be determined as soon as possible.
- **The Case Processing Procedure**
  This procedure involves the quick and non-bureaucratic processing of customer complaints with the goal of remedying the customer's concern in a way that is convincing to the customer. Whether or not the regaining of the customer's satisfaction is successful is decided in the context of the case processing procedure. A company can only truly win back those customers who receive a solution to their problem that in their eyes is convincing. In this instance, the social competence of customer contact personnel is important, since coping with highly emotional conflict situations may often be required.

- **Feedback Procedure**

  In the context of this important checking procedure, the complainants are questioned concerning their satisfaction with how the process of dealing with their complaint went, as well as to how satisfied they are with the result. Again, timeliness is of utmost importance here, as a dissatisfied customer needs to have their needs met as soon as possible.

- **Information Collection Procedure**

  The fourth procedure in complaint management consists of acquiring information that can be used for future enhancement or alterations to the processes integral to the rendering of services, and relevant individual features of services. On the basis of an exhaustive analysis of its customer complaints, a company can discover what particular weak points and problem areas arise, with regard to their rendering of services.

CHAID: An Effective Predictive Segmentation Tool

In order to achieve the highest levels of customer retention, firms must be better able to understand which descriptive features of their customer base are most associated with customer loyalty and long-term customer relationships. One such segmentation tool is **CHAID** (**chi**-squared **a**utomatic **i**nteraction **d**etection). The chi-square test evaluates statistically significant differences between proportions for two or more groups in a data set. First, a logistic regression should be run to determine which variables are the most valid predictors of the dependent variable. Then, the CHAID algorithm can determine the best segmentation based on those variables. In a recent study, CHAID was utilized to determine what specific demographic components best determined the probability of a customer obtaining and using loyalty cards during their relationship with a given company (Galguera et al, 2006).

CHAID is a preferred method of customer segmentation since the results are relatively easy to interpret, and can be more easily communicated to top management than some of the other segmentation applications. CHAID is used when there is a dependent variable, which can be compared relative to a set of independent variables. CHAID looks for a relationship between the dependent variable and each of the independent variables, with the ultimate aim of selecting a set of independent variables and their respective interactions that best predict the dependent measure. CHAID produces a classification system similar to that discussed in Chapter 2 (Decision Trees). This decision tree framework itemizes how certain sets formed from the possible independent variables differentially predict the dependent variable.

The CHAID process allows for the review of each independent variable in isolation to see if any of the categories represent a significant predictor of the dependent variable. In the aforementioned study, the dependent variable was the possession of a customer loyalty card, while independent variables consisted of sex, age, urban versus suburban dwelling, education, and other factors. The goal of CHAID is to break up the group of independent variables into subsets until the variables that are most statistically significant are determined. This is done by the partitioning of each independent variable using the same algorithm that was applied to the entire data set, in an effort to strip down the independent variables as much as possible. CHAID diagrams can be thought of as a tree trunk with progressive splits into smaller and smaller branches. The initial tree trunk would consist of the entire population, and the subsequent branches would be the various independent variables. In the earlier cited loyalty card example, the initial tree trunk was the survey-respondents that had a loyalty card of some kind, and the successive branches were groupings based on age, education levels, etc. Once the most statistically significant of the possible predictors was determined, that specific variable could then be further broken down relative to the other variables in the study. If age was the most statistically significant variable, then age could be further broken down based on other factors such as the level of education, or urban or suburban residence. In the study, it was determined that loyalty cards are most likely to be used by customers under the age of 22, who are college educated, and live in urban settings. It was also determined that loyalty card use was much less effective for customers over the age of 55. The study was conducted in both the United States and Spain, and it was determined that the results were the same in both locations.

CHAID can thus be used to segment, via algorithms, a customer base in terms of their probability of purchasing a given product or service. As has been discussed earlier in the chapter, being able to successfully retain customers depends greatly on a company's ability to understand the reasons for a customer's purchase behavior. The better an organization understands their customers, the more effective it can be in its marketing expenditure for existing customers, as well as for potential customers. By appropriately segmenting the customers based on the aforementioned study, companies may decide that marketing loyalty cards to customers over the age of 55 does not lead to the desired increase in purchasing for that segment of the customer base. In lieu of this information, valuable marketing expenditures could be wasted using a 'one-size fits all' marketing scheme.

Questions for Discussion

1. List and elaborate on the importance of the five categories of causes of commitment.

2. Discuss the primary advantages of an effective customer retention program at your company or university.

3. Explain why an effective customer orientation program must precede a successful customer retention program. What might be possible problems of offering a strong retention program as the first step?

4. How might the tools of customer retention be utilized in your company or university? Are there any strategies that were discussed in the chapter that would not be feasible for your organization?

5. Consider the last time that you experienced dissatisfaction with a product or service that you purchased. Did you complain? If not, why did you fail to complain? If you did, discuss how your complaint was handled, and what the firm might have done differently to improve the situation.

Chapter 6

Customer Value

Chapter Objectives:

- *Discuss the transaction versus relationship approaches to customer value.*
- *Assess the strengths and weaknesses of the Calculation of Customer Profit Contribution (CCPC) model.*
- *Explain customer-oriented process cost calculation.*
- *Discuss the concept of customer lifetime value (CLV).*
- *Elaborate on the three phases of the Customer Value Development (CVD) model.*

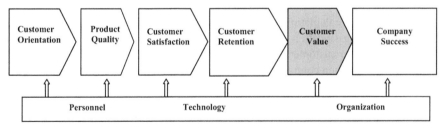

Figure 6.1: Approaches to acquiring customer value

Detailed knowledge with regard to customer profitability, as well as the behavior of the customer within the value added process, is basic as far as the development of a sound CRM strategy is concerned. A company is only in the position to increase its value as a company in the long term once it knows its customers, can influence customer behavior, and only if it invests in its profitable customers with precision (Rapp, 2000, pp. 83–84). It certainly does not make any sense for a company to compete on price for all of its customers. The task of the company simply lies in concentrating on the profitable customers (Schmid, Bach, & Österle, 2000, p. 35). Only companies that implement an effective CRM system will be able to assert themselves against the competition in the long run (Krafft & Marzian, 1997, p. 104).

Approaches to Acquiring Customer Value

As will be discussed in the next few pages, there are numerous approaches to acquiring customer value. The key for many organizations is to define the perspective that will define value as it relates to their customers. Some companies may value increasing their market share for a given product or service, and are thus more focused on achieving a critical mass of transactions in order to reach their targeted performance levels. Some small community banks thrive on this concept, often to the detriment of their larger competitors (at least temporarily). A small organization could decide that their definition of customer value is best exemplified in the level of market share that the firm achieves. From a CRM perspective, however, firms should instead focus on the profitability of entire relationships, rather than simply on the profitability of a given transaction.

Once the focus is moved from a transaction-oriented approach, to one based on customer relationship profitability, there are numerous perspectives with which to view a firm's portfolio of customers. The first approach to customer value that we will discuss in detail relates to the profit contribution for a given customer. From there we will discuss the approach relating to a customer's process cost calculation, and then we will discuss the concept of customer lifetime value (CLV).

Calculation of Customer Profit Contribution

The goal of the calculation of the customer profit contribution (CCPC) is the gathering and classification of costs, revenues, and impairments to revenue, which are attributable to customers or to segments of customers (Schulz, 1995, p. 105). These results are then contrasted against the sales profitability. The remaining gross surplus is a clue with regard to how much the consumer has contributed to company success. A precondition of CCPC is the so-called allocation. This means that each customer is assigned a customer account number. All future costs and proceeds that have to do with the customer will be classified according to this customer account number (Köhler, 2000, p. 423).

The frequent differentiation into fixed-and service-dependent variable costs, in product-oriented analysis within a single-tier calculation of profit contribution, is not considered to be the decisive criterion of accountability when determining customer profit contribution. Here it has much more to do with the specifics of the customer relationship, which in many cases can yield fixed costs within a given time period (for example a listing fee, which a customer receives). In Figure 6.2 an approach to CCPC is presented (Köhler, 2000, pp. 423–424).

As the basic set-up of the CCPC presented above shows, the case of customer-oriented product costs diverges in strict principle from individual costs calculation. The calculation of variable unit costs is performed by a single-tier profit contribution calculation, which is taken over from the product calculation. The argument can be asserted here, that without this utilization of capacity, a reduction of these general variable costs would arise, if the pertinent customer orders were not present. In the literature on the subject, there is the opinion that variable product costs should also be subtracted from gross proceeds. Accounting in full for manufacturing and

Customer Gross Surplus Per Period
– Impairments to Proceeds
= Net Customer Proceeds Per Period – Costs of Products with Reference to the Customers (Variable Unit Costs are Product Calculation Multiplied by the Purchase Volume)
= Customer Profit Contribution I – Clearly Defined Customer Contingent Costs of the Assignment (e.g., Equipment, Shipping, and Handling)
= Customer Profit Contribution II – Clearly Defined Customer Contingent Visiting Costs (e.g., Costs of Customer Incentives) – Special, Relative Individual Costs of Customers Per Period (e.g., The Salary of a Special Key Account Manager; Engineering Help; Mailing Costs; Interest on Outstanding Active Debts; Costs of Customers at the Trade Level; Cost of Having Offered Advertising Help; Listing Fees and Similar Costs)
= Customer Profit Contribution III

Figure 6.2: The basic set-up of a Calculation of Profit Contribution (CCPC) (Kohler, 2000, p. 424)

even original costs has the consequence that fixed costs not directly caused by the customer are also prorated (proportionately assessed) (Köhler, 2000, p. 424).

Aside from the addressed difficult questions related to the division of costs, there are further critical points with regard to the assessment and preparation of a CCPC. As is, the CCPC only has an alibi function, for use when no organizational measures for a stronger target group orientation are forthcoming. The CCPC can also lead to poor decisions, when costs attributable to customers or to a customer segment are not assigned according to the principle of cost causation. In addition, an assessment of customer relationships which is purely centered in the present, and on the basis of the CCPC, can harm the company, because then management is not taking into account the retention period of the customer as part the company's regular clientele, resulting in concentration on customers with a high customer profit contribution, who in fact may only remain as part of the regular clientele for a short time.

Certainly there are also many advantages to a CCPC. It allows for focused guiding of segments on the basis of a strategic, target group-oriented approach. Furthermore, it leads to more transparency in relation to customer specific profit contribution and revenue contingent factors. As a guiding instrument it can also be implemented to improve segment specific yield contribution. Another positive aspect of CCPC is that, since it is an aid in the decision-making process, it can be used in the optimization of financial resources and as an argumentation and reconciliation instrument (Schulz, 1995, p. 108).

Finally, on the basis of CCPC results, the company is in a position to assess the current profitability of its customers. In turn, it can be determined, in relation to profitability, whether future investments in particular customers or customer segments are justifiable. Thus, not all customers are good customers in terms of meeting profitability targets.

Customer-oriented Process Cost Calculation

It is characteristic of process cost calculation procedure to more precisely allocate the areas of general cost units (customers) on the basis of individual processes (Schulz, 1995, S. 109). It is based on the basic idea of a full calculation of costs procedure, but it differs from the full calculation in the way general costs are allocated. While in full calculation of costs overhead charges are schematically portioned out, in the procedure of process cost calculation, general costs are schematically allocated in a manner that spans different areas. The conventional divisions of fixed and general costs are expressed as codes. These codes determine the internal service costs and encode them with the customer's cost unit, as a reference value according to the input involved. As a foundation, all processes are identified, which for example, pertain to customer A. In addition, all cost drivers that relate to the processes have to be defined, and the amount of cost drivers must be established. An individual process could, for example, represent the processing of orders, shipping, invoicing, or complaint processing. The following example of a calculation should serve to clarify customer-oriented process cost calculation:

On the basis of the information process cost calculation, a company can set-up and optimize its procedural organization. Additionally, high process cost customers can be identified. As a consequence, the company can give up these customers in order to reduce fixed costs. In this way, the process cost calculation is of help in strategic considerations by providing orientation. A determination of customer value in the strict sense is not possible (Köhler, 2000, p. 426). A primary focus is to attempt to segment the profitable customers and to build on those relationships.

Process: Invoicing

Process Costs Per Period
(Process Contingent Stipends and Deductions for Office Equipment): €300 000

Process Amount Per Period: 20 000 Invoices

Process Cost Rate = $\frac{\text{Process Costs}}{\text{Process Amount}}$ = $\frac{300\,000}{20\,000}$ = €15

If customer A has given rise to 120 invoices in the period, his assigned portion in invoicing costs is €1,800.

**Figure 6.3: Fundamentals of customer-oriented process
cost calculation (Kohler, 2000, p. 426)**

Customer Lifetime Value

The above discussion on calculating customer value was focused on the present. With the help of past values, a situation analysis is led to a particular point in time. The future trend of the customer relationship is thereby not taken into consideration. In the German literature, customer life value is specified as a long-term value or a prospective lifetime calculation. A characteristic of the calculation of long-term customer value is that in addition to the value of a customer being calculated on the basis of short-term sales turnover or profit expectations, the customer's specific period of time spent as part of the regular clientele, is also factored in (Schulz, 1995, p. 195). Here the total length of a customer relationship is studied from its beginning to its projected end (Köhler, 2000, p. 437). The actual customer value is found out with the help of the capital value method. In this method, at the beginning of the customer relationship all future receipts of payment, and expenditures, are estimated and totaled. The possible length of a customer relationship is projected on the basis of mean values. Finally all sources of revenue are discounted with the company's own rate of interest at the current date. Qualitatively assigned amounts can also factor into the calculation, in that potential revenue sources are multiplied by their probability of occurrence. Because the projected length of a customer relationship is of such significance, the possibility of customers leaving for the competition and customer group scenarios are also factored in (Zezelj, 2000, p. 15). A calculation of CLV is useful for winning new customers and also within existing business relationships. From the present point of evaluation, it is possible to observe in two directions:

- Looking back, 'is data' serves to determine past-related customer profitability. As a possible means of determination, the already discussed CCPC may be of use.
- Looking ahead, the calculation of the CLV supports projections of prospective customer value, which arise out of future, continuous transactions.

These two ways of observing are highly correlated. The distinction lies in the fact that the value that has already been siphoned off from the past (retrospective value) is deducted from the future value (prospective value). At any rate the future value— as is usual in dynamic investment calculations—is limited to the flow of payments, so that suppositions about definite payment properties of revenue and costs are concluded. In the context of the simplified supposition that the cash flows all accrue at the end of a period, the calculation formula for prospective customer value reads as follows:

$$CV = I_0 - O_0 + (I_1 - O_1)q^{-1} + (I_2 - O_2)q^{-2} + (I_3 - O_3)q^{-3} + \ldots + (I_n - O_n)q^{-n}$$

CV   = prospective customer value
I   = incoming money
O   = outgoing money
q   = 1 + a, where 'a' is the adequate target rate
n   = last observation period of continuous customer relationship
E0, A0 = payment flow falling in present point of evaluation

The estimation of future, customer specific outgoing and incoming money, proves to be a problem of practical implementation. At the same time similar, very positive, developments in various industries can be established, like for example, the decrease of customer-specific costs with increasing length of commitment and rising sales profitability. This positive tendency is included in the CLV calculation. Certainly working with multi-period investment calculations contains significantly more estimation accuracy than single-period calculations. It is therefore advisable to regularly calculate customer profitability retrospectively, so that the '*is*' values can be compared with the projected values. Then, any differences can be spotted early on and, if necessary, a revision of the customer value determination can be carried out (Köhler, 2000, pp. 437– 439).

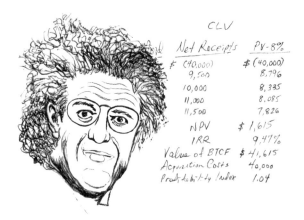

In some industries, such as financial services, the projected length of a customer relationship is more readily apparent via statistical modeling. For example, in the commercial banking industry, most firms calculate the effective life of a loan, which is another way of saying the length of time that a loan stays on the bank's books from origination until it is paid out. This is substantially shorter than the amortization on the loan, given that borrowers have a tendency to either seek other financing sources, could sell the business or investment asset, or could opt to pay the loan out early. Another financial services industry example of the use of statistical modeling to determine the projected length of the customer relationship is the insurance business. Most of us are familiar with actuarial tables that help to predict the longevity of a customer given prevailing physical conditions. These tables would play a large part in developing a model of customer development, and could serve as an example of how other industries could begin to calculate the relevant lifecycle of their customer relationships.

Customer Lifecycle and Customer Mindset

John Kenneth Galbraith has said, 'A man in imminent danger of being hanged is little worried about catching cold. There is no point in eliminating a minor source of uncertainty if a major one remains' (Galbraith, 1967, p. 221). When determining CLV, the most important uncertainty to clarify is that of the mindset of the customer. As we have discussed in earlier chapters, the better that a firm understands their customers, the more likely the firm will be able to surprise the customer with features that keep them satisfied relative to the competition. The customer mindset determines customer behavior. Customer behavior directly determines the length of a customer's association with the firm. This association is known as the lifecycle of the customer.

There are various stages of the customer lifecycle. The first stage is the acquisition stage, when a customer first decides to conduct business with a given firm. The second stage is retention, which was discussed at length in Chapter 5. This stage involves a firm being able to maintain profitable relationships with their customers via consistently meeting and exceeding their expectations. A third stage in the customer lifecycle is that of development, when a firm attempts to broaden their business with their existing clients. This is a key component in attaining profitable, valuable customer relationships. The fourth stage is defection, which is something that all firms wish to avoid. Sometimes defection is unavoidable, and a good question to ask is whether a customer defection is due to a permanent or a temporary change in the customer's situation. Some products and services may be purchased by those customers that are within a certain age, education, or income level, and the defection may not necessarily be as a result of rejecting the firm, more than simply aging out of a particular demand behavior. This should be a consideration when calculating the lifetime value of customers. Obviously, customers do not necessarily have to follow each step in succession, as a dissatisfied customer may opt to stop doing business with a given firm after their first transaction. In such situations, if the firm had spent more time understanding the benefits that a customer desires, there might not have been such a gap between the product or service offered, and what was expected by the customer. Thus, a key component in calculating CLV is the mindset of the customer.

The customer mindset is defined as everything that is in the customer's mind concerning the firm (Berger, et al, 2006, pp. 156–167). Since the customer's mindset determines customer behavior, it is of paramount importance for a customer-focused company to understand as many aspects of the customer's mindset as are possible. While marketing does help to shape the customers' opinions about a given brand or company, firms must strive for finding the proper balance between marketing expenditure and firm profitability. If too many marketing dollars are spent on a per-customer basis, the profitability of the firm could erode. Once again, it is clear that having good intelligence concerning the desires and expectations of the customers will improve the profitability and duration of the relationship between the firm and the client.

The mindset of the customer can best be described using the 'five As' as is itemized below:

- awareness
- association
- attitude
- attachment
- advocacy

Awareness is here defined as the ability of the customer to recall the brand, and to generally recognize the firm's products and services. Association deals with the customer's perceptions of the uniqueness, strengths, and benefits of a product or service. This influences the customer's attitude concerning the product or service. A positive attitude is defined as having a positive opinion with regards to quality and satisfaction of a product or service. Attachment deals with the level of customer loyalty. Do the other components of the customer's mindset lead to a continued relationship or a defection? The components of the customer's mindset also impact the level of advocacy, which is the extent of recommendation of the product or service to other potential customers.

Each of these components can be positive, negative, or neutral. In Chapter 3, we discussed the Kano model, which is a methodology that can be used to assess the desires and expectations of the customers. What is apparent is that negative attitudes, associations, and advocacy can seriously impact the reputation of a given firm. Since a key component of an enduring profitable relationship is trust, the challenge of all companies is to achieve the highest levels of performance possible in each of the 'five As' for the firm's targeted customer base. Tools such as the Kano model, and other customer-inclusive panel discussions are key to being able to understand the mindset of the customer, which is a driving factor for predicting their future behavior, as well as the length and value of the relationship.

Customer Value Development

In connection with the determination of customer value, it is necessary to investigate the calculated financial contribution of individual customers or customer groups in a more differentiated way. Such an analysis allows for deriving well-founded decisions with regard to behavior toward customers or customer groups. Customer Value Development (CVD) is an approach to analyzing customer value and for the deriving of customer strategies. The analysis consists of three constructively coordinated phases or portfolios, which are described below.

Customer Value, Customer Satisfaction Portfolio (Phase 1)

In the first phase of the analysis, the calculated customer value and customer satisfaction of the respective customers or customer groups, are placed in relationship with each other (see Figure 6.4). This presentation communicates information about from which customers the company obtains high or low revenue, and to what extent the customers are happy with the company's performance.

In the first quadrant (A) are found customers who are satisfied with the performance and with whom a high customer value has been achieved. This represents the ideal situation. In Figure 6.4, 50 percent of customers are found in this quadrant. The situation in the second quadrant (B) reveals customers who are satisfied, but who result in low or even negative revenue (deficit) for the company. The goal with these customers has to be to raise the customer value. As depicted in Figure 6.4, 20 percent of the customers are classified in this manner. The third quadrant (C) describes customers who are presently unhappy with the company's performance and who are generating a low customer value for the company. In this situation it needs to be ascertained to what extent the company should attempt to divest itself of these customers, which represent ten percent of the customer base of the firm. In most cases it is practically impossible to increase the customer satisfaction as well as the customer value. This is a result of the fact that raising customer satisfaction is as a rule almost unobtainable without increasing the level of expenditure. While it would seem unthinkable to some that this many of a firms customers are providing a low customer value, remember the adage of not being everything to everyone. One of the key components of CRM is to determine which customers provide long-term profit potential, and which do not. The fourth quadrant (D) contains customers who yield a high customer value and who are not, or not very, satisfied with performance. As Figure 6.4 shows, this category represents 20 percent of the firm's customers. Here arises the fear that these customers might seek out an alternative to the company, for example changing to another provider. The goal is necessarily to increase customer satisfaction and as much as possible to maintain the customer value. Before a definitive strategy for the customers or customer groups can be determined, there needs to be more knowledge concerning which features of services or products are important to the customers, which costs the individual product features require, and to what extent possibilities for optimization exist with regard to these features. These specific goals are addressed by the following two phases in the context of CVD as shown in Figures 6.5 and 6.6.

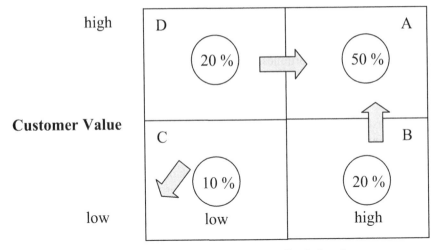

Customer Satisfaction

Figure 6.4: Customer value, customer satisfaction portfolio

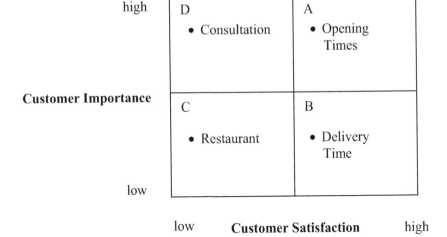

low   **Customer Satisfaction**   high

Figure 6.5: Customer importance, customer satisfaction portfolio

Customer Importance, Customer Satisfaction Portfolio (Phase 2)

In the second phase, a differentiated investigation of the respective customers or
customer groups within the different quadrants of this phase is conducted, with regard
to the importance and satisfaction of individual product features (see Figure 6.5).
From this presentation, it can be deduced which features are in need of corrective
action. The product features that are relatively unimportant to customers, but are

features that they are however, very satisfied with currently, offer the opportunity of lowering costs (as is shown in quadrant B). As far as product features that are important to the customers are concerned, and with which they are dissatisfied, there arises the necessity of seeking to raise the level of satisfaction (as is shown in quadrant D).

In the context of a study for a commercial enterprise, it is shown for example that a customer group that is for the most part satisfied with the services, but which displays a low customer value, is also unhappy with consultation. This service is, however, very important for the customer group (see Figure 6.5). The central question now is to what extent is it possible to raise satisfaction in this area and how to organize the costs such that customer value is increased? Of relevance here is the potential for optimizing individual product features in relation to the respective customers or customer groups. The answer to this query is dealt with in the third phase, or in the cost allotment, optimization potential portfolio.

Cost Allotment, Optimization Potential Portfolio (Phase 3)

In studying the question of to what extent there is a possibility of raising customer satisfaction, and of increasing or maintaining customer value, the cost allotment for individual features is correlated with the optimization potential of the respective product features (see Figure 6.6). This analysis can also be applied to individual customers or customer groups. If a particular feature is important to a customer, then the task is to find out if there is a possibility of lowering costs and/or of increasing productivity. In the context of the above-mentioned study for a commercial enterprise, it is apparent that the dissatisfaction with consultation can be traced back to a lack of

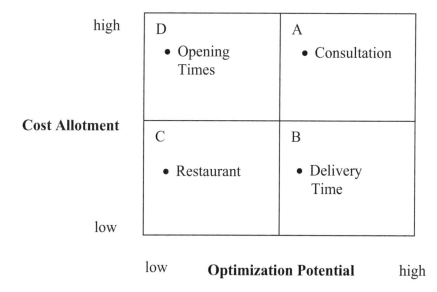

Figure 6.6: Cost allotment, optimization potential portfolio

professional know-how on the part of sales personnel. By way of a training program for the sales personnel, the quality of consultation could be considerably improved at relatively low cost. The optimization potential of this feature was relatively high, with regard to it having a large portion within the total provision of services cost allotments (quadrant A).

In the context of CVD, it is especially apparent in the analysis of customers with a low customer value and only slight customer satisfaction (see Figure 6.4) that a company is not in the position of being able to improve product features which are important for, and which are found unsatisfactory by, the customer, without increasing the level of costs. In this situation the only and final action to take is for the company to divest itself of these customers. The establishment of professional relationships between customers and a company entails that the company will profit from the relationships in the long term. The implementation of the three phases described above provides a well-founded and comprehensible basis for the formulation of specific customer strategies.

By analyzing the three phases of CVD, a firm can begin to determine the specific product or service features that are contributing the most to customer satisfaction, while at the same time comparing these features to the cost associated with the offering, as well as the potential of increasing the efficiency with which these features can be provided to the customer.

Questions for Discussion

Does your organization have a transaction or relationship orientation to the customer? Does your firm espouse the relationship focus, but act according to the transaction focus? Provide specific examples in your answer.

1. Does the forward-looking component of the CLV model seem appropriate for your company or organization? If not, what are some reasons that it would not apply? Then provide details as to ways that the CLV model could be implemented.

2. What are the benefits of the CCPC model? Are there any weaknesses in this approach?

3. Assess the strengths and weaknesses of the customer-oriented process cost calculation model. How might the weaknesses be alleviated?

4. Describe the three phases of the CVD model. Make sure to comment on the link between customer importance, customer satisfaction, and customer value in your answer. How would this model be applied to your organization?

Chapter 7

Company Success:
Customer Relationship Management
and the Balanced Scorecard

Chapter Objectives:

- *Understand the importance of the Balanced Scorecard in achieving company success.*
- *Explain how the Balanced Scorecard relates to international strategy in the global economy.*
- *Elaborate on the four perspectives of the Balanced Scorecard.*
- *Describe the value chain model as it relates to the fulfillment of customer wishes.*
- *Discuss the cause and effect chain in the Balanced Scorecard.*

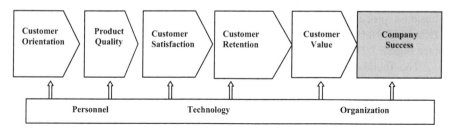

Figure 7.1: Company success: the Balanced Scorecard

In the preceding chapters, it has been demonstrated that CRM is an integral approach. Each of the components discussed, whether they be customer orientation, product quality, customer satisfaction, customer retention, or customer value, are all very important for the success of the firm. Along the way it has been repeatedly shown how key figures (indexes) for directing the establishment of long-term and profitable customer relationships, can be determined within these individual phases of CRM. These indexes can be integrated into the Balanced Scorecard concept developed by Kaplan and Norton (1997). A successful integration involves attributing central importance to the customers' perspective, and including some of the described indexes in their approach. Through combining the Balanced Scorecard (BSC) with

CRM, organizations can gain a solid basis for directing stable and profitable customer relationships, and for achieving company success.

The Balanced Scorecard

The starting point of the BSC developed by Kaplan and Norton, was a criticism of the excessive financial emphasis of the American system of controls. From examples such as the return on investment (ROI) of the DuPont ratio analysis system for assessing shareholder value, the predominant financial indexes were the rubric dictating the assessment and leadership of management and companies.

Financial indexes have the considerable disadvantage of being past-oriented as a rule, and suffer a delay in their availability for use. A firm will be limited in its ability to analyze cause and effect, and to maneuver in the face of negative developments. Often top management is left in ignorance as to whether measures which have been decided upon in the context of company strategy, will contribute to the achievement of objectives.

A future-oriented company, however, requires continuous information concerning the current situation within the company and with regard to moment-to-moment market occurrences. Financial indexes do not offer the breadth of information required by the management. The BSC represents a solution to this problem. Understood as an evaluation sheet, it has as its task the presentation of a balanced spectrum of indexes that enable the comprehensive guidance of the company. The BSC supplements the financial indexes of past performance with the driving factors of future performance. At the same time, the objectives and indexes focus company activity according to four perspectives: the financial perspective, the customer perspective, the internal business processes perspective, and the learning and development perspective (Kaplan & Norton, 1997, p. 8). These four perspectives form the context of the BSC (see Figure 7.2).

The foundation of the BSC concept is the company vision. This has to be formulated by the company management and should answer the following question: How does the management see the company in the future? From there the company strategy is developed. This aspect should be attended to very carefully, assuring that all future steps are derived from it. In Chapter 1, we covered the various international strategies that a firm can pursue, and the BSC should be considered as a method of achieving success for the company. On the basis of the business strategy developed by top management, objectives can then be broken down into the individual perspectives. Goals will be defined depending on the perspective, and in turn corresponding indexes will be assigned, whereupon guidelines and necessary measures and initiatives can be formulated within the individual perspectives.

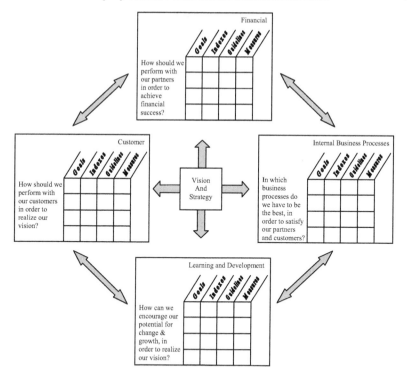

Figure 7.2: The four perspectives of the Balanced Scorecard (Kaplan & Norton, 1997, p. 9)

The Four Perspectives of the Balanced Scorecard

The Financial Perspective

The first of the four perspectives of the BSC (see Figure 7.2) includes traditional fiscal goals like profitability or growth, as well as the corresponding financial indexes like sales growth and cash flow. These quarterly and yearly indexes are extremely important in the context of the BSC for the assessment of operational business activity. However, financial goals should not simply be transmitted from the company as a whole to the individual business units. Similar to how strategy is established, financial goals should be separately determined for the business units. In fact, strategies should be developed for at least three different levels of the corporation. In Chapter 1 we discussed the various corporate level strategic possibilities. Strategies should also be made at the business unit, as well as the functional level. Business unit strategies focus on the particular line of business, rather than the company as a whole. A business unit may strive for being a leader in cost control, via a differentiation strategy, or possibly by developing a niche focus. Differing strategies and goals will be necessary depending on the business unit's phase of the product life cycle.

The financial perspective is the basic reference point for the following three performance perspectives. Thus, monetary indexes are seen as a foundation in the scorecard also. The goals and the transformed measurement values of all perspectives exist in a cause and effect relationship with each other. In the context of an optimally arranged scorecard, it should be possible to see how changes within the other perspectives work themselves out, on the basis of the financial performance values.

The Customer Perspective

In the customer perspective (see Figure 7.2), the company should very clearly define its target customer groups and markets, which are most important for future business.

As a general rule, customer needs diverge from each other within the various market and customer segments. It is very advantageous to clearly differentiate these by classifying them according to price, product performance, product functionality, image or reputation, service, and time. In this way, a company can, for example, determine whether the customer's decision to buy was purely motivated by the price, or whether the quality of the product and the extra services offered were the decisive factors that won the business. By questioning customers concerning the above-indicated criteria, it is often quickly established how significant it is to formulate definite customer segments.

On the basis of the identified target segments, goals and indexes can be developed. In their study, Kaplan and Norton came to the conclusion that there were two index groups that were implemented by companies. One group describes the so-called 'basis indexes' or 'core indexes' like customer satisfaction, market share, and customer loyalty, which are also causally interconnected. The close connection to CRM is here especially of note (see Chapters 3 and 4).

In the second group, all indexes are collected which could be identified as performance drivers, or 'differentiators' of customer outcomes. These represent instruments which can more firmly commit a customer to a company, and with which customer satisfaction and high market share can generally be attained. The indexes of the second group have the important function of describing that value being offered, which represents the summary of company services performed for a customer.

Kaplan and Norton (1997, p. 63) have demonstrated that values offered depend on the various industries and market segments, but that they also have certain characteristics in common, like for example, service characteristics, customer relationships, image, or reputation.

A firm should work out an individual offer of value that corresponds with customer wishes, which can then be translated into the customer perspective of the BSC. On this basis, goals and indexes can be formulated, in order to meaningfully layout the relevant customer segments.

Figure 7.3 depicts the causal connection of various core indexes in the customer perspective. The illustration is an important one to consider. As you can see, all of the various core indexes, such as customer acquisition, customer satisfaction, customer loyalty, customer profitability, and market share of the firm are interdependent. The circular nature of the illustration implies that there are not necessarily successive

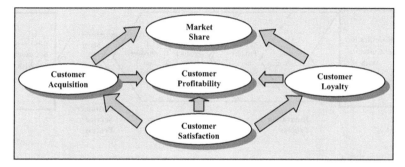

Figure 7.3: The casual connection of core indexes in the customer perspective (Kaplan & Norton, 1997, p. 66)

steps to achieve one particular goal. The pursuit of being a customer-oriented company is a continuous and ever-improving mission for any organization.

The Internal Process Perspective

The internal process perspective (see Figure 7.2), which concentrates on the operative processes of a company, is of particular significance. Many companies have only just begun to identify value-creating processes during the course of process cost calculation. Thereby process-specific costs are made transparent, and conclusions can be drawn regarding efficiency and effectiveness. What new thoughts in focusing on process does the BSC present?

Conventional concepts concentrate on identifying, optimizing and controlling already existent processes. A thorough analysis serves the purpose of discovering which processes in no way contribute to the creation of value, which therefore can be eliminated. The scorecard approach compliments this idea, in that it formulates a preparedness to find new processes, necessary for the optimal fulfillment of customer and shareholder standards. The determination of these goals results from the first two scorecard perspectives. These constitute the basis of the internal process perspective.

Kaplan and Norton (1997, pp. 90–92, 97–102) emphasize that from the balanced BSC, goals and indexes for the internal process perspective of explicit strategies can be derived toward the satisfaction of shareholder and customer expectations. This top down process can reveal completely new business enhancing modes of operation. It supports the management in the identification of processes necessary for bettering performance with regard to customers and shareholders. In this vein, goals and indexes should be formulated in the internal process perspective part of the BSC, which guarantee a successful implementation of company strategy. If, for example, a company discovers that a customer places a lot of importance on the support and services.

As you can see from Figure 7.4, during the innovation process, both market identification and the formulation of the product and service offer are conducted. As

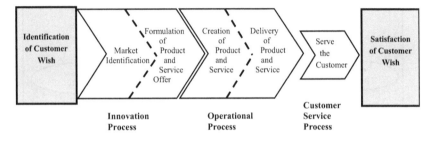

Figure 7.4: The generic value chain model (Kaplan & Norton, 1997, p. 93)

was discussed in Chapter 1, one component of developing a successful international strategy is determining the distinctive competence of the organization. During the innovation phase, it should be determined what market to serve and what products to offer based on the distinctive competence identified. During the operational process, both the product itself as well as the delivery method of the product or service are created. This can also be linked back to our discussion in Chapter 1. Since two other important components of international strategy are the scope of operations as well as resource deployment, both of these necessary ingredients for success are determined in this phase. The final phase of the value chain model involves the customer service process. During this phase, firms that are engaged in a CRM environment will deliver the product or service to the customer in an effort to meet the customer's desires. As we discussed in Chapter 1, the hope here is that synergy will be created via cross-selling other products and services to the same customer base in an effort to boost customer retention and company profitability.

The Learning and Development Perspective

This perspective is of a forward-looking nature, and concentrates on the company as a growing, learning organization, consisting of a linkage of personnel, systems and processes. This relates to the concept of worldwide learning that was discussed in Chapter 1, and represents a sustainable competitive advantage in the global economy. The goal here is to develop an organization that offers a high standard of communication and information (see Figure 7.2).

The BSC supports this process through the development of goals and indexes describing the performance and potential of the organization. Along these lines Kaplan and Norton (1997, p. 121–123) assert that there are three central constituents in the implementation of a balanced report:

1. Staff or individual employee potential.
2. Information systems potential.
3. Motivation, empowerment, and goal orientation.

As a preview of the determination of indexes with regard to the customer perspective, three potential indexes can be presented: Employee satisfaction, personnel trust, and employee productivity. The determination of these indexes, considered by Kaplan and Norton to be core indexes indicating performance, can for example, be achieved on the basis of employee surveys, from viewing employee turnover rates, or via the revenue per employee.

Another main component of the learning and development perspective is information systems. These are extremely difficult to measure, but they supply for the employees a comprehensive overview of customers, internal processes, and of the financial consequences of their decisions. In prior chapters, we have discussed some methods utilized in the banking industry for tracking customer information. The important thing to remember is that the ability to track the prior experiences of your customers allows for not only the ability to analyze the past. It also allows the future-oriented firm to predict what may occur in the future.

The Meaning of the Cause and Effect Relationship

All indexes in the BSC should share a cause and effect relationship with each other, since only the integrated strategy that results from this can be conveyed effectively. For example, ROI behaves like an index of the financial perspective according to increasing sales figures, but is also contingent on customer satisfaction, which is an index of the customer perspective. Satisfaction of customers is influenced by the product quality standard. Quality related indexes are a part of the internal process perspective. A higher standard of quality can in turn be the result of an intensive training program for the employees, or of a continuous program of educational improvement. These aspects belong to the learning and development perspective part of the balanced report (see Figure 7.5).

The fundamental idea of the BSC is to create an index structure that links corresponding goals and indexes, thereby producing an integrated system. If the financial figures do not add up to expectations, then the causes are to be sought in the customer perspective, the internal process perspective, or in the learning and

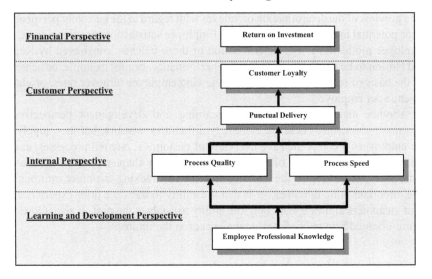

**Figure 7.5: Cause and effect chain in the Balanced
Scorecard (Kaplan & Norton, 1997, p. 29)**

development perspective. According to Kaplan and Norton, the causal chain of all scorecard indexes should be linked to financial indexes.

Kaplan and Norton (1997, pp. 28–29; 147–149) warn that current restructuring programs or management approaches like total quality management (TQM) or reengineering often do not have any relationship to financial performance, and as such are absolute ends in themselves. If a company does not see any success coming out of its alteration programs, this can lead to disappointment and disillusionment. It is necessary, therefore, that any measures taken in the field of internal action are linked together with a result, whether they are negative or positive. This is the only way a constructive learning process can result.

In observing the cause and effect chain of the BSC (see Figure 7.5), the strong relationship between it and CRM is evident. Both approaches compliment each other in that the indexes defined, and the strategies derived in the context of CRM, can or should be incorporated into the integrated system of the BSC. By integrating them, management is supplied with sound information to help guide the development of enduring and profitable customer relationships.

Questions for Discussion

1. Explain how the BSC enhances a firm's ability to create a successful global strategy. Then elaborate on how the BSC is most suited to the CRM approach.

2. Discuss the value chain as it relates to the components of international strategy. Then choose a product or service and outline how the innovation, operational,

and customer service processes can be utilized in order to fulfill the wishes of your target consumer.

3. In a short paragraph, write down the key components of a successful CRM program for your organization. Be sure to include commentary concerning each of the chapters covered in this book in your answer.

4. Explain why the financial perspective of the BSC is the foundation from which the other perspectives are grounded. Also elaborate as to how each of the four components must be dependent on each other for success.

5. Devise a high-level BSC for your organization. Make sure to include all four perspectives in your analysis.

Chapter 8

Challenges for Global Customer Relationship Management

Chapter Objectives:

- *Discuss the challenges facing successful CRM implementation efforts.*
- *Elaborate on the characteristics of an effective change management program.*
- *Compare and contrast the 'top-down' approach of organizational sponsorship with the 'bottom-up' approach.*
- *Discuss implementation issues with Global CRM.*
- *Elaborate on which international strategies and competitive advantages are compatible with CRM.*

The Primary Challenges Facing Successful Customer Relationship Management Implementation Efforts

In this concluding chapter of the book, the authors would like to discuss the current and future challenges regarding the implementation of a successful and viable global CRM system, as well as the common problems experienced in CRM implementation at the domestic level. As the primary audiences for this book are current and future business executives, as well as educators, discussing issues that have been problematic for others is good medicine to help ensure that similar problems can be avoided regarding CRM implementation in the future. On a positive note, over US$80 billion is spent globally on an annual basis on CRM, which is more than three times the average of just five years ago. Thus, CRM is here to stay, and corporate decision makers should take careful note of the topics covered in this book, to ensure that the knowledge gained from reading this book is not lost when it is applied in practice. Unfortunately, upwards of two-thirds of CRM projects have been viewed as failing to achieve their objectives based on industry reports (Kale, 2004).

This should lead us to ask why so many CRM applications are supposedly failing to live up to the expectations of the firms that are implementing CRM programs. The answer may be gleaned from the following quote from the Danish philosopher Søren Kierkegaard:

Let us imagine a pilot, and assume that he had passed every examination with distinction, but that he had not as yet been at sea. Imagine him in a storm; he knows everything he ought to do, but he has not known before how terror grips the seafarer when the stars are lost in the blackness of night; he has not known the sense of impotence that comes when the pilot sees the wheel in his hand become a plaything for the waves; he has not known how the blood rushes to the head when one tries to make calculations at such a moment; in short, he has had no conception of the change that takes place in the knower when he has to apply his knowledge.

As discussed in Chapter 1, a key to the success of business enterprise in an age of globalization is the achievement of sustainable competitive advantages. As should be apparent from the preceding chapters in this book, establishing and maintaining profitable customer relationships should certainly be seen as a competitive advantage. Organizations that successfully have implemented CRM have been those that have included a broad, cross-functional collaboration in their businesses as early in the process as possible. Successful CRM implementations have also focused the efforts of their company in learning how to best understand the knowledge that is required in order to retain, grow, and delight their customers. As should be evident from the quote in the paragraph above, those organizations that have not been successful in CRM implementation have been those that were unable to turn the platitudes into a realizable company strategy.

Over the last few years, there have been a plethora of articles and publications, in both popular and academic press, concerning the pitfalls of CRM implementation. The most often cited reasons for such failure are itemized below:

- ineffective change management;
- lack of top-level executive support;
- lack of customer vision;
- lack of understanding of customer lifetime value;
- lack of cross-functional teams in implementation/planning;
- seeing CRM purely as technology;
- long and over-budget implementation;
- underestimating difficulties in data mining and data integration.

These supposed pitfalls may possibly look familiar. The majority of the pitfalls in CRM implementation have already been discussed in preceding chapters. For example, we have devoted Chapter 6 to the considerations of CLV. We have devoted pages in Chapters 2 and 5 to the issues associated with data mining and data integration. And we certainly have spent the better part of the book making a case for the benefits for achieving (as well as the pitfalls for not achieving) a customer vision for your organization. The first two bullet points, ineffective change management and lack of top-level executive support, are the two most common reasons for CRM implementation problems. These can be seen as root causes of trouble, with the symptoms appearing as increased time lines for CRM implementation, higher budget costs due to the increased length of the implementation effort, missed milestones and fewer realized benefits. We will now discuss the two most common reasons for

CRM program troubles with references for further reading. Then we will discuss the strategic issues involved in the pursuit of a global CRM strategy.

Ineffective Change Management

Change management is defined as a strategy that supports personal and organizational transitions (Petouhoff, 2006, p. 48). This support should be focused on cultural as well as technological change, which is a primary implementation problem at the corporate level. Many organizations, that for one reason or another see CRM as purely a technology, are often willing and able to offer training on the use of the new system, but may not be as ready to handle cultural factors within the organization that may impede success. One cultural factor is the resistance to ownership of something new or innovative by some employees. If employees (not to mention customers) are involved in the process of creating the CRM system, there are more chances for success. But it is often difficult to include each and every employee in the organization in the creation process, thus there will be a need to reduce the level of initial objections that are typical when changes occur.

The management style of managers at the supervisory level is an important determining factor as to whether CRM implementation efforts will be successful. Since employees often have an inherent aversion to change, these objections could be increased depending on the management style within a business unit. If a manager is more likely to admonish the members of their staff for either failing to follow the new CRM process, or for following it incorrectly, the resistance to change could be much more pronounced. Since one of the key assets of a company is its people, the longer it takes for the company's employees to embrace a new system, the more likely it is to fail. Some readers will recall that the founder of TQM, W. Edwards Deming, has stated that the admonishment of the workforce has no place in a quality environment (Besterfield, D., Besterfield-Michna, C., & Besterfield, G., 1998). Since the pursuit of quality and the goal of customer satisfaction are related, it should be no surprise that this form of management is anathema in this setting as well.

Thus, another aspect of a successful change management program is an internal marketing initiative. The firm should plan to 'sell the vision of change' as early as possible, in an effort to obtain the maximum level of internal customer (employee) acceptance for the new CRM program (Kale, 2004). As we have discussed in preceding chapters, the benefits of focusing on the wishes and desires of the customer will become apparent, especially when one considers that the alternatives being pursued by companies that are not customer focused can have disastrous consequences! How many of us would remain loyal to a firm if we were not treated with respect, and if our opinions for improvement were not taken into consideration? This same thought process should be applied to the employees, since an organization's people can literally make or break CRM initiatives. The internal marketing program should be integrated into each step of CRM implementation process. In other words, from the earliest discussions of the benefits of a CRM program, all the way until the new initiative becomes a reality, the internal customers should be kept apprised of the benefits of the new approach.

In order to effectively communicate the message in a change management program, a mix of social, organizational, and individual factors must be utilized in an effort to increase the perceived usefulness of the system for the employees, as well as to increase the perceived ease of use of the new technology (Avlonitis & Panagopoulos, 2005, pp. 355–368). Perceived usefulness involves employees being able to see how the new CRM platform will allow them to increase their sales volume. If a sales employee is able to have access to pertinent customer data concerning purchasing history, the acceptance of the CRM technology may be much quicker. If the employee also perceives the new system as being easy to use, and something that will not slow them down on a daily basis, then the prospects of acceptance increase significantly.

Social factors concern the influences in employee performance due to supervisors, peers, and competitors. If the internal marketing initiative concerning CRM can improve the knowledge base of the employees, there will be less reason to initially reject the new procedures using the bandwagon approach to decision making. Organizational factors that allow for better chances of success for a change management program must include adequate training of all employees in how to use the new system. Managers must be trained in addressing employee objections, as well as in the methods that allow for the creative learning process to flourish. Employees should receive similar training, in an effort to create the levels of trust required for a well-functioning team. Individual factors include a firm understanding of the computer experience and innovativeness of its staff. If a company realizes the benefits of a customer CRM orientation, but fails to realize the level of sophistication of its employees, implementation efforts will suffer. Thus, key ingredients in successful change management programs involve setting accurate expectations of their employees' involvement, increasing the levels of user participation as early in the process as possible, and providing adequate training for all employees.

Another recent study also showed that successful CRM implementation requires linking the style of management with social and structural factors within an organization (Osarenkhoe & Bennani, 2007, pp. 139–164). The authors contend that the core dimensions of CRM strategy implementation can be summarized as the 'five S's': structure, staff, style, systems, and schemes. The most appropriate structure for a successful implementation is a team-based structure. As was noted earlier, not including cross-functional teams in the planning process has typically led to failures in CRM implementation. The cross-functional nature of the organizational structure leads to the second dimension of this implementation framework, that of staff. As we have discussed in an earlier section, the employees of a firm can make or break any strategic effort, and CRM is no exception. The third component mentioned in the study was the style of management, which is of paramount importance to success. Systems is the fourth component in the 'five S' approach. Successful CRM implementations involve establishing relational systems such as the BSC, supply chain management systems, and customer-focused order fulfillment systems. The last part of the framework involves schemes. These include programs that support a customer relationship framework, such as loyalty and retention programs, and internal and external marketing communication that values the relationship between the firm and the customer.

In summing up this section on change management, another recent study helped to shed light on the fact that a firm may have various levels of change resistance, especially when cross-functional teams have not been utilized to determine the processes affected by CRM (Bohling et al, 2006, pp. 184–194). The sales, marketing, and finance areas of the firm may have different objectives, and different feelings toward the best methods to satisfy customers. When beginning a CRM project, all of the business processes in an organization must be reviewed to determine which are the processes that are most likely to be improved with CRM technology. The customer-oriented organization must collect data on all customer interfaces, and must map out the point of contact between the customer and the firm, wherever this might occur. Since technical complexity alone is seldom the problem in a successful CRM program, and since the problems with change management are compounded when the CRM initiative is organization-wide, it is all the more important to link CRM strategy with the overall marketing strategy of the firm. In order to do that, there must be a strong commitment to CRM at the highest levels of the organization.

Lack of Top Management Executive Support

It has been said that relationship management is one and the same as the process of implementing it (Osarenkhoe & Bennani, 2007, pp. 139–164). Put another way, the means do not justify the ends. The means are in fact the ends in the process of occurring. If a firm is attempting to achieve a customer orientation, but stumbles along the way, the impact to the customer will be apparent. The goal of any CRM initiative should be to change the focus away from product life cycles, to customer lifecycles, as was discussed in chapter six. Firms that do not understand this face an uncertain future in an ever-increasing global economy where customer relationship management will be a sustainable competitive advantage for those firms who are able to be successful. Another primary facet of this success is in the area of upper-management support.

As we have previously discussed, organizational leaders must embrace the fact that all people are wired to resist change. This is the first step toward a successful CRM implementation effort. The CRM process must be a 'top-down' approach, or the implementation effort will not be successful (Kale, 2004). Top management should participate in risk mitigation meetings as early as possible in the planning of a CRM system. If upper-management understands the risks of not moving to a customer-centric viewpoint, CRM can be a sustainable competitive advantage. Studies have shown that CRM initiatives that were from a 'bottom-up' approach have tended to be more tactical in nature. Rather than viewing CRM as a strategic enabler, bottom-up approaches tend to view CRM as purely technology or as a sales tool. Since these approaches typically originate in a specific business unit within a company, there are usually many more implementation problems when users outside of that originating unit are involved in the implementation.

If the 'CRM champion' in the organization is at the corporate or upper-management level, it is more likely that the goals will be linked to organization-wide, tangible benefits, rather than goals of a narrower scope. These tactical goals could be counter to the goals of another group. For example, if an organization simply views CRM as a technology initiative, a situation could arise where data is being captured not for the purposes of improving products or services for the firm's customers, but to purely make the organization more efficient. While organizational efficiency is certainly a goal to strive toward, efficiency should not be achieved to the detriment of the customer experience. Organizations that are focused on lowering cost regardless of the impact to the customer's mindset, are by definition non-customer-focused organizations.

In yet another link to the TQM philosophy, the goals as established by upper-management for a CRM program must not only be linked to tangible business benefits; they must also be measurable. The 'top-down' approach is more likely to combine employee and customer objectives in an effort to achieve market share gains and an increase to shareholder value. It is also more likely to be able to align CRM goals with key stakeholder groups, namely the customers. The 'bottom-up' approach has proven to not be as successful in terms of balancing long-term goals with short-term aspirations (Bohling et al, 2006, pp. 184–194). Oftentimes, these goals are cost related, and CRM programs sponsored by top management are typically better equipped in making these important decisions. From the beginning of the initial planning stages and for long after implementation, firms with a customer focus must have accurate data concerning the revenues and costs of serving their customers, regardless of where they are served. While activity-based costing studies can help determine cost drivers, the involvement of upper-management is required in order to ensure that all of the company's efforts are appropriately aligned. Upper-management may also be in a better position to ensure that the provider of the CRM solution has the ability to control the costs of implementation both during and after the new process is realized.

What should be apparent by now is that the commitment of upper-management is required in order for success. This plus an effective change management program has been the primary reasons for the success of CRM initiatives in the recent past. Not having these two key components has also led to CRM failures.

The CRM Technology Purchasing Decision

Now that we have discussed some of the primary pitfalls associated with CRM implementation, it will be helpful to discuss the best approach for managers in selecting the CRM technology platform which best meets the needs of their organizations. As we have made clear in the preceding pages, the first step in the CRM technology purchasing decision is to clearly define the requirements of CRM and the objectives of your business. Since seeing CRM purely as technology is one of the primary pitfalls of CRM implementation, corporate leaders must realize that obtaining a new CRM technology platform is not a panacea. Making the wrong decision could lead to a costly and inefficient system that will not meet company needs. In order to best understand the needs of the entire organization, it is advised that cross-functional representation be achieved as early as possible during the CRM technology purchasing decision phase. Some of the requirements that must be considered include the functional requirements of the chosen CRM technology, the integration requirements in order to allow for the CRM technology platform to seamlessly integrate with existing company technologies, as well as cost and budgetary requirements. In order to most accurately calculate these costs, the costs of training and support for the CRM technology must be considered. Additionally, firms should identity goals such as return on investment and the desired productivity improvement as part of the first step.

The next step in deciding on which CRM technology platform to purchase, is the creation of a list of vendors that match the criteria determined by the organization. As a general rule, managers should consider vendors that have a proven track record in successful CRM implementation with organizations that have similar CRM technology needs to the purchasing manager's organization. As part of the vendor selection process, managers will want to speak with a given vendor's existing clients, in an effort to obtain information concerning how successful the implementation went, as well as how good the vendor's support was following the initial implementation. Companies that have experienced successful CRM implementations are those that require their vendors to provide specifics upfront as to how they will meet the firm's business objectives. Additionally, as part of the vendor selection process, all costs must be clear, so firms can avoid exceeding their budgets owing to a lack of communication concerning what specific features will require additional cost during the CRM technology implementation. Purchasing managers should attempt to obtain discounts wherever possible, especially given the competitive environment of the CRM technology services provider industry.

As part of the open communication process of vendor selection, once the list of prospective CRM technology providers has been shortened to the top contenders, purchasing managers should plan on visiting the vendors, as well as having the vendors visit with the company in order to provide demonstrations of how the CRM technology will most benefit the purchasing manager's organization. A key component in these meetings is for the managers to view the CRM technology in the eyes of their customers. While two goals of CRM technology implementation are increased productivity and net profit, another goal must be the maintenance of the 'customer experience'. Any CRM implementation effort that materially alters the level of customer service or the quality of the product offering will seldom lead to success.

Finally, when negotiating with the chosen CRM technology provider, purchasing managers must make sure that they consider where the organization is heading in the foreseeable future, so that the vendor selected is able to grow with the organization, rather than providing a technological solution that only meets the current needs of the organization, and may become obsolete in the immediate future. Successful CRM technology implementations involve management discussions of the time horizons for the initial implementation, as well as the future needs of the organization, all before the final contract is signed.

Going Global: A Strategic and Central Approach for Customer Relationship Management

In the first chapter to this book, we outlined some common international strategies, as well as some common sources of sustainable competitive advantage in a global economy. The first sustainable competitive advantage that we discussed was global efficiency. As should now be apparent, location advantages can play a central role in a successful CRM implementation for a multinational firm, but the operational efficiencies cannot be such as to hinder the customer service provided by the firm. Location advantages, and other means of achieving global efficiencies, must be such that still allow local responsiveness. The second sustainable competitive advantage discussed at the outset of this book was multi-market flexibility. A customer-oriented organization must be responsive to their customers, wherever they operate, so this strategy would appear to be conducive with CRM. Moreover, the third sustainable competitive advantage, that of worldwide learning, is also highly compatible with CRM. The examples provided in this book suggest that having a true customer focus in every action that a firm makes would also have to be considered a competitive advantage in today's global market.

CRM Across National Boundaries

Corporate leaders and academics have begun to inquire as to the implementation issues associated with CRM on a global scale (Ramaseshan et al, 2006). The goals of global CRM are now clear: the ability to acquire, retain, and develop (via cross-selling and up-selling) customers across national boundaries and cultures. Since CRM is by definition a customer-focused methodology, the open question at this point is whether the differences experienced when conducting business in different countries will require any modifications to the CRM platform. Depending on the severity of the differences in operating environments for a given firm, there may be some modifications necessary due to different customer expectations as well as drivers for satisfaction in multinational settings. Managing cultural differences at the organizational level, as well as those at the customer level are of paramount importance if a multinational firm is to have any success in a customer-oriented strategy. By focusing on local differences, a firm can effectively meet and exceed the desires of the customer. This makes the collection of data extremely important, as well as the creation by upper-management of an organizational culture that values creativity, learning, and the sharing of information. These are the fundamental values of an organization with a transnational strategy, as was discussed in Chapter 1. Unless a firm is operating in international markets with a high level of congruity, a total home replication strategy, or even a global strategy, is inconsistent with CRM. The home replication strategy attempts to place a 'one size fits all' approach to all markets based on how things are done in the home market. The global strategy orientation attempts to do the same standardization based on the one strategy that is expected to work the best in the most markets worldwide.

In our prior discussions of data mining efforts, as well as that of loyalty cards, it was shown how vital it is to be able to appropriately segment the customers based on their probability of future purchasing behavior based on their past preferences, as well as how well they fit into the targeted demographic that is most likely to behave in a certain way.

In addition to differences at the customer level, multinational firms must also face a myriad of challenges outside of the customer dynamic. Factors such as the competitive environment, technological infrastructure, trade barriers, political systems, and legal regulations all vary in different jurisdictions of the world (Ajami, Cool, Goddard, & Khambata, 2006). Each of these factors makes a completely standardized approach to CRM very difficult, depending on the level of disparity among the markets where a given firm operates.

In terms of technology, the levels of infrastructure development worldwide are very different. These differences could make the costs associated with data collection very high, and could also impact the quantity and quality of the information available. Thus, companies that wish to employ a customer orientation worldwide may find that it is very difficult to do this on a standardized basis given the differences in technological sophistication.

Global CRM is also impacted by differences in markets. Thus far, the majority of CRM applications have been undertaken in developed countries of the world, although CRM penetration rates in Asia have been increasing in recent years (Ramaseshan, Bejou, Jain, Mason, & Pancras, 2006). International trade and urbanization levels can also impact the success of Global CRM strategies. Many trading blocks such as the European Union are forging increased levels of integration and harmonization in terms of business operating environments, and some industries such as financial services, are involved in levels of integration that far exceed that of the European Union. For example, the Bank of International Settlements has required that all large, internationally active banks participate in the Basel II Accord, which details how banks should risk-rate their loan portfolios in an effort to standardize the amount of capital that is held back due to portfolio risk. Even given this level of integration, some industries may find that there are barriers to trade that can certainly affect a standardized approach to CRM strategy. Some Asian nations, such as China and Singapore, are only now loosening their prohibitions of having foreign-owned financial services companies. As regards international trade agreements, there are many bilateral agreements that are complicating business operating environments, so it appears that there will continue to be a duality of increased integration at the multinational level, along with a further preponderance of bilateral arrangements that may keep the waters muddy for multinationals looking for global integration across operating environments.

Organizations would benefit from better understanding cultural differences among the various markets in which they serve. There have been many attempts at classifying cultures based on geographic proximity or other high-level variables, but organizations must understand that relying simply on generalizations concerning cultural differences will not lead to sustainable competitive advantage. Organizations that are truly customer focused must strive to understand the mindsets of their customers, and this involves understanding the various components that make up the customers identification with the firm, product, or service offering. Global CRM can also be impacted by the aforementioned social and cultural factors. Numerous studies have shown that there are differences in how people behave depending on their culture. One well-known model of cultural analysis is Hofstede's Five Dimensions (Hofstede, 1991). This classification system views cultures in the context of a social orientation, a power orientation, an uncertainty orientation, a goal orientation, and a time orientation. Social orientation reflects a person's beliefs about the relative importance of the individual and the groups to which that person belongs, and is typified by the two extremes of individualism and collectivism. Power orientation refers to the beliefs that people hold about the appropriateness of power and authority differences in hierarchies such as business organizations. The two extremes in this category are power tolerance, exhibited in cultures which are more willing to question authority, and power respect, which is seen in cultures that are more willing to accept power based on position (and hence are more hierarchical). The last three of Hofstede's dimensions include the feelings that people have regarding uncertain situations (whether they accept uncertainty or in fact avoid it), the manner in which people are motivated to work toward different types of goals (whether they be aggressive, more materialistic goals or passive life quality goals), and the extent to which members of cultures adopt a long-term outlook versus a short-term outlook on work, life, and their patterns of consumption.

Western values tend to show that individuality, self-interest, and immediate gratification are more likely to be apparent, while Asian values, as well as other parts of the world, may more often tend to resemble delayed gratification, and a more collective viewpoint. Some scholars have suggested that cultures with a group orientation may be more apt for repeat purchases, than those societies that exhibit more individualistic behaviors. Given these cultural differences, companies with a global CRM strategy may need to consider different marketing approaches depending on where they are conducting business. The loyalty cards enjoyed in western societies may not be as important as the sincerity of service for some other areas of the world. This clearly shows how important it is for a firm to know their customers. Since it is especially hard to generalize that all people in certain parts of the world behave in the same manner, a good global CRM strategy will entail programs and metrics that allow the firm to know their customers, wherever they may reside.

Another area of departure in a global CRM initiative concerns differing legal systems and regulations. We have already discussed some of the differences in business operating environments produced by international trade agreements. Another issue of concern for all companies with a customer orientation (global or domestic) is the increasing anxiety of some customers as it concerns the privacy of their personal information. There are certainly varying degrees of acceptability for data collection processes worldwide. In the United States, for example, there is less apprehension concerning the sharing of personal consumption habits via the survey methods discussed in this book, than there has historically been in Europe. This is another example of where differences due to national boundaries may cause the need for altering some of the tactics used in CRM schemes.

CRM Practices Across Cultures

Now that we have covered some of the basic challenges in implementation of CRM across cultures, are there any generally accepted guidelines for which cultures tend to follow specific behaviors? In our study of loyalty programs that compared the US and Spain, it was found that loyalty programs currently in the United States tend to be based more on quality than on profitability (Galguera et al, 2006, pp. 459–479). It was also found that multinationals based in the United States tend to use a more standardized approach to CRM strategy, than European multinationals do. European firms are more likely to exhibit a more customized approach (Ramaseshan et al, 2006). One possible explanation for this could be the cultural and geographic proximity of countries in Europe, as opposed to the United States.

   The proximity of so many national boundaries in Europe could also help explain the fact that studies have shown a higher level of privacy concerns in Europe, relative to the United States. Additionally, US firms tend to have more unused data than that of European companies. One of the most notable CRM implementation problems from the United States is seeing CRM as purely technology. It has been reported that US firms that exhibit these tendencies are more apt to pursue the most expensive technology for their CRM efforts, while firms from Germany and Scandinavia tend to focus their CRM expenditure primarily on building customer loyalty and in customer retention strategies. These generalities may help shed light on how a firm could benefit from having a transnational strategy that encourages information sharing within the firm, and are a helpful starting point for firms in their quest to pursue a CRM strategy in our increasingly global business environment. A cultural focus, if done correctly, can help to broaden the focus of CRM strategies beyond the domestic, local market, and can help customer-focused organizations create a sustainable competitive advantage in all of the markets that they serve throughout the world.

Questions for Discussion

1. What are the most common pitfalls of CRM implementation and how can they best be avoided?

2. Outline an effective change management system that will produce a successful CRM implementation for your organization.

3. Elaborate on why upper-management support is crucial to the success of a CRM implementation effort.

4. Discuss the complications and benefits to be achieved by pursuing CRM on a global scale.

5. Why are failed CRM implementation efforts seldom due purely to technology?

APPENDIX
Case Studies on
Customer Relationship Management

Case Study 1

Customer Satisfaction at Paradorn Bank

G. Jason Goddard
Wachovia Corporation, USA

Paradorn Bank is a newly created financial institution located in Bangkok, Thailand. The small, community-oriented bank was formed in 2004, when three executives at Asia World Bank saw a need to meet the needs of a very profitable, yet small, niche market in the Greater Bangkok area. Three years ago, Lucas Kim, a senior Commercial Lending Officer at Asia World Bank, along with Khaosai Khaokor, Head of Asia World's Thailand wealth management office, decided that the time was right to leave their executive positions at Asia World Bank, and to seek start-up capital to form the new community bank. Lucas and Khaosai asked the then head of Thailand Operations for Asia World Bank, Danai Kittikasem, to join them in this new venture. All three executives felt that their larger, former employer had lost touch with its customers in Bangkok, as the large bank applied the same lending criteria to customers in Thailand as it did throughout the continent of Asia. Lucas, Khaosai, and Danai felt that a bank which catered to these same clients with whom they had developed relationships over the years, and to whom they provided a more personalized service, would be very successful. In the aftermath of the Asian Financial Crisis, many commercial clients in Thailand had expressed an interest to them in dealing with a locally owned and operated bank, rather than one which made many of its financial decisions in another part of the world.

Following a year-long period of raising the necessary capital and achieving the necessary regulatory hurdles in order to open their first branch, Paradorn Bank was open for business in June of 2005. Given the strengths of the new bank's leadership, Paradorn Bank began with a specialization in personal lending, as well as fulfilling the needs of small commercial loan customers. The bank's initial loan portfolio was small, but the desire was to increase their exposure to their existing customers over the next few years. Many of the former clients of both Lucas and Khaosai felt that the service levels that had been achieved by Asia World Bank in the past had deteriorated since their departure; yet, it was these former client relationships, cultivated in the past, that were instrumental for the bank to begin to gain market share in the Bangkok market by the middle of 2006.

Paradorn Bank's early mission was to acquire as many profitable relationships as possible from Asia World Bank's Bangkok offices. Given the operational expertise of Chief Operations Officer Danai Kittikasem, the bank was able to track from its very beginning the profitability of its deposit relationships relative to the amount of total credit outstanding for each of its customers. Given the limited scope of the new firm, the methods of such data collection were manual in nature, as opposed to having a more automated format for collecting the data. At the end of each month, Danai provided a report summarizing the total average monthly deposit balances for each of the Bank's customers, along with a summary of the loan profitability over the same period.

Lucas Kim, the CEO of Paradorn Bank, knew that the reliance on the manual reporting was acceptable to the bank while it was still in its nascent stage, but the movement to a more automated reporting process was critical as the bank grew its customer base. Of equal concern to Lucas was the fact that the manual reporting process did not effectively capture customer complaints or suggestions for improvement that would allow the bank to meet the needs of its existing clientele, or prepare them for a successful relationship-oriented marketing campaign to achieve even greater market share gains in the Greater Bangkok area.

Lucas asked Khaosai Khaokor, Paradorn's Chief Credit Officer, for a report, which addressed the current methods for gauging customer satisfaction levels at the bank. He asked Khaosai for the report rather than Danai, as Lucas had known Khaosai for a longer period of time, and felt that Khaosai would not have a vested interest in making the customer satisfaction results higher than they were in reality. Lucas was happy to learn that there was a method of measuring the satisfaction for the bank's customers, and that the same methodology had been in place since the first day of the company's existence.

The Customer Satisfaction Survey

Khaosai's report provided a brief description of a customer satisfaction survey that was included as a part of Paradorn Bank's loan closing documentation package. The report stated that during the first year of the bank's existence, the five-question survey was completed by over 80 percent of the borrowers who closed loans at Paradorn Bank. Branch personnel were instructed to carry out the five-question satisfaction survey in person immediately following the loan closing. Once the loan documentation was completed, each customer was asked to rank the following five questions on a scale of from one to four, with four being the highest and best ranking. Below is an itemization of the questions contained in Paradorn Bank's Customer Satisfaction Survey:

- How satisfied are you with the location of the branch?
- How satisfied are you with the friendliness of the branch personnel?
- How satisfied are you with the terms of the loan agreement?
- How do we compare with other banks?
- Please rate your overall satisfaction with Paradorn Bank.

During Paradorn Bank's first year of operation, the survey was completed over 100 times. Khaosai did not have the data on hand to determine how many of the surveys were completed by the same borrowers, but was sure that each survey represented a distinctly different borrowing experience at Paradorn Bank. A perfect score was achieved in over 70 percent of the surveys. A perfect score is defined as achieving the highest ranking on each of the five questions in the survey. Given the success rate of obtaining surveys, Khaosai decided to implement the survey as part of the annual performance review for branch personnel. Any employee that achieved an average customer satisfaction survey score of 3.6 or higher would require preferential consideration for annual merit increases and bonuses. This was the equivalent to a 90 percent satisfaction score on the survey. Khaosai noted that other competing banks had disclosed that their surveys have achieved results far below this level, so by setting this as a goal, the bar was set very high.

As Lucas reviewed the report, he noted the average scores for the surveys compiled so far: 3.3 for the branch location question, 3.4 for the branch personnel friendliness question, 3.5 for the loan agreement terms question, 3.1 for the comparison with competitors question, and an overall score of 3.5 for satisfaction with Paradorn Bank question. While Lucas was happy with the results of the survey, he was having trouble reconciling the high scores with the bank's recent inability to increase market share in the greater Bangkok area. While the bank had experienced early success in terms of market penetration, growth had flattened out over the last few months. He attributed the low score for the first question and the flat growth curve with a need for more branches. Since many of Paradorn Bank's customers came from prior banking relationships achieved by the company's leadership at Asia World Bank, it may be the case that the sole branch location of Paradorn is not extremely convenient for all of the bank's current customers.

Lucas was also concerned that the answers being obtained in the surveys would be skewed upwards by the new policy of rewarding branch personnel for achieving high customer satisfaction survey results. Lucas was concerned that branch personnel would be sufficiently motivated for obtaining high merit increases and bonuses, and would ask the customers to provide a perfect rating rather than simply obtaining the answers as provided by the customers. When Lucas confronted Khaosai about this concern, Khaosai stated that his mechanism for judging whether the survey results were inflated was to compare the level of perfect scores with the current level of 70 percent. If in the future, perfect survey scores were obtained far in excess of 70 percent, then ratings inflation may in fact be present.

Lucas considered increasing the survey questions to include inquiries about deposit account satisfaction, and also reviewed the possibility of including a section for comments for the borrowers. Since Paradorn Bank offers both depository services and lending products, Lucas felt that the lack of discussion in the satisfaction survey about deposits was causing the results to be less meaningful on an overall basis. Lucas also discussed the idea of including an open-ended section in the questionnaire with Danai and Khaosai, and all three managers felt that having the ability to read a customer's comments would better help them in their future targeted marketing plans.

A last area of concern to Lucas was the fact that the lowest score on the survey results so far was the question that compared Paradorn Bank to its competitors. Since many of Paradorn's initial customers had come from Asia World Bank, these customers might have scored the other questions in the survey higher as those questions represent the primary reasons for their movement to the newer, smaller organization. Lucas was sure that the comparison question was being ranked consistently lower as the larger banks provided a much more extensive service offering than did the smaller firm. Including open-ended questions in the survey might help to better determine the areas where Paradorn Bank could improve in the near term. By listening to the desires of their customers, Paradorn Bank could better position itself for continued growth.

Measurement of Employee Performance

Paradorn Bank was also concerned with the satisfaction of its employees. In terms of other mechanisms for rating the performance of branch personnel, during the first year of the bank's existence, the employee evaluation system at Paradorn Bank was very subjective. Due to the reliance on manual reporting, and given the focus on gaining market share during the first year of operation, there was not an effective means of stack ranking employees relative to each other at the branch level. Within the last six months, Lucas Kim implemented a more quantitative means of evaluating the branch personnel. Lucas felt that something that he could successfully measure was the total processing time between when a customer applied for a loan, and when the eventual loan decision was made. This was done by comparing the date of the loan application with the date of the communication between the retail banker and the customer. Lucas also felt that he could effectively measure the total volume of loans and deposits obtained by an employee on a monthly basis. Since the amount of loans and deposits obtained by the branch was evaluated monthly, Lucas felt that it made sense to add a volume-based judgment criteria for all of the branch personnel as well. Lucas knew that the continued reliance on the manual reporting process would cause trouble as the bank expanded into different branch locations, but he felt that the current size of the organization was appropriate for the manual tracking of customer response time data.

Each morning, Lucas was provided with a report detailing loan requests that either came in the previous day, or were still in process at the bank. Branch personnel were judged on the percentage of the time that they responded back to the customer within 24 hours, within 48 hours, and within 72 hours. Lucas felt that a response time longer than 72 hours was unacceptable under any circumstances. He managed this process by making the discussion of this 'pipeline report' part of the daily branch meetings that were held at the start of each business day. This meeting informed the branch personnel which loans had to be processed during that particular business day, was a forum for any questions that the employees had of the management team and was a team building exercise to maintain the level of employee excitement that was key to the bank's success.

There were eight employees working in Paradorn Bank's sole branch location. Three employees were responsible for direct lending and deposit acquisition, three employees were tellers, and two employees were customer service representatives. The eight employees had not all been with Paradorn Bank since its inception, but Lucas felt that having the branch staffed a little heavily at present would improve the overall service of the bank, and would allow for smoother future expansion into more branch locations. Lucas felt that his daily updates to all branch personnel concerning the status of loan processing requests, would ensure that everyone in the branch would understand the importance of achieving quick loan processing times.

When Lucas first implemented the new policy, one of the lenders voiced concern over the fact that they considered the daily updates to be a form of micromanagement previously not seen at Paradorn Bank. Another lender voiced concern over the fact that the tellers should not be privy to this information, as they did not have the means to control the loan processing time. One of the bank tellers complained that they felt that only the lending staff should be judged on a volume basis, as the primary role of the teller was customer service. As time progressed, Lucas felt that the initial reactions against his new policy had ceased, as he did not hear any further complaints on the matter during the morning meetings. Based on the feedback received, Lucas decided that it was appropriate to measure the tellers and customer service personnel based on the total volume of customers that each employee serviced during a given month. By coupling this performance measurement with how the lenders were measured, Paradorn Bank could achieve an even higher level of customer satisfaction than was reported previously.

Lucas had a lot of other ideas for improving the customer satisfaction at the bank, and most of his ideas concerned ways of increasing the productivity and efficiency of the employees. As Paradorn Bank expanded into multiple branch locations, Lucas envisioned having the employees ranked relative to each other on a weekly basis in terms of their production, so that all employees would know how they measured up to others in the same job function. He considered offering additional monetary incentives annually to the top-producing employee in each job function. In the future, he envisioned group team-building events outside of the branch environment, but this would have to wait until Paradorn Bank expanded. One program that Lucas thought was worthy of immediate implementation was the '*Make the Prospect a Customer*' program. In an effort to increase the bank's customer base, Lucas wanted to begin offering rewards to the employees that were able to attract the most new customers, whether it was via the opening of a deposit account or a new loan at Paradorn Bank. Lucas also felt that by sponsoring sporting events such as the Thai national football team's games at nearby Rajamankala Football Stadium in Bangkok, the bank could expand its customer base greatly. The key for Lucas was to motivate the employees for success. By instilling a competitive spirit among the branch personnel, and by increasing the brand recognition of Paradorn Bank in Bangkok, Lucas felt that the overall performance of the bank would certainly improve.

After Lucas had reviewed Khaosai's most recent customer satisfaction report for the third time, he wondered if it made sense for Paradorn Bank to hire an outside consultant in order to further improve their program for measuring customer satisfaction at the company. This was a crucial time in the development of the small bank, and he wanted to make sure that all options were considered to ensure a successful future in a highly competitive industry.

Questions for Discussion

1. What are the primary weaknesses in the measurement of satisfaction at Paradorn Bank?

2. What are the primary benefits to be achieved by moving from the current manual data collection model to a more automated approach?

3. If you were a consultant hired by Paradorn Bank to aid them in the preparation of a targeted marketing campaign in the near future, what changes would you make in their current data collection strategy?

4. Does the method of employee evaluation help or hinder the bank's customer satisfaction goals?

5. What other recommendations would you have for this new company in order for them to be successful in the future?

The Case of Discovery[1]

Hanne Nørreklit
Aarhus School of Business, University of Aarhus, Denmark

Lennart Nørreklit
University of Aalborg, Denmark

Brief Presentation of Discovery

Discovery was established in 1992 in Urbana-Champaign, Illinois, USA. One of the founders is the present president and owner Fred Kersten, who is educated in fine art and sculpture. He started the company together with two others. They quit their jobs, moved into a house all together, and then they started the company in the basement.

The company has been a leader in providing microcomputer boards and systems to the original equipment manufacturer (OEM) and value added reseller (VAR) marketplace. The business currently occupies a 30,000 square foot facility that includes manufacturing, engineering and corporate offices, employing approximately 90 people. Expansion has outstripped the microcomputer industry with revenue growth of approximately 60 percent per year for the last five years. The company has been ranked among the 200 fastest growing privately held small companies in the U.S.A.

In the microcomputer boards industry, there are two big competitors and ten smaller companies. The two big competitors have 80 percent of the market. The ten small have 20 percent. Discovery is one of the ten smaller companies.

Since its establishment, the strategy of Discovery has changed from being a custom-minded company to being a market-oriented firm. This has changed the composition of its customers. Today, their customers are found in industry, hospital, military, and research and development areas. The goal of Discovery is now to increase orders in the contract market. Discovery has changed from customized products to more standardized products. The primary competitive advantages of its products and services are high quality, speed and cost efficiency.

The production plant is quite new, as the company moved to the existing location only a few years ago. In their new facilities, they have production capacity five times higher than what they are producing currently, with the same equipment. They only need to have more employees, which was a primary motivation for their move to the new location. They can deliver within one week, and ship right away. The Sales Department wants the orders delivered at once, but this is not realistic.

---

[1] This case is based on actual events. Only the names have been changed.

The Engineering Department develops new products and adjusts the products sold to fit the specific situation of the customer. The development of the products has changed to be more oriented toward the market needs. Earlier, the products were more engineering-oriented. It is very important for the company to keep up with technology advancement, especially given the strong competition from Asia in its industry. A few years ago, in 2003, there was an occasion where the development of a new product was not finished at the right time—this caused a serious crisis for the company. It is important to finish the product at the right time because of the very short lifecycles of the products, and the need to keep up with the technology in the industry.

During the crisis, the computer market was still recovering from the dotcom crashes, and Discovery had to change its structure by reducing the number of employees from 96 people to 72. The company had to face reality. It turned out that people had hired other people to do their jobs.

Recently, Discovery has expanded the sales and marketing function and the company now intends to automate their production with computer-aided design (CAD), and other technologies.

Growth and the Financial Position

Total growth of sales from 2000 to 2006 is 2,580 percent (see Table CS2.1).

Table CS2.1 Financial indicators 2000–2006

Fiscal Year	Sales $1000	g(S)* %	Assets $1000	g(NA)** %	Profit RONA***
2006	41,820	31	18,980	14	5%
2005	31,760	57	16,505	94	7%
2004	20,145	141	8,470	118	5%
2003	8,345	101	3,885	58	2%
2002	4,150	34	2,470	125	10%
2001	3,090	97	1,100	68	9%
2000	1,570		660		11%

* Growth rate of sales; ** Growth rate of net assets; *** Return on Net Assets.

However, the financial position is very weak in the company. To illustrate this we apply Donaldson's formula[1] for self-sustaining growth to evaluate long-term growth. The formula for balanced growth is:

g(S)   **= r(RONA + d(RONA-i)), where:**
g(S)   = growth rate of sales
RONA   = Return on net assets
r   = earnings-retention rate
d   = debt-equity ratio
i   = after tax interest rate on debt

For any given set of values for the goals r, d, and i it is possible to calculate the self-sustaining growth values for g(S) for any presupposed value of RONA.

Donaldson's formula makes it possible to evaluate the validity and consistency of the goals of a company. If, for example, the turnover planned in the budget will bring about a decrease in the equity/debt ratio then this is not a sound goal. According to Figure CS2.1, the company has grown with 100 percent or more for three of the six years we analyzed, but the company has only earned 11 percent or less profit in these years. That means, according to Donaldson, that the company has favored the goal of growth much more than the equity ratio. The result being that Discovery is now in a weak financial situation.

Total growth of assets from 2000 to 2006 is 2,797 percent. The fact that total growth of assets is higher than total growth of sales means that the company's efficiency in using its assets to create sales has decreased. Ceteris paribus, this should lower the self-sustaining growth rate with the same difference as that between the total growth of assets and the total growth of sales. The difference is eight percent. We have not taken this into account in Figure CS2.1, which shows Discovery's self-sustaining growth. We can conclude, however, that a decrease in the efficiency of the assets makes the situation of Discovery's financial position look even worse than portrayed in the figure below.

Suppositions on the Financial Goal System of Discovery

R   = 1 i.e. all earnings are retained in Discovery
i   = 6 i.e. average interest on debt is 6% after tax
d   = 1 i.e. equity is 50% of total assets—normal in the USA
d   = 9 i.e. equity is 10% of total assets—fairly close to the goals realized in Discovery

SSG1: If r = 1, i = 6, d = 1 then g(S) = 2RONA - 6
SSG2: If r = 1, i = 6, d = 9, then g(S) = 10RONA-54

---

1   See Gordon Donaldson, 'Financial Goals and Strategic Consequences', *Harvard Business Review*, May–June 1985, pp. 58–9. For deduction see Appendix.

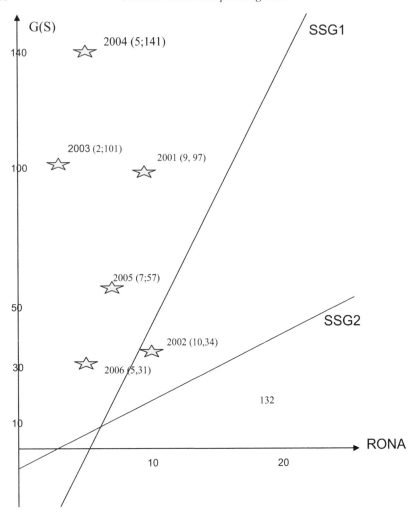

Figure CS2.1: Discovery's financial growth
Note: The units on the x-axis are expanded compared to those on the
y-axis—otherwise this figure would become too disproportionate. This
may be felt misleading because both axes represent percentages.

Organization and Management Thoughts

The organizational structure of Discovery is line and staff structured—see Figure
CS2.2.

In on-site interviews, the president and managers of Discovery discussed the
history, the policies, and their perceptions of the firm. It is a general opinion in
the firm that the coordination between the departments is poor and that it has been
better. The only ones who do not talk about it are the president, Fred Kersten, and the
Director of Sales and Marketing, Gilbert Null.

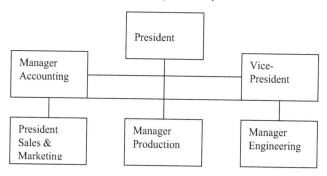

Figure CS2.2: Formal structure of the organization

Fred Kersten, President (41 years old)

I am educated in fine art and sculpture. I started the firm together with two others. We quit our jobs, moved together in a house, and then we started the firm in the basement. We had together 50 thousand dollars when we started. We were earning a total of 50 thousand dollars a year in the beginning.

After a while, the two others got tired and left the firm. I continued alone. I received money and guarantees from my mother, my former boss, friends, etc. Every time I could get one dollar the bank would lend me one dollar. The bank took half of the risk in that way. The others left the firm just before it began to take off.

I learned by running the firm, that the most important thing for the firm to survive is the cash flow as opposed to the profit. Discovery had at that time a lot of customized orders. Since the orders were produced to special customer needs, I required that the customers pay in advance. In this way, I found a solution to the cash flow problems of the firm. The bank could not understand how we could expand 60 percent a year, have a profit of US$10,000, and not have to incur further bank loans. The philosophy was to make a break-even cash flow any way possible. We had to pull ourselves up by the bootstraps if we were to be successful.

I was engaged in developing the products, but mostly I took care of the sales function. I had an accounting firm to make the financial arrangements. During the early growth phase of the firm, I hired a sales manager; after that I got an accounting manager and a production manager, and for the moment I am trying to obtain an Engineering Manager.

And then, he said, 'My job is to stop people from fighting.'

I feel very closely related to the sales and marketing function, and I listen carefully to the information about the market which the sales representatives provide. I always ask the sales representatives how to improve the firm. The sales forecast is based upon their information. I have taken care of the sales from the early days of the company. Therefore, I have an understanding of the market, as I can understand reasons for sales declines. If I had been more production oriented, I think I would have fired the sales manager. I agree a lot with the marketing president. He is an entrepreneur type too. I like him. I think that he is too much of a marketing man, and not a sales person. He has not been in the field and I don't think he likes the salesmen. He is tough, and does business as if he had no feelings.

I want sales growth. Don't you see! I am a small man, but I want to make the firm as big as possible. But I don't want to go on a trip and come back without any money. I have to make a profit. Perhaps I want to make a good profit, and then sell when it stops. I think I want to be in the firm for the foreseeable future. I am a little scared of not continuing. I want my freedom, but you are not always free since you always have to relate to others. I want to keep on top, or else I will feel lonely. When you get older you get to be more of an advocate type.

We are dealing with the professional companies more and more. I think the employees have followed the changes, so they are able to deal with the new customers. The fact that we have standardized the production has made it easier for our production and engineering team. We make changes to customers, but it does not matter to the production team whether the customer wants it in red or blue. The engineers find it difficult to cope with anything unknown, as they have to know what to do and what to count on. For that purpose the Sales Department is making sales forecasts

The accountants are good at making profit and loss statements and balance sheets, but they have no feeling for the cash flows. They are not creative people; they don't understand the finance side, as they only understand accounting. They are so depressing to talk with; they always think the worst will happen. They think that all projects are bad. When you ask them why, they just say that their figures show too small of a profit. They don't have the understanding of cash flow. And they cannot find out how to stretch the payments. They don't know anything about timing. They always have to pay at the right time. Accountants define equity as having money in your pocket. What they don't understand is that if you get money in the beginning of the week and you have to pay it out in the beginning of next week, and if you do that every week, then you have equity too.

In the relation to the bank you have to pay at the right time. You have to do what you promise. The bank trusts us. I asked the bank if they want a conservative budget or something realistic. They told me that they want a realistic, optimistic budget. They are making adjustments for the optimistic view in their judgments. They anticipate that a budget will be a little optimistic. The accountants have not understood this fact. But that's okay, they have to be pessimistic, we expect it.

Mr. Kersten recently started a firm in Chicago together with two others, in an industry other than computers. He wants to start up some more companies in the future. He also considers the possibilities of starting a new firm with a higher technology than that of Discovery. Possibly, a firm making medical-related products or perhaps something software related.

At the moment, Fred uses all of his energy to find a way to secure cash flow in the firm:

The manager of sales and marketing and I try to make a cash flow system. The bank is looking at the profit, but that is not important, what really is important is the cash flow.

Furthermore, one of Fred's plans is to make a sales firm with the manager of sales and marketing and some other sales people as his partners, and with the manager of sales and marketing as the president. Another plan is to make an engineering firm because Fred thinks that it will become possible to employ engineers if they become co-owners of the firm. He has not enough capital himself to let other people have shares in Discovery without losing control. The intention of the plan to construct the new companies is that it should solve the cash flow problem for Discovery.

Chuck Berry, Manager of Production (35 years old)

The manager of production was appointed to Discovery two years ago. He has a degree in business administration, and has been in the workforce for eight years. The production department is organized professionally and is efficient. The capacity is managed rationally, and the department is able to cope with future development.

The manager of production has learned by experience that it is impossible to use the sales forecast because it is too unreliable. Therefore he makes his own sales forecast. Furthermore there are too many urgent orders demanded by the sales department. He thinks that the customers run the firm, and that the sales department thinks too short-sightedly. The manager of production has problems with the engineering department because it is unorganized. The engineers are not incompetent but, he thinks, the firm must appoint a chief engineer who can stand the pressure from the sales department, who can make a priority of orders and projects, and who can make better plans.

Gilbert Null, Director of Sales and Marketing (33 years old)

The director of sales and marketing has degrees in engineering and business administration. He came to Discovery one and a half years ago. He started as marketing manager; after a period he was promoted to director of sales and marketing. The director of sales and marketing has proven abilities to plan strategic developments and to create high volume contracts. It was his idea to change the strategy by going into the contract market. He has succeeded in getting the organization to accept the new strategy. The managerial philosophy of the director of sales and marketing is 'to kick people in the ass'. He does not communicate much with the personnel employed at the factory; he gives orders, but otherwise he only communicates with the president, the sales representatives, and the customers. For example, one of the employees said, 'He just gives an order. He says, "I want this....", and then he turns around.' He is not concerned with the relationship between the sales department and the other departments. Generally, he states that all personnel are incompetent; he thinks that the skills of the employees in the firm are poor. The skills of the sales representatives are poor, because they cannot make sales contracts. He likes to work together with Fred, but he believes he is a weak manager. Gilbert believes that the accountant at Discovery is not qualified enough, and he feels that it is stupid that the manager of accounting uses full cost in price setting. The director of sales and marketing has told the accountants to change the figures so he can get information about the variable costs. He then calculates the prices himself. It is his policy that Discovery shall take all the orders they can get without losing money, i.e., all orders with a price above variable production costs; it is his intention not to lose an order due to the price. As an exception he thinks that the manager of production is actually doing very well. He believes that the production department was unorganized two years ago, before the production manager came to the firm.

Gary Johnson, Manager of Engineering (45 years old)

The manager of the engineering department has been in the firm for ten years, i.e. almost from the beginning. He has a degree in technical engineering. He is the manager of ten employees. He is developing and planning the new products, designing projects, and standardizing software and hardware. The manager of engineering manages informally, according to reason and common sense, and is able to get the engineers to work despite not very optimal conditions. Thus the sales department uses the engineering department to develop the products and to make the necessary changes in order to customize them. The sales department tells the manager of the head of engineering what they want, and then he tries to deliver. If the sales department changes their priorities, which happens often, then the engineering follows sales in changing their priorities too. The sales department gets angry if the engineering department does not immediately supply what they want. The manager of engineering feels no problem in relation to the production department and he tries to do what the accountants want. He likes to follow the technological development and see what new things happen. On the one hand, he does not like to manage— he would like the firm to get a new manager for the engineering department who can organize things better. On the other hand, he does, as a matter of fact, like to be manager because it gives him better possibilities to follow new technological developments. Remarkably, he does not say anything negative about anyone.

Orville Clark, Manager of Accounting (38 years old)

The manager of accounting has a business degree; and he has been employed for two and a half years now. He communicates with the manager of production due to the fact that they cooperate in building accounting and production systems. Otherwise he only communicates with the other managers about figures. He is always very busy because as he expressed:

> I am constantly going after the fires to blow them out; as the accountants can see all the problems and what is going wrong in the firm. I would like to close down the firm for a period of three months so that we could obtain the necessary time to organize the firm to make all things go more smoothly. I think it could be a good idea to see what would happen with the cash flow over the next few years. That's my plan, but until then I am still going to be chasing after the fires. It is difficult because of the uncertainty in the sales forecast and all the other things. We have to stop the fires. The manager of production has problems. Before the cutbacks the manager of production could be more flexible, when the sales people pressed orders through. He had extra capacity to handle it, but now he does not have the manpower and the necessary materials are not available, which implies that the planning becomes confused. Before we could deliver within two weeks, now we can only deliver within 30–40 days, and the customer is not satisfied.

It means a lot to the manager of accounting to please the president. However, he and the president do not communicate very well with each other. As an example: the president told him that he and the director of sales would need to make a new cash flow system. By saying this, the president actually meant that they needed to find a new way to finance the company's operations. The accountants thought that Fred wanted him to make a new cash flow information system, thus he called the bank to get ideas for a new way to report the cash flows. Recently, the manager of accounting told the president that he did not want to be a financial manager, but that he wanted to remain as an accountant only. It should also be noted that he does not know that the director of sales and marketing has lowered prices.

Peter Parker, Vice-President (52 years old)

The vice-President has an engineering degree. He has been engaged in Discovery since 1994. His job was to design and construct the products of the firm. For a period, he was manager of the engineering department. Now he is the vice-president and mainly concerned with producing manuals for and technical descriptions of Discovery's products. The managerial skills that Peter Parker possesses are of the inventive type—at this point he has a very good reputation. He is apparently not interested in playing a leadership role or in displaying management skills. When asked the question, 'What do you think about the future of Discovery?' his remarkable answer was, 'Nothing, I don't know anything about it.'

Questions for Discussion

1. Describe and evaluate the strategy employed by the president. Is the strategy sustainable?

2. Is the president a good manager?

3. Describe and evaluate the organizational structure and leadership at Discovery.

4. Describe and evaluate the management controls used by Discovery.

5. What changes in the strategy would you recommend?

6. What changes in the customer orientation system would you recommend?

Appendix

Deduction of Donaldson's Self-Sustaining Growth Equation

The formula for balanced growth is:

g(S) = r(RONA + d(RONA-i))

Symbols used:
g(NA)= growth rate of net assets
g(S) = growth rate of sales
RONA = Return on net assets
r   = earnings-retention rate
d   = debt-equity ratio
i   = after tax interests rate on debt
NA = Net assets
E = equity
Ç = debt
O_s = result before interest but after tax
R_s = after tax interest amounts on debts

Presupposition: g(S) = g(NA)

Derivation of the Equation
Growth of assets = growth of equity + growth of debt
$g(NA) \times NA = r((O_s - R_s) + d(O_s - R_s))$; d=Ç/E, debt-equity ratio
$g(NA) = r((O_s/NA - R_s/NA) + d(O_s/NA - R_s/NA))$
$g(NA) = r(RONA - R_s/NA + d \times RONA - d \times R_s/NA)$;
                    RONA=O_s/NA
$g(NA) = r(RONA + d \times RONA - (1+d) \times (R_s/NA))$
$g(NA) = r(RONA + d (RONA - [(1+d)/d] \times (R_s/NA)))$;
        and $[(1+d)/d]=[(E/E+Ç/E)/Ç/E]=$
            $[((E+Ç)/E)/(Ç/E)]= [(E+Ç)/Ç]=NA/Ç$
$g(NA) = r(RONA + d (RONA - [NA/Ç] \times R_s/NA))$
$g(NA) = r(RONA + d (RONA - R_s/Ç))$; $R_s/Ç = i$
$g(NA) = r(RONA + d (RONA - i))$;
 g(S) = r(RONA + d (RONA - i)); g(S)=g(NA)

Gordon Donaldson, 'Financial Goals and Strategic Consequences', *Harvard Business Review*, May–June 1985, pp. 58–59.

Case Study 3

AB Swedish Lumber[*]

Hanne Nørreklit

Aarhus School of Business, University of Aarhus, Denmark

The general managers of our yards are primarily focused on the next order. They hold a short-term perspective; but if we buy a yard and pay 20 million for its goodwill, then it is a disaster if we get a manager who is not capable of handling that goodwill. The managers are administrators of goodwill and we need more future-oriented indicators of the results of our profit centers.

These are the words of the Deputy Manager of the AB SWEDISH LUMBER-Prof Division. He believes that AB SWEDISH LUMBER needs long-term performance indicators and strategic measures that can assess and operationalize the strategies of the group. That is why he is considering implementing a system similar to that of the Balanced Scorecard (BSC). In order to ensure that the decision will be made on a sound basis, he has carried out an analysis of the group. The results of the analysis are presented below. Section 1 presents the formal strategy of the AB SWEDISH LUMBER-Prof Division and its planning and reporting system. Section 2 presents the management models of the local yard managers, as well as the division manager, and the managers' assessment of the BSC.

AB SWEDISH LUMBER-PROF

AB SWEDISH LUMBER-Prof is a division of the Swedish group AB SWEDISH LUMBER. The division sells a varied set of products to professional customers in the lumber industry. The group consists of five divisions which each have their own business area. The development of group financial results appears in Table CS3.1 In recent years, the group has performed well, but it ran a deficit in 2002. The years up to 2002 were unsatisfactory because of an economic decline.

The AB SWEDISH LUMBER-Prof Division consists of a number of lumber yards throughout Sweden. The yards are organized as 45 autonomous profit centers, each with its own general manager. Each profit center has been strategically limited to its own business area. Apart from that, however, they enjoy considerable freedom. The general managers of the lumber yards are responsible for sourcing, sales, the choice of product mix, the day-to-day management, etc. Investments have to be approved by the center. The group has made a framework agreement with approximately 350 of its largest suppliers, which deliver 80 percent of the goods purchased by the group.

---

[*] This case is based on actual events. Only the names have been changed.

Table CS3.1 The development in the financial results of AB SWEDISH LUMBER

Million S.CR.	2002	2003	2004	2005	2006
Net turnover	31,785	24,190	30,605	30,705	32,885
Year's group results	-620	170	745	765	750
Group equity	3,460	3,490	5,295	5,915	5,915
Return on equity (%)	-7	4	15	14	13
Equity ratio (%)	20	25	33	37	37
Investments	415	245	750	710	1,600

Each lumber yard manager may freely choose which supplier(s) to buy from, and is also free to enter into more favorable agreements with suppliers. Similarly, the yards may freely trade with internal or external suppliers.

Information technology and administrative affairs, such as bookkeeping, accounting, and budgeting, as well as IT development, are centralized functions performed at the corporate headquarters. The group tries to strike a balance between (i) joint, monitored and controlled administrative routines and (ii) the competent local management of sales and marketing with fast, efficient, well educated, and non-bureaucratic decision makers with access to market intelligence which is always up-to-date. The group headquarters offers courses to all members of staff throughout the group. As young people are very keen on supplementary training, having a program is actually a good idea. It serves the function of providing a sense of security and an increased level of employee satisfaction. The yards may decide for themselves whether they want to participate in the courses. Similarly, they can choose whether they want to be ISO certified. Powers and responsibilities have been considerably decentralized.

In many ways, the managers of the lumber yards are very different, but they also have some common characteristics. The following is a typical profile: the manager ha his lower secondary school leaving with examination; he did not like going to school he became a carpenter's apprentice; he enjoys his freedom and making the decision himself; he has met typically concrete challenges openly and successfully.

The strategy and Planning Process of AB SWEDISH LUMBER-Prof

As is evident from Appendix A, the planning and reporting system of AB SWEDISH LUMBER-Prof is fairly comprehensive and formalized. The long-term planning an budgeting are a bottom-up process. The lumber yards plan and perform tasks, and th corporate headquarters monitors them. The division management needs informatio that is sufficient to perform the monitoring function.

The general strategy of the business unit AB SWEDISH LUMBER-Prof is revised and formulated every third year. It may briefly be described as follows:

Financial strategy
The lumber yards of AB SWEDISH LUMBER are to produce the highest return on investment in the industry and to have 'balanced' financing of their growth. The group is to show financial strength through its willingness and ability to pay and to have precise administration and payments systems. In addition, it has to be able to bear credit risks.

Customer strategy
The strategy of AB SWEDISH LUMBER-Prof is to be the market leader. The lumber yards of AB SWEDISH LUMBER-Prof are to be the leading (largest) suppliers to professional customers. They are to deliver quality; their deliveries have to be reliable and according to plan; they must have efficient and well-assorted collection depots and stores; and they have to stimulate the professional customer's unplanned consumption. The aim is to build long-term relationships by representing the best traditions in the industry and by upholding stable and long-term working relationships.

Supplier strategy
AB SWEDISH LUMBER-Prof wishes to have stable and sustained relations with its suppliers and to make use of internal suppliers of purchases and administration to the extent that this is rational. It wishes to build long-term supplier relations where working with the suppliers is more important than 'squeezing' them. The purchasing committees are solidly rooted in the yards and the division management is not directly involved. If it is possible to derive an advantage from doing something centrally, then that is where it will be done; otherwise it will be done at the lowest level.

Internal processes strategy
Holding stocks of a wide customer-adapted range of goods is a vital function if the unplanned consumption of customers is to be stimulated and if the yards are to satisfy the customer expectations from a well-assorted supplier in the local area.

The lumber yards of AB SWEDISH LUMBER wish to have rational and reliable routines and to be able to keep and attract competent staff. The business procedures are to be supported by information technology, which is in fact managed centrally by the division. A new IT system was introduced a couple of years ago, which was very tough. The personnel manager believes that it was fortunate that the introduction took place during a recession; otherwise, there would have been a risk that some of the employees would have left. In the case of administrative affairs, the principle applies too, that if doing something centrally creates an advantage, then it will be done there, otherwise it will be done at the lowest level.

Performance Measures and Reporting

Appendix B outlines the monthly reporting. The yards are measured on the basis of their profits after 1 percent interest per month on capital invested has been deducted.

The rate of return required is a minimum of 14 percent. This is the ideal measure, but in fact some yards have a rate of return of 40 percent while others have less then 14 percent. Rates above 14 percent are considered a motivation for success, while rates below are considered a danger of failure. In addition, the division requires 40 percent of gross profits for personnel costs—this percentage depends on whether the yard has its own transportation company.

Some years ago, debtors were a very real problem, and some of the yards suffered immense losses:

> Prior to 2002, we were measured in terms of rate of return. At first, it was 11 percent, then 14 percent and finally 18 percent. Some of the yards exploited that because they could get 22 percent from their debtors. To some, it was a very close thing—they suffered huge losses. After that, we managed to get the debtors under control. We introduced a credit maximum, so that debtors of more than S.CR. 250,000 are referred to the division manager. Debtors who are of acceptable financial condition are rebuked by the division manager, and everybody else has to give an explanation. We have become very skilled at shortening our accounts receivable turnover rate: at the time the average credit period was 105 days, today it is down to 36.

In addition, the stock turnover ratio is measured since the lumber yard managers are not being held responsible for liquidity.

The monthly turnover is the 'early warning' signal because, unlike what is the case in manufacturing firms, it is impossible to measure the volume of orders received. The division conducts joint market surveillance. Measuring the market is a problem, however, what should be included? For example, the division sells wooden shoes, but should it include all shoe stores? Similarly, statistics cover counties, but the yards cut across counties. So guesstimates are used.

As regards customer satisfaction levels, the methods used for measuring them have not included anonymous surveys (this also holds of staff satisfaction levels). Although it is not something which is said explicitly, the organization sets great store by individuality—and this everybody knows. Mass marketing is not appreciated—it is like sending formal invitations to your friends. So, instead, the organization uses person-to-person marketing. In fact a recent survey shows a reciprocal relationship between customer satisfaction and profitability; i.e. the yards with lowest customer satisfaction are the most profitable.

The division manager regularly meets with the local yard managers—some three or four times a year—and the agenda includes items such as the debating of the plan, the follow-up of the plan, and the motivating of efficiency and performance. The meetings also ensure that buildings are not neglected. The manager sees the buildings and how the stores, etc., present themselves. In addition, the people who evaluate the condition of the buildings sometimes also attend the meetings. It was in this connection that the concept of the 'black book' developed because the division manager notes all agreements in a black book.

The targets that the yard managers set themselves are ones that they are able to reach, and they are not allowed to present either optimistic or pessimistic budgets. The division manager's view is that budgets have to be realistic and that anything else is unprofessional. If a yard is not doing well, it will be placed under surveillance until it has recovered.

Commenting on the performance evaluation of the division, the personnel and marketing manager said:

> An experienced management team can assess the results of the yards. To be able to follow developments, it is important that the figures are an inherent part of one's nervous system. You have to know how to interpret the figures on the basis of your subjective knowledge of the yards. For example, some yards have their own trucks and others lag behind with their invoicing.
>
> We measure some relations and focus on some areas. Then, when we measure something else, we shift our focus. We use the concepts of management control measures and information measures. Management control measures are the ones we focus on. We want to have sufficient information to feel confident that we know enough about how things are going. It shows strength in a leader if he says 'no' to getting some information. There are things we do not want to know (a) because we do not know what is good and what isn't, and (b) because we do not know what to do about them. We have decentralized responsibility.
>
> The yards are very dissimilar. Some are scrupulously tidy and others are messy. If customers prefer orderliness, they will probably leave the messy ones and turn to our competitors instead, and those who do not require an orderly presentation will turn to us and vice versa. We do not see the difference from the results.
>
> Knowledge about staff satisfaction is really not something that we are interested in. We would not know how to use the information provided in a staff satisfaction analysis. What is good? We provide our employees with motivation by increasing their responsibilities. We give them a certain degree of freedom and we assume that the managers do the same. Maybe it would be a good idea to find out whether the staff thinks that they have an interesting job. We get our information the opposite way: if somebody calls and complains, we will get the message and do something. The strategic key issue is whether they have an exciting job—and that goes for both managers and staff. Many of our staff could be potential managers. Because of takeovers, we have a lot of potential managers.
>
> Where things are not going well, we make use of therapy. We have our Top 45 rankings: the yards at the top get very little attention but we are in close contact with the ones that are not doing too well.

The Lumber Yard Managers' Conception of Management Control and Performance Measurement

According to the lumber yard managers, the financial targets can be reached in numerous ways. They do not want to be standardized. They are business people and not administrators.

> We are very dissimilar and arrive at the same results in numerous ways. You cannot just make a checklist and say that this and that will lead to success. It would not do if we were identical. The differences make us visible. The yard has to have a soul. You build up a business. The concept of uniformity is fine for McDonald's—it is like a textbook case. If the customer concept is a given thing, then there will be someone at the register who complains. Creative people do not want to be standardized.

There are 45 yard managers. Some are stout, some slim, some aggressive, others calm. Our differences are an asset. Some managers create a balance in the division, while other managers act like spearheads. If you have to report too many specifics to the group management, then they need an administrator. The job is interesting because it is independent. I see this as my yard. If the company sent me a pile of documents and forms, I would leave. Each yard has to have the freedom of action, otherwise you need administrators and not business people. Of course, some things have to be centrally organized.

The Management Model of the Lumber Yard Managers

The lumber yard managers are all engaged in making customers satisfied. Each addresses their customer segments in their own way. They all emphasise control by means of informal personal relations. However, they seem to accept the prospect of qualitative measures if these are adapted to each yard and everyone is allowed to make the decisions himself. To provide a sampling of the divergence of management styles at AB Swedish Lumber, three managers were interviewed. The three managers interviewed were Mr. Strid, Mr. Jönsson, and Mr. Deergaard. Below follows a description of the management philosophy of each of these business people.

The philosophy of Mr. Strid is that the yard must be in close contact with its immediate environment. The customers have to be within 'a horseshoe's distance', that is, it has to be possible to get back and forth in one day by horse carriage. A clientele that is close by will be loyal to the business, but if you move beyond that distance, business gets price-driven. Mr. Strid has numerous small customers. He does not dare have customers who owe millions of Swedish crowns at a time: the risk involved is too large.

Mr. Strid has recently rebuilt his firm. Today the building is customer-oriented, the office area now being on the side where the customers enter the building. The partitions and shelves are 1.20–1.40 meters high, so that a customer entering will always be able to see that there is somebody in the office. The idea is that if an employee has sent a customer an offer some days ago and then sees the customer then he addresses him and asks how things are going. So the sales representatives are now also doing fieldwork in-house. One of the old buildings could have served as a staff canteen, but then the staff would have been away from the customers. The staff would have chatted on their way to and from the canteen; but, the way it is now, the customers can enter the staff canteen. The duty of the staff is to serve the customers and some customers were beginning to find the firm too snobby. By explaining to the customers why things are the way they are, Mr. Strid and his staff tried to convince the customers that they are not snobby. Mr. Strid listens to his customers and trie to behave like them and dress like them. He does not want the firm to become any larger now. If it is to become larger, others will have to take over.

In Mr. Strid's opinion, it is important that any member of the staff knows the customers of the firm, because the entire organization has to sell. The driver, for example, cannot drop the goods in a pool of water—if he does, everything will b wasted. Mr. Strid sees no need to have the business ISO certified as long as it has staff with the right mentality. The firm has to have staff that are perceptive and pu their emotions and internal commitment into their work. The ability to deliver can be judged on the basis of the storekeeper's ears. Mr. Strid does not care much for paper and reporting systems and does not always see information technology as a blessing. Information technology should first and foremost be service-related and not run the business. The customers need fast service and the firm needs people with a bit of life in them. One success criterion is that people have fun; otherwise the customers will not feel good. IT people think in other terms and listen in a different way.

One managing clerk and one storekeeper are in Mr. Strid's employ. His door is always open. To him, management means putting his own thoughts and ideas properly through to other people. His employees should have some charisma, have responsibilities, and make decisions. It is acceptable if they make mistakes, but they do not have to repeat them. If there are any problems in the firm, they are dealt with, and colleagues largely serve as supervisors too. Mr. Strid feels bad about firing people and he is glad that he feels that way—particularly when elderly people are involved. When he has to fire someone, he talks to that person and uncovers the root cause. He has found that people are often relieved to get to talk about their problems. Indeed, most people know whether they are successful or have problems. In fact, he thought that one person to whom he talked would give up entirely, but that person flourished. Mr. Strid asks people whether they are lucky—he believes that this is a success criterion. He does not think much of business consultants and teachers. They are people who could not be put to use in business. Using a consultant is a sign of poor management.

Mr. Jönsson believes that the lumber yard should be a sanctuary for his customers. It is enough that they have trouble with the taxing authorities, they do not need to have trouble here too. Some customers turn up eight times in a day and others once a week. Of course, the firm could impose a service charge, but Mr. Jönsson does not want to do that. He gives his customers some latitude but that does not include credit policy.

Mr. Jönsson does not believe in customer satisfaction analyses:

> They would tell us that our prices are too high and our service levels too low. Keeping an eye on customers who disappear is important, but there may be a reason for it. If, for example, a customer squeezes us too much, we will let that customer slip away. Personal relations are important—you have to cultivate your customer relationships. Our relations with our customers are personal relations, and we do not want them to be ruined by sending them some impersonal questionnaire. The sales representatives visit the customers with whom they best relate. If the rep is sufficiently active, that is okay—if he is not, we will kick him out. The amount of work the reps manage to do varies a great deal: Peter Hansen manages to do a lot—he is rather confused—but the customers like him.

Mr. Jönsson gives priority to selling. He does not believe in oversimplified explanations of why a business is doing well. For example, he does not want boards to lie at an oblique angle because he does not want crooked boards. In other places, however, where boards lie at an oblique angle, the business is running well because the customers are used to crooked boards. Mr. Jönsson focuses on waste and on doing things properly. The lumber yard is ISO certified and ought to record errors and leakages, but it does not. The results of the business are influenced if there is stock theft, shrinkage, or if there is an accident with the forklift truck. If someone has an accident with the truck, the others will needle him a bit. Mr. Jönsson believes that social control is important. He listens if there is any gossip and is not afraid of an open dialogue. In a conflict between two members of staff, for example, he has had to tell them what they had said about each other. He believes it is important to take problems seriously so that you can learn from them. He talks to his employees and tries to influence the common attitude toward things. If some people cannot be convinced, you have to remove them.

Mr. Jönsson is open-minded about new ideas. But we do not think alike and things have to be adapted to each yard. His view is that everything has to be comprehensible, down-to-earth, and concrete. Mr. Jönsson believes that more measurement devices are in the pipeline, but he would like to suggest new ideas himself. He likes to influence development. 'I prefer to invent sliced bread myself—we want things to be up to us. Of course, one wants to increase one's own value.' Mr. Jönsson believes that they used to be more involved in developments. Anyway, the way he sees it, the people at the headquarters are people with whom you can talk.

Mr. Jönsson likes the monthly reporting, which he himself has contributed to designing. The yard managers receive the figures of the entire division so that they can compare figures. Mr. Jönsson uses this as a source of inspiration for improvement. In his yard, for example, carriage costs are fairly high, so he has begun to analyze the issue.

Mr. Deergaard has been the yard manager for the past three years. His job was to turn a deficit into a surplus. The results at the time were negative and nobody was happy. It was necessary to expand the customer base. He used some focus areas formulated in his ten laws. They contributed to creating a good customer base and in two years the sales turnover rose from 1,075 million crowns to 1,500 million. Net profit results rose from 5.5 million crowns to 39 million according to official figures. He believes the figure will be 50 million crowns, but he does not want to say that aloud because then he will have to increase his budget.

Mr. Deergaard would like the yard to measure customer and staff satisfaction because that would rank him among the top five. Such measures would show even better results than the financial indicators. But he does not think that they should be required of everyone.

Mr. Deergaard performs his own form of customer satisfaction analysis. He visits the customers of the yard in January and February. He puts on his dark blue jacket, makes speeches, and gives away champagne. The 25 best customers receive a bottle of champagne to give to those on their staff who they believe have earned it. This means that there is some competition to become the best customer. On such occasions, Mr. Deergaard asks whether the customers are satisfied, what they think of the people who serve them, etc. In addition, Mr. Deergaard takes into consideration whether customer no. 52 has a lot of potential. If so, he visits the customer to talk to him and to ask what his firm can do better.

Something similar happened with a large customer who owed 3.4 million crowns when Mr. Deergaard took over. Mr. Deergaard paid a visit to the customer and told him that he did not want to allow credit. The customer had no problem understanding that: he had been using the yard as his bank. The customer has now paid down his debt in instalment payments, and only 100,000 crowns are still outstanding. After his visit, Mr. Deergaard informed the division manager of his conversation with the customer, so that he would not hear about it indirectly. In connection with his arrival to the firm as its manager, Mr. Deergaard says:

> When I arrived, the yard was in a state of crisis. I had to get the staff to smile, make them get a haircut and make them clean their nails. I felled a few trees so that it became possible to see that this was the yard. I have pulled down walls so that we could see each other—it is much better when you can see people. I fired a few—among them, a bad-tempered porter who drove our customers away. I put a customer services officer on the staff, who was in charge of pinpointing customers we were about to let down. Before procedures become a routine, they are just rules, and before they become a routine, it is entirely feasible that our customers will be let down. I put a sign on each door that said, 'Welcome'—the customers are our guests.
>
> In addition, I introduced phone measures. We had 400 calls coming in daily. People were on the phone, waiting, and they hung up because they could not reach anybody. In brief, there were a certain amount of customers who wished to buy goods and who were waiting. So I singled out two employees to be in charge of answering the phone. They were allowed to let it ring no more than twice before picking it up. Of course, I could have said three times, but that would have become four. Just because we pick up the phone, people believe that we are much quicker than we actually are.
>
> I changed our opening hours, so that we are now open from 6 a.m. until 4.45 p.m. We have 25 customers coming in between 6 and 7 a.m. People think it is expensive. Our staff work in shifts during the five business days and they get compensation—for example, time off in lieu of payment. We have customers who come because we are open between 6 and 7 a.m.
>
> We have come to agree on the rules here. I am the supervisor. They do not break the rules to be evil. If they do, something is wrong. For instance, our working day begins at 8 a.m., so we arrive at 7.50 a.m. and I arrive at 7.40 a.m. If someone repeatedly arrives at 9.10 a.m., then we have a talk about that. I ask that person why they are late and whether they are prepared to come at 8 a.m. If they are not, then this is not the right job for that person.

Mr. Deergaard attaches great importance to agreements and rules, but apart from that he leaves much responsibility with the individual employee. He treats his staff in the way that he would like to be treated himself. There are numerous ways of doing things. Everybody would like to have some responsibilities but the extent of responsibilities that they would like to have varies. If the driver of a forklift truck runs into something with pallets on the truck, then the storekeeper wants to know about it. It will be recorded because the yard has been ISO certified.

Mr. Deergaard believes that the yard managers learn from each other in their own quiet ways. Mr. Deergaard learns a great deal from Mr. Larson (another yard manager). He likes Mr. Larson even if it does take him a couple of days to come up with an answer. The division has a network that goes in all directions—and the division manager takes ideas to the top.

The Lumber Yard Managers' Conception of the Division Manager's Management Model

The division manager's management model is very important to the management control of the lumber yards. The yard managers talk enthusiastically about him and his informal and direct management style. The way they characterise him is described in what follows.

Mr. Strid sees the division manager as a person with a vision who does not interfere much. Two or three months may pass without their talking to each other. The division manager pays a visit some three times a year and stays for a couple of hours. Mr. Strid gives the following examples of how the division manager allows the managers certain degrees of freedom:

> I once established an industry unit. The division manager said, 'It will not succeed. I would not do it.' I was allowed to anyway, but it did not succeed and shortly afterwards we had to close it down.
>
> I had noticed that a firm in a town nearby was having trouble. So I sent a short note to the division manager and recommended that we should buy the firm—and he said okay. You just have to write a short note in this company to suggest an idea. But the degree of freedom is directly proportional to earnings.

According to Mr. Strid, the division manager has great impact. If he says something, then the yard managers believe in it, because if he says something, then there is a reason.

It is also Mr. Jönsson's opinion that they have a good division manager. The division manager is good at expressing himself and rarely talks nonsense, although he is not always particularly diplomatic. Here is one example:

> Once when I was fighting over a customer with Haas Carpentry, which is a sister lumber yard, the division manager called me and said, 'That is the customer of Haas Carpentry.' Then he hung up.
>
> I have only been annoyed with the division manager once. That was when I was a yard manager at Jönköping. We had a maid in the house, which was right next to the lumber yard. I had not seen that our maid had hung the laundry in the carport right next to the shop, but the division manager's wife had seen it. So he mentioned the laundry problem to me. That made me annoyed with him.

Mr. Jönsson says that the division manager knows the yard managers' judgment well. For example, he knows how they assess a customer's creditworthiness. Once when the division manager was paying a visit, Mr. Jönsson said that one customer had equity of 225,000 crowns. The following year, when they spoke about that customer again and Jönsson mentioned a figure, the division manager opened his black book, looked at it and said, 'Yes, that is true.' If things are not going well, the yard manager has to make an agreement with the division manager about what is to be done. The division manager does not want any unsuccessful yards.

In Mr. Jönsson's opinion, a manager who dictates too much deprives the staff of its responsibilities, 'It would be a rude awakening if a technocrat were to enter these premises. It would affect both our earnings and our good spirits.'

Mr. Deergaard believes that, if there are difficulties, the firm always focuses on the issues and never looks for a scapegoat. The division manager is in a class of his own. When he arrives, he walks through the firm, assessing the situation, and gets an impression that cannot be communicated via e-mail. If there is a mess somewhere, the division manager does not say that there is a problem. He says that there is a slight problem with orderliness. When the division manager is paying Mr. Deergaard's yard a visit and they reach an agreement about something, the division manager says, 'I will write it down in my book.'

Mr. Deergaard explains that if something is not covered by the rules, then all you need to do is to pick up the phone and you will make a joint decision. Only very rarely does the division manager say, 'I will not allow you to do that.' Instead he says, 'The decision is yours.' In the group that Mr. Deergaard came from, simple things were made complex. At AB SWEDISH LUMBER, complex things are made simple. For example, the division manager says, 'Remember that each time you write you are forcing 60 people to read it.' The division manager does not want things to be pompous and he has no secretary. He does not want to be bothered by these things.

When things were at their worst in the yard that Mr. Deergaard was with before joining AB SWEDISH LUMBER, they had to complete the largest number of reports ever. When the yard was taken over by AB SWEDISH LUMBER, it was given peace to work. The division manager thought that the staff would object to being taken over by AB SWEDISH LUMBER, but nobody did; on the contrary, everybody was looking forward to leaving the bureaucracy.

Mr. Deergaard does not believe that it is possible to handle the job better than the division manager. Nobody is afraid of him. The only thing that annoys Mr. Deergaard a bit is that the yard managers are the division manager's boys—whether they like it or not.

The Division Manager's Description of His Own Management Model and His Assessment of the Balanced Scorecard

Below follows a summary of the division manager's own description of his management model and his assessment of the BSC.

According to the division manager, he steers the company by keeping it in front of him instead of behind. That is the way he has learned to handle the situation. He pieces everything together in pictures and includes only what he thinks is important. He believes that you cannot know quantitatively whether an organization is moving in the right direction. He is able to observe qualitatively by looking at the surroundings and how people are acting. He can see that the firm is getting worse, but the yard managers are free to walk the plank.

Speaking about his management method, the division manager says, 'When I meet with the lumber yard managers, I talk to them about procedures. They have described their plans and I ask them what they have not described. What are you afraid of? If there is a problem, I ask them what they feel like doing about it and then they find the solution.'

One example of this management style relates to a yard in which a newly employed person brought with him a turnover of 15 million crowns. The interests of buyer and seller sometimes merge because the newly appointed staff brings with them a portfolio of orders. The sales turnover in the yard amounted to 120 million crowns. The yard manager called and said that the new appointee wanted his annual salary to be 250,000 crowns higher, but that would mean that his salary would be higher than that of the head clerk, Karl Johan. The new man might leave if he was not paid more. The following conversation ensued:

> The division manager: 'What was the sales turnover that the new man brought with him?'
> The yard manager: '15 million crowns.'
> The division manager: 'What is your profit on that?'
> The yard manager: '3 million crowns.'
> The division manager: 'How much more do we have to pay him?'
> The yard manager: '250,000 crowns. But what about Karl Johan then?'
> The division manager: 'Yes.'
> The yard manager: 'Oh, well.'

The lumber yard manager then made his decision, and Karl Johan did not leave. Here is another example:

> A few years ago, we introduced a new EDP system. We almost broke our necks on that. It was terrible. One of the lumber yard managers posed a problem. He was really angry. He told everyone from Malmö to Umeå about how terrible it was. Then I said, 'We have that system. It has to work. If it does not, we will separate the sheep from the goats.' Then he said, 'I have gotten the message.' I had to say, 'Now the party is over.'
> We discuss things, and afterwards a deal is a deal and we stick together. Some people in the Prof Division are unable to make a decision. I am not. Yesterday they discussed the whole day. Then I said, 'What is our decision?'" The difference between centralized and decentralized management is very subtle. People have to try something and make some mistakes—not too many mistakes though.

The division manager further comments on his philosophy as follows:

> Honesty is the best policy. Life is easy: you just have to say what you think, then you do not have to remember all sorts of things. If you make a mistake, you just have to apologize. When we prepare our budget, we have roast turkey. This year it was exactly one week before Thanksgiving. What they served was like what you get out of the oven the day after—a black carcass. We called the chef and showed him the carcass. He was very nice, but they did not do anything about it. They should have offered us something else. If only they had just given us the chance to remove the bad feelings. We will not be back next year.

The division manager has learned these techniques from his mother, who has always been very direct:

> The other day, for instance, she called me and said that she had arranged a family get-together. I said I could not come because I would be travelling the next day. 'When are you leaving?', 'Early in the morning.' 'When?', 'At 10 a.m.' That is not particularly early. And then I came, of course.

Not much has been entered in the black book—only about one page per yard manager:

I write down the agreements we make. I do not write much. Nowadays, I can remember most of it.

I know what is going on. Some have long-term customers, but the long-term customers are not the ones who win the orders. For example, a yard manager at Karlstad sold primarily to long-time customers. I asked him to stake more on new customers and sell for half a million more. He did not want to. So I had to find another employee. For some time, they were supposed to work in parallel, but that did not work out, and the older person had to leave after a year. He reached the sales turnover target, but it was against his convictions. The new manager has more drive. At first, things were not working out particularly well, but now he leans on his colleague at Varberg. You need to dare to have faith.

I do not know how a success measure such as delivery time is supposed to be used. We have growth targets—we need to be able to keep pace with the industry. A demand for more efficiency may lead to poor net results.

According to the division manager, a large number of the measurement factors included in the BSC are ones which any proper manager has to consider in connection with his planning:

They may be items such as delivery precision, good professional service, orderly areas, and two managers who do the hard work. The BSC looks trustworthy, but it is not all that simple. NN1 is a firm north of Stockholm. It is in an impossibly remote location, but the customers are used to going there. If it were measured against the factors of the BSC, it would fail against many of them. Others would fail, too. I do not want to travel around to all the yards with that as my reporting system. I will continue with my method. I cannot say what would happen, if it were introduced. Some would leave. It would be disruptive.

From 1998 until 2000, I was the head of a firm that sold directly to consumers. There you needed a business concept. Some wanted things to run like here, but that does not work in such a place. Some people want to march in serried ranks, they fit with some types of business; others want to choose for themselves and fit with other types of business.

The center prepares directives and instructions. They would like more of it, but the intervention of the system has to stop somewhere. The straight path ruins too much. It standardizes the managers.

The division manager does not believe that it is useful to relax and let everything drift:

You have to work for something. We have included that in our plans for the next few years. We had a party at which we celebrated our good results in our best clothes. My thinking was that after the party we would have to put on our work clothes. So next year we want improvements; if they cannot deliver them, then we want three reasons why they are losing ground and three ways in which they can improve matters. We have had to press them for an answer. This is something I want to deliver before I retire. They have to put in an effort to be more successful. Our competitors only do some exercising until they get tired. We continue even after we get tired. We stick it out. Our competitors only continue until they get tired—although with some of them it takes a long time for them to get tired.

The personnel and marketing manager found the following job satisfaction factors in a book: responsibility and influence, variation, and a job with substance, experiencing oneself as important, social relations as well as information and communication. We have been so brave as to include them in the framework of our plans. We are committing ourselves when we include them there.

I write to the lumber yard managers to ask them what they want their salaries to be. I write on paper with no letterhead. There is no need for that tool of power. Only five times has there been a complaint. But I just say: if you want to take the hard line, then I will as well. We are equals. If you want to push me around, then I will push you around. I do not want to use the fine polish. We have talked about a bonus system, but if we are to introduce one, then the lumber yard managers have to be fully and exclusively responsible for all influences on their results. Not everybody on the board agrees with me.

We have a reciprocal evaluation procedure. The managers have to say something about me and vice versa. Only useful information should be given; anything else will not do in an information society. Then we can always party afterwards.

The division manager believes that he is using a harsh form of management:

Some have had a pain in the stomach and have been unable to sleep. Some of them feel insecure because of my style. They think I have got something on them, but I have not. You can exert management control in different ways. But it is not the right model for me. The board is afraid of this. It is not something others can learn. I do not want to be followed around by a trainee. The lumber yards are used to meeting with me alone, so I am not buying that. Tomorrow, I will be 59 years old: I cannot promote propositions that I do not believe in. You have to use the gifts with which you were born. The human aspect is important. That is why we are here. If they want a radical change, then I am leaving. That is what I will tell the chairman. I cannot live with having a trainee. I have always worked on my own. The personnel and marketing manager is the ladies' boss. I am worried about the generational change. I am afraid of destroying our culture. You cannot rebuild that.

Questions for Discussion

1. Describe and evaluate the strategy employed by AB Swedish Lumber.

2. Describe and evaluate the management style employed by the division manager.

3. Describe and evaluate the management control methods used by AB Swedish Lumber.

4. Is there a difference between Swedish and American management styles?

5. Why are the yards with the lowest customer satisfaction the most profitable?

6. What changes in the management control systems would you recommend?

7. How would an implementation of a BSC influence the company?

8. Would your suggestions differ if the company were located in the US and not in Sweden?

9. Evaluate the strengths and weaknesses of the firm in the following areas: customer orientation, product quality, customer satisfaction, customer retention, customer value, and company success.

Appendix

Planning and Reporting at AB SWEDISH LUMBER-Prof

Long-term planning

The planning procedure at AB SWEDISH LUMBER-Prof appears in Appendix A Every third year, a long-term plan is prepared (LTP). In the LTP, the lumber yard managers present their goals and visions, opportunities and threats, their market position, an evaluation of their resources, and their plans of action. There is a separate plan for each yard and its financial consequences in each of the three planning years are estimated. The planning process is controlled by the planning guidelines and by a division conference at which the general vision and strategy of AB SWEDISH LUMBER-Prof is presented by the executive board of the division. Appendix B provides an outline of the planning activities and the timetable. The three-year plans of each lumber yard are discussed 'thoroughly and in detail with the local managers, so that they become a tenable and agreed management control instrument both financially and in terms of marketing.'

The good ideas in the LTP are usually realized over the first one or two years. When things were not too good, some projects had to be postponed. These are carried out now.

Risk Management

Risk assessment is not a formalized part of the management control of the lumber yards, but there is an explicit requirement that each lumber yard has to have a contingency plan in case its sales turnover drops by 30 percent: I prepare a 10-year investment budget for operating equipment (forklifts, trucks, etc.). I prepare them so that our investments can be equally distributed over the years and so that our level of depreciation does not exceed what we can cope with even in times of recession. You have to be able to run a business in bad times—to be able to cover the costs of rent and operating equipment.

Budgeting

The budget is prepared annually in October/November. It includes the financial consequences of the detailed planning session. In connection with the budgeting process, the lumber yard managers have to prepare analyses concerning:

1. the market and market share of the yard;
2. its present customer volume;
3. the potential of its present customer volume;
4. its potential customer volume;
5. the storing space needed;
6. its mix of stocks;
7. the personnel required;
8. its organizational development;
9. its development as regards special costs, joint costs and necessary assets.

The management of the local yard summarizes the various analyses and takes care of the preparation of the final detailed plan or marketing action plan, which is to form the basis on which the targets envisaged are to be met. The plan of the management has to include specific targets for any activity areas and describe the staff's share in meeting the targets, to the extent that the staff members are involved.

Accounting

Each month, year-to-date accounts and budgetary controls are prepared for the division management by the lumber yards. The reporting required from each yard appears in Appendix C. The corporate headquarters prepares a summary report which gives the results of each yard with respect to each of the items listed in Appendix C. A copy of the report is sent to each lumber yard manager, which allows them to compare their own results with those of the others. The accounts and accruals are prepared by the division administration, while the lumber yard managers prepare a report on reasons for any deviation from the budget. Over the year, three estimates of the annual results are prepared. Estimate 0 is prepared in connection with the accounts for the first quarter of the year. At this time, the budget is five months old. Estimate 1 is prepared in connection with the semi-annual report, and estimate 2 in connection with the budget meeting for the following year.

Appendix A

Planning process at A.B. SWEDISH LUMBER - Prof. Division

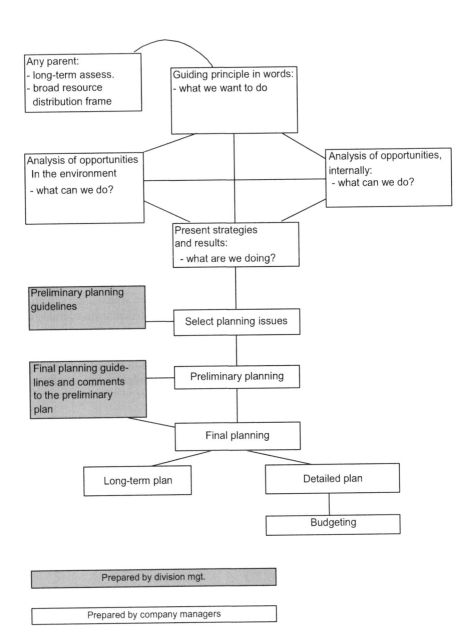

Appendix B

Timetable and Activity Plan for the Long-Term Planning at AB SWEDISH LUMBER-Prof

Time	Planning activity
February	Division conference with division managers and yard managers
March–June	Local preparation of plans, analyses, etc.
March	Staff meeting with formulation of visions and planning issues
April–May	Special planning issues and actions are agreed with the division manager
15th May	Tables with market descriptions, etc. are delivered to the secretariat
Mid-June	Corporate headquarters distributes tables to be used for calculating any financial consequences
15th August	The plans are submitted to the executive board
Mid-August–mid-Sept.	The joint plan for AB SWEDISH LUMBER-Prof is prepared and each business plan receives preliminary approval, which is simultaneously the approval of the draft budget for the following year
Mid-October	The AB SWEDISH LUMBER-Prof plan is submitted to the group management
November	The joint plan of AB SWEDISH LUMBER-Prof is submitted to the board of directors

Appendix C

Monthly Report at AB SWEDISH LUMBER-Prof

Result	Realized	Budget	Index	Year-1	Index
Month's sales turnover Total sales turnover Gross profits					
Staff expenditure Contribution margin I					
External staff expenditure Transportation Advertising Store and shop Office expenses Premises excepting internal rent Total external costs Contribution margin II					
Bad debts Depreciation Contribution margin III					
External financial revenue Yard contribution					
Internal rent Internal financing Month's result					

Balancing items	Realized	Budget	Deviation.	Year-1
Inventory Stock turnover ratio				
Debtors Days of credit				

Key figures by employees	Realized	Budget	Year-1
Sales turnover Gross margin Staff expenditure Result of main activities Pre-tax result			

The Case of Leban, Inc. and the Croatian Frozen Packaged Foods Market

Masoud Kavoossi

Howard University, Washington D.C., USA.

Aram, a Division of Leban, Inc.

Leban, Inc. is a national food and agricultural cooperative serving family farms from the East Coast to the South. Leban processes over 10 billion pounds of milk annually and markets more than 300 dairy products across the US and around the world. Leban is owned by and serves more than 7,000 producers worldwide, and approximately 1,300 local community cooperatives. Leban's food products division, which is primarily concerned with dairy products, sells to supermarkets and food service establishments across the US and in more than 12 countries. Leban is governed by a 12-member board of directors, which is elected by the entire membership. Leban employs more than 6,000 people and operates more than 200 processing, manufacturing, warehousing, and distribution facilities across North America, Europe, and Asia.

Leban's 2006 annual sales were approximately US$6 billion. At year-end, the company had total assets of US$1.1 billion and total equities of US$837 million. They are a leading marketer of dairy, frozen beef and swine feed, alfalfa seed, plant food, and crop protection products in North America. Aram, the international frozen food division of the firm, was established in 1997 following a US Trade and Development Agency (USTDA) request for proposals and award for Croatia. The USTDA's purpose is to advance economic development and to promote US commercial interests in developing and middle income countries via the creation of partnerships between US companies with proven success strategies and overseas project sponsors. The goal of the USTDA is to provide for the creation of stable, sustainable market conditions in areas of the world that need improvement. This is achieved by implementing rules, standards, and other best practices that have proven to be successful in more developed economies. Local Croatian firms were beginning to suffer from competition from imported food products, and were losing market share. Croatian consumers viewed local producers as being poor in quality and customer-focus as the products were not attractively packaged. This is where the USTDA and Leban were able to provide assistance. In the creation of Aram, Leban's leadership felt that a true opportunity existed for significant market penetration for Aram, and for overall sector improvement in the Croatian food processing industry. Leban's management wants to take advantage of the first mover advantage to expand its market share and also to increase the firm's diversification. Since the conclusion of the war and the independence of Croatia in 1995, the country has been able to maintain stability, and experience economic revitalization due in part to its growing service sector, which now accounts for the majority of the country's gross domestic product, as well as an industrial sector dominated by shipbuilding, chemical production, and food processing. Given the Croatian government's commitments to economic liberalization, Leban's US based management team felt that the time was right for a meaningful, long-term foray into the Balkan state.

Aram's objective in the Croatian market is to increase growth in local food markets, by primarily focusing on the frozen meat and dairy segments. Leban proposed a demand-driven approach for Aram based on a 'Seal of Quality in Customer Relationship Management'. The quality seal approach is a customer-centric methodology that strives to provide the highest levels of quality to customers. Aram's premise is that in order to gain market share in a market where quality is an issue, that the acquisition of long-term, profitable customers can be quickly achieved via a quality-based strategy. The leadership at Aram believes that quality is the key success factor in world frozen food markets. By providing the best quality, the firm can achieve its profitability targets. They feel that the effective managing of customer relationships can serve as a source of competitive advantage now and in the years to come.

The Croatian Frozen Packaged Food Marketing Activity

The Leban 'brand' has established itself in CRM with a 'seal of quality' for US consumers. Establishing the Croatian Seal of Quality program is faced with some challenges, however. The first challenge concerns enabling the existing food processors in the country to meet the need for improved quality standards that play a large part in the success of Aram. Concomitant with this issue is the challenge of establishing a system to verify high standards and best practices in Croatia. Since a primary aim of the USTDA was the replication of proven best practices in an economy in need of improvement, a large hurdle for the firm will be to change the mindset of local industry competitors, who have simply not been communicating their successes or failures with other competing firms. If the food processing sector in Croatia is to improve, the local firms must be willing to work together for the good of the domestic industry.

A further problem concerning implementation of the 'seal of quality' will be in developing a system that awards retailers that meet high standards with a 'CRM quality seal'. Since no effort such as this has been attempted in Croatia before, the consumers may not recognize the importance or the significance of having their products stamped with the 'CRM quality seal'. Thus, there will be a need to promote these retailers, and the seal, via a national campaign. Aram executives felt that a good opportunity to capitalize on Croatian national pride would be to select as their spokesmen two members of the 2006 Davis Cup world champions: Ivan Ljubicic, and Mario Ancic. Both of these professional tennis players are well regarded in Croatia, and were key in leading the Croatian team to victory in the Davis Cup in

2006. Should either of these well-known sports stars be available for endorsement, Aram's management felt that the consumers would certainly equate 'quality' with either of these individuals, thus helping to ensure a successful marketing of the CRM quality seal concept to the Croatian market.

The Seal of CRM Quality program can lead to impressive results. Company management projected that Croatian meat product sales could triple, and that dairy sales could increase by 45 percent in two years. Having the best product on the market, as well as effective marketing efforts could provide significant market share increases over the next two-year planning period. Aram's leadership has outlined a three-phase process for success in Croatia. These phases will now be discussed in an executive summary format.

Phase 1—Build Industry Awareness and Support

The first step in the CRM seal of quality implementation process will be to conduct consumer preference surveys to determine attitudes towards local food retailers. As mentioned earlier, the primary reason for Aram's entry into the Croatian marketplace was for the purposes of improving the overall performance of the food processing sector. Only by understanding the needs and desires of the consumers will any improvement be made.

The next step in building industry awareness and support is via consulting with industry leaders to make them aware of the challenge facing local processors. Since the food processing industry does not operate in isolation, the leaders of other segments of the Croatian economy, which depend on the success of the food processing sector, should be included in the discussions. Given the importance of this industry to the overall performance of the Croatian economy, Aram's leadership in Croatia plans on casting a wide net in order to get as many leaders from industries with ties to food processing as possible. Certainly leaders from agriculture, storage, and transportation will be included at a minimum. Once a base of industrial leadership can be created, the next step will be to establish a working group, with frequent meetings, to further assess the current state of the industry, and to establish a common approach to the problem of poor quality and a lack of customer focus in general in Croatia.

Once a macro-level view of the impacts of poor food processing on the competitiveness of the Croatian economy can be better understood, the next step in creating awareness of the need and importance of improvement would be to broaden the base of support by bringing in as many of the local food processing companies as possible. Work to establish an industry wide organization, which can eventually own and manage the process of certifications for quality standards in the Croatian market.

Phase 2—Establish Standards For Awarding the Seal of Quality

After broad-based industry support has been generated, the next step is to determine what standards for quality are realistic and achievable for the Croatian market. Aram's leadership would like to implement the same standards for achieving the seal of quality in Croatia that are necessary in the US, but the initial feedback from the

USTDA was that this may not be feasible, at least over the short term. Aram's plan of action is to start this process by evaluating the existing local food quality standards, and then to compare them with US and European Union standards. Depending on the variance in terms of quality, which may be significant, Aram will then set a realistic goal for achievement of the seal of quality in Croatia. Drazen Vlasic, President of Aram in Croatia, envisions that within three years, the standards for food processing quality in Croatia will mirror those in the US and in Western Europe.

Vlasic feels that a key ingredient for success in the establishment of the seal of quality will be in establishing a mechanism that the public will trust. If Aram can realize the quality improvements thus far not seen consistently in the Croatian food processing industry, there will be significant monetary rewards for both Aram, and the domestic companies, as customers will seek only the products that have the quality seal of approval. In order for the seal of quality initiative to be successful, the process must be seen as being independent of retailers. If Croatian consumers felt that the quality seal was simply a marketing gimmick, then the odds for success would diminish greatly. Additionally, government owned and operated retailers may not have the public trust either, so there may be a need for a new, privately owned, CRM consulting group in Croatia to fill this void. Vlasic is not sure whether it makes sense to hire an outside CRM consultant, or to simply create a strategy similar to what has been successful in other markets. He has had conversations with Leban executives in the US recently concerning whether it makes sense to outsource this project to proven global CRM service providers, or if Vlasic and his team should handle the implementation from on the ground in Croatia. If the decision is made to seek a global service provider for assistance, the result could be either disaster or the creation of a core group of firms that have the 'quality seal' in the Croatian market. This will help to establish a base of acceptance that will appear in many outlets throughout the Croatian economy, as long as the global service provider attempts to include the key participants in the system as early on as is possible.

On the other hand, if the decision is made to keep the CRM seal of quality project in-house, the Leban executives see three alternative approaches available to choose from regarding internationalizing the firm's core CRM activities. The first alternative, when keeping the project internal to Leban, is to seek a standardized approach based on its US model. This would have the effect of lower overall costs, but given the differences between the US and the Croatian economies, Vlasic wonders if this is a viable strategy. Another alternative, which may be recommended by Aram's parent company, is the use of a country-specific approach (otherwise known as a multinational approach). The third alternative that Vlasic can see being chosen is a standardized approach, where Leban attempts to standardize its overall CRM policies and its quality seal processes on a global scale.

Given the known timeframe for a decision as to the overall corporate strategy on CRM to come from Leban's US based executive team, Vlasic has decided to plan out the third phase in the implementation process for the seal of quality. This phase would be required regardless of the overall strategies employed by Aram.

Phase 3—The Process of Awarding the Seal of Quality

The first step involved in determining which Croatian firms are eligible for the seal of quality is the physical plant inspection. It is highly likely that there will be a need for significant renovation of the facilities, especially early on in the process. Based on the prior experience of Leban, Inc., and based on information gleaned from meetings with industry leaders in Croatia, the next step should be to determine the physical characteristics to be examined, and to establish a checklist that is acceptable to all potential applicants. Once an agreeable basis for inspection has been achieved, a working group that is trusted by all involved should be established in order to conduct plant and store inspections.

The second step in this final phase of implementation of the quality seal is periodic store visitations. The working group must agree in advance on a protocol for the random, unannounced store visitations. The public at large can be made aware of the inspections, so they can realize that the Croatian food processors are making a strident effort to improve, which will help to establish brand loyalty around feelings of nationalistic pride. The system of inspections should be a random process, which will help to ensure that the stores are thorough in their record keeping, and that the element of corruption that sometimes plagues food and restaurant inspections in other parts of the world will not be experienced in Croatia.

Once the methods and processes of inspection for quality have been established, norms for color, taste, smell, and appearance of the food, as well as standards of excellence in customer service should also be established. Drazen Vlasic realizes that while the quality of the product is important, so is the buying experience of the customer while shopping at the retail location where Aram's products are sold. Drazen envisions the creation of a two-page scorecard that lists all of the factors associated with a quality-minded provision of frozen packaged food in the Croatia market. The scorecards should be filled out by a pre-approved group, which includes members of the general public, to ensure that the standards of quality improvement are assessed in an unbiased manner. The end result is to have each member of the group individually score the store's performance on a rating sheet, and then the results will be averaged to determine which stores meet the standards to achieve the seal of quality from Aram. Once the competition has been assessed, the final step of the process is to award the seal of quality to all firms that are able to pass all of the tests in quality assurance.

Questions for Discussion

1. Which of the three alternative approaches to internationalization of the firm do you recommend?

2. What are the challenges for each choice?

3. Perform library research to determine Croatia's current market trends. Focus your efforts on the food processing industry, as well as the current state of the economy.

4. Describe the key success factors for Aram in Croatia.

5. Provide a one-page outline of a scorecard that should be used to inspect the quality of the food processing manufacturing plants, transportation systems, and retail outlets in Croatia.

Customer Orientation at Tesco[1]

Gerhard Rabb

Ludwigshafen University of Applied Sciences, Germany

Starting Position of Tesco

Tesco History[2]

Founded in 1924 by Sir Jack Cohen, Tesco today has to be considered one of the most successful state-of-the-art food retailers in Great Britain.

Since its inception, Tesco has been characterized as an innovator in its industry. In the 1930s, Tesco opened the first self-service grocery stores in the United States. The opening of the first superstore (90,000 square feet) in Great Britain, and the introduction of so-called trading stamps in the 1960s, could be called further milestones in the successful history of the company. Trading stamps were stamps accumulated by customers upon purchase, and once they had obtained a certain amount of the stamps, they could be traded in for cash or gifts. By introducing the trading stamps, Tesco was able to avoid the matching of other retailers' prices and offered lower prices to its customers. Over the following years, it quickly became clear that the superstore idea was the key to future success in the food retail busness. Therefore, since the opening of the first superstore in 1967, Tesco has continued to build new superstores.

In 1985, the 100th superstore opening was celebrated. Furthermore, Tesco decided to ensure future business by changing its strategy; by starting to act in the marketplace as a quality-oriented vendor rather than a price-oriented business. For that reason, in the 1980s Tesco successfully enlarged its product range and customer basis, improved the equipment and presentation means of its stores as well as its service. One measure within the scope of this repositioning was the introduction of the so-called 'Healthy Eating Initiative', which provided customers with nutritional information on Tesco's own brands. Tesco was the first major retailer who offered this service to its customers. Retrospectively, this repositioning provided the basis for Tesco to become the internationally successful, quality- and service-oriented commercial enterprise that it is today.

---

1   Following Fend, Lars & Fiala, Brigitte (1999): TescoTesco—Efficient Consumer Response beginnt beim Verbraucher! in: A. Meyer, L. Fend & M. Specht (eds), *Kundenorientierung im Handel*, pp. 121–145. Frankfurt am Main: Deutscher Fachverlag. All quotations refer to this book, except when indicated.

2   Company History. http://81.201.142.254/companyInfo/history; 20.05.2003.

In the 1990s, an increasing number of discounters implementing a low-price strategy entered the market. Coming along was the trend that people tended to buy staple food at the discounters in particular, but went to the superstores to get the quality goods. Therefore, by launching price-focused product lines like 'Value Lines' or 'Unbeatable Value Pricing', the food retailer extended its strategy by adding the low-price element to its quality and service focus. In order to extend its market position, Tesco furthermore introduced new store cocepts (Tesco Metro, Tesco Express, and Tesco Extra) and customer-focused initiatives. By launching the first customer loyalty card in 1995, Tesco once more broke new ground in food retailing. In this way, Tesco not only offered benefits to regular customers, it also gained important information about its customers and their needs. Customer services like grocery home shopping, customer assistants to make shopping more comfortable, and financial services via Tesco Personal Finance in cooperation with the Royal Bank of Scotland were introduced as well. By 1995, Tesco had become the most successful food retailer in the United Kingdom, and had a dominant market share of 16.5 percent.

Tesco Today[3]

By consequently focusing on its customer-oriented strategy, Tesco managed to grow from a domestic retailer to an international group. Today (2003) Tesco employs 296,000 people and operates 2,291 stores in ten different countries worldwide (1,982 stores in the United Kingdom; 309 stores in Ireland, Hungary, Poland, Czech Republic, Slovakia, Thailand, South Korea, Taiwan, and Malaysia) and takes the fourth rank in the IGD[4] Rating, right below Carrefour (France), Wal Mart (USA), and Auchan (France). In 2003, the food retailer was able to achieve an increase in profitability in each part of its strategy. The Tesco strategy comprises the following four elements:

- Core UK Business: Still being the core market of Tesco, the company successfully further extends its market share in the UK by consequently realizing its customer-oriented strategy, providing cheaper prices as well as offering broad choice, convenience, and great value.
- Non-food Business: To strengthen its position in the market, Tesco recently started adding non-food items to its range of products, ranging from toys, sports equipment, clothing, and home entertainment products to furnishing, electrical, and cooking equipment. By offering value and the best selection, the food retailer managed to reach a market share of five percent in a market worth £75bn in the UK by 2003. In the future, Tesco aims at achieving an equal market share in both food and non-food.
- Retailing services: To stay competitive, Tesco adapts its products and services according to the changes in the customers' shopping habits. In that context,

---

3   The   Tesco   Strategy.   http://81.201.142.254/companyInfo/businessStrategy.
asp?Section=2; 05.20.2003. Tesco—Our Markets. http://81.201.142.254/presentResults/
results2002_03/Prelims/Report/site /our_markets; 20.05.2003.
4   IGD is a independent research, information, and education provider for the food and grocery industry.

Tesco Personal Finance was founded in 1997 (in cooperation with the Bank of Scotland) offering different financial services, a Visa card, and insurance. As of 2003, Tesco Personal Finance had 3.4 million customer accounts, offers a range of more than 15 products and services, and achieved a profit of £96m in 2003. In 2000, the company's rapidly growing e-commerce ('Tesco.com') business was launched including Tesco's home shopping business. Three years later, Tesco became the leading grocery e-tailer worldwide with a profit of £12m.

• International: To ensure a long-term growth, the Tesco strategy furthermore provides expansion plans for entering growth markets in Asia and Central Europe for instance. Since the opening of the first stores in Taiwan in 2000, Tesco was able to increase its total percentage of revenue outside of the UK to 45 percent at the end of 2002.

The successful implementation of its company strategy enabled the Tesco Group to once more increase sales by 11.5 percent from £25,654m in 2002 to £28,613m in 2003. The Group's 2003 pre-tax profit grew by 14.7 percent to £1,401m (£1,221m in 2002). With an amount of £23,407m, the UK sales traditionally make up the major part of Tesco's sales (+7.9 percent in 2003). Moreover, Tesco was able to further develop the European market in 2003 and increased sales up to £3,032m (+22.5 percent) and pre-tax profit up to £141m (+56.7 percent). With a rise in sales of 45.5 percent, to £2,174m and an increase in pre-tax profit of 144.8 percent to £71m, Tesco was able to realize an enormous market growth in Asia[5] as well.

The Individualized Loyalty Concept of Tesco as a Competitive Advantage

Lifelong Customer Loyalty as Major Aim

In times of hyper-competition and increasing demands made to enterprises in regard to a simultaneous optimization of the 'magic triangle' of quality, costs, and time, reaching the objective of high customer loyalty has to be considered a decisive determinant for the success of a business. In the long run, only companies that are able to earlier, better, and more broadly fulfill their customers' individual needs and desires will be successful. This not only implies an early detection of the different requests and wishes, but also an adequate realization of customer orientation by each employee every day. Today, both have to be regarded as great challenges for a business.

Tesco faces these requirements by first of all concentrating on its own employees and their permanent career advancement as well as further training. Furthermore, Tesco has been consequently and systematically analyzing customer information for a long time. The data material received is used to obtain detailed information for a well-directed and effective customer orientation. This information offers valuable clues to specifically address the different customer segments and to offer products

---

5   Profit and loss account. http://81.201.142.254/presentResults/results 2002_03/ Prelims/Report/site/profit_and_losses; 05.20.2003.

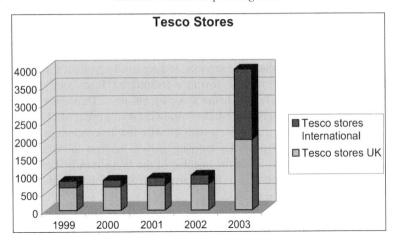

Figure CS5.1: Number of Tesco stores 1999–2003

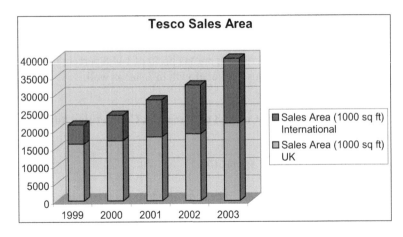

Figure CS5.2: Tesco sales area 1999–2003

and services matching the customers' permanently changing individual needs. Generally once a company would like to increase its customer loyalty, the following questions have to be taken into consideration:

- What does a customer expect of a loyalty concept?
- What are the success factors for such a concept, so that the customer will be loyal on a long-term basis?

Taking these basic questions into account, Tesco developed four different answers:

- becoming acquainted with the customer;
- actively identifying and understanding the customers' individual needs;

- remembering the customer;
- appreciating the customer.

This shows that it is by far not enough to just welcome the customer after entering the loyalty program. It generally is decisive that such a program is not only used to communicate the existing products and services of the company, but to determine and implement the customers' individual needs. Against the background of these requirements, today's very complex customer demands the increasing individualization of the needs as well as the intensification in competition have to be considered great challenges for an enterprise. The aim is to encounter the customers and their demands as personalized and individualized as possible, but by also keeping the costs down. How Tesco managed to cope with this trade-off will be described in the following section.

In terms of a broad orientation regarding the customers' needs, Tesco tracks an integral approach to surveys and the use of customer information. The major aim of this approach is to follow-up each of the above-mentioned requirements when having any kind of customer contact. Owing to the structure of Tesco, these contact possibilities are manifold.

If Tesco succeeds in realizing those principles in all stores, and to adequately encounter the customers via the various contact possibilities, a long-term commitment by the buyers to the company is very likely.

Data Analysis

An important prerequisite for customer orientation, besides surveying the relevant data, is an adequate analysis and utilization of the data. In contrast to the survey of the data needed, the processing, interpretation, and application of the information as well as the implementation of appropriate consequences in particular usually raises difficulties. Companies typically confine themselves to collecting and providing the data instead of spending more time and effort on analyzing and interpreting it. By accurately and succinctly processing and interpreting the data, Tesco applies a much more integrated approach and therewith tries to avoid the errors that are often made in practice.

In addition to this integrated approach, Tesco utilizes a rather extensive method of surveying the relevant data and therefore makes use of the increased straightforwardness, allocation, and usability of the information coming along. The company not only uses internal information, but also external data gathered from research institutes. The result is a combination of very differentiated data structures that enable Tesco to effectively partition the different customer, product, and distribution segments.

In order to provide a better understanding, Tesco's integrated approach is pointed out in the following graph. The internal information (e.g. data on transactions, data on customers, or the use as a store of specific information), which is mostly collected via the Tesco Club Cards used by more than 8.5 million customers, form the basis of the whole evaluation process. In addition to the internal data, external information on demographic as well as consumer trends, branch-specific and demographic developments, lifestyles, and locations is utilized. Based on such a detailed stock

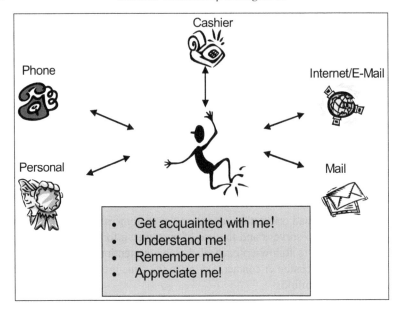

Figure CS5.3: Tesco's manifold contact possibilities for surveying customer information (following: Fend & Fiala, 1999, p. 128; own translation)

of information, an effective segmentation regarding different customer groups, distribution channels, and products could finally be conducted.

Loyalty Cube

Generally Tesco aims at a better and deeper understanding of the customers' demands. To realize such an efficient customer orientation, Tesco determined the following three variables:

- The transaction data are the first variable, which is generated by offering the Tesco Club Cards. The point of time, the frequency, and the value of a purchase are examples of such transaction data.
- The 'share of wallet' has to be considered the second variable, since it provides information on the share of the total demand of consumer goods that a customer satisfies at Tesco stores. Generating this kind of information is by far more difficult than the first category of variables. Therefore, results of market research institutes are primarily considered in that context.
- The commitment or identification of the customer regarding the company has to be called the third determinant. Instruments employed to receive information on this topic are interviews, interrogations, and also the evaluation of coupons used at Tesco stores.

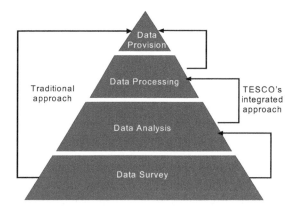

Figure CS5.4: Tesco's manifold data management (following: Fend & Fiala, 1999, p. 130; own translation)

The result of the simultaneous consideration of these three variables is very detailed and meaningful information on the customer structure of Tesco company. Being in possession of such important data concerning the various existing customer segments and the very different demands, wishes, and expectations coming along is a decisive prerequisite for an effective customer orientation.

One-To-Many-Approach

Based on the identified customer structure, so-called customer clusters are now formed. This in turn enables Tesco to provide very specific and individualized marketing instruments corresponding to the demands and desires of each individual

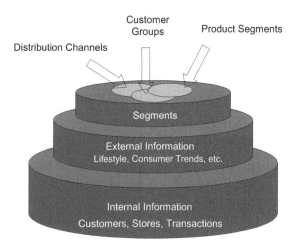

Figure CS5.5: Tesco's broad data basis (following: Fend & Fiala, 1999, p. 31; own translation)

cluster. For that reason, specific, cluster-related marketing goals, strategies, and measures are put forth.

In the following section, some specific examples, which show how revealing the surveyed data in regard to the formulation of specific Tesco measures is, will be described:

- Basket of goods gives information on the current family status.
- Buying school equipment indicates that customers have kids in school.
- Diapers in the basket of goods shows that offspring have arrived in the family.

Being in possession of this information, the creation of specific and individualized offers becomes possible. This not only brings about a direct increase in sales, the customer also feels recognized and personally appreciated. A rise in customer loyalty therefore is an indirect consequence. Since it is a key to a company's success to learn and understand from the surveyed data how, why, and when the customer acts, it is worthwhile for Tesco to undertake the enormous costs for specific loyalty measures for 8.5 million customer card owners.

In the context of its customer orientation strategy, Tesco tracks several approaches that will be described in the following section:

Members Canvass Members

In the context of the 'Members canvass Members' program, Tesco organizes topic-centered events, which then take place in specific subsidiaries (e.g. cheese &

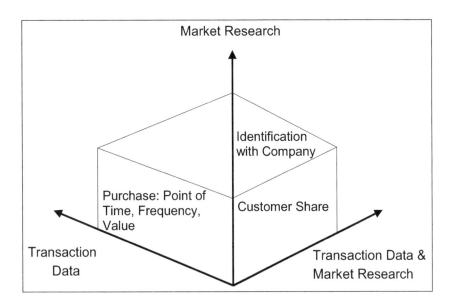

**Figure CS5.6: Tesco Loyalty Cube (following: Fend
& Fiala, 1999, p. 32; own translation)**

wine, hair care and cosmetics). By arranging these events corresponding with the specific interests of the customer clusters addressed, not only existing customers are provided with a benefit. Tesco furthermore aims at attracting completely new customers in the context of such an unusual setting. For that reason, Tesco customers are invited to bring friends or family. The success of such concepts becomes clear taking the following numbers into account: about 40 percent of the people brought by existing customers also satisfy their demand for groceries at Tesco.

Customer Mailing

The customer mailing is a major factor of success of Tesco's 'One-To-Many-Approach'. It consists of 65,000 content-wise different, personalized letters that are sent to the 8.5 million customers. By making use of the detailed knowledge about the several customer clusters, each customer feels addressed individually, although Tesco actually does not appeal to each customer separately. Customer mailings as a method to create and increase customer loyalty first of all has to be considered an instrument that is rather effective for Tesco in its accomplishment, but also makes the customer feel appreciated. Furthermore, customers could deal with the offers and rewards at home, in a quiet and well-known environment, where there is enough time and leisure to consider the offers at their leisure.

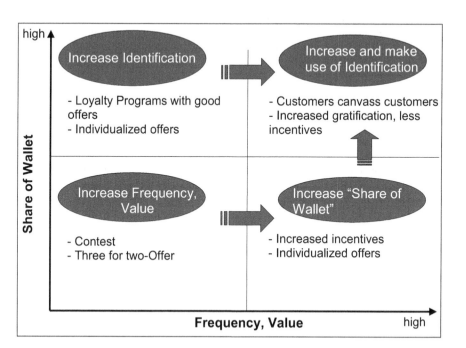

Figure CS5.7: Strategies and measures for Tesco customer segments
(following: Fend & Fiala, 1999, p. 138; own translation)

Clubcard Magazine

Similar to the customer mailings, Tesco also compiles the *Clubcard Magazine* according to the needs and interests of the individual customer clusters.

Generally, the network existing between the Tesco stores effectively supports the company's marketing activities. Via this network, each store manager is able to get detailed information about the customer portfolio of the particular store and therefore a detailed picture about the customer structure. This enables the manager to effectively plan purchasing and realize adequate marketing activities.

Employees

The training of the employees has to be considered a further significant instrument in the context of customer orientation. All employees, independently of their position, have to go through the 'First Class Service' program. The main parts of this program are:

- products
- presentation
- processes
- people

Each employee has to look at each of the four parts with the eyes of the customer and provide adequate suggestions. Moreover, employees are informed about the content of the loyalty program in detail. Thus, the employees are able to better serve customers on a daily basis as they are more familiar with the needs of the customer clusters.

Final Remarks

The present case study aims at demonstrating how important detailed customer knowledge is in times where direct marketing, that is the direct addressing of customers, has to be considered a decisive competitive advantage, especially when compared to ineffective mass mailing campaigns. This fact gains even greater importance given today's high prices and product similarities. The possibility to address customers faster and more individually than the competitor does (by considering their expectations and needs) opens up important possibilities to gain a competitive advantage, especially in retailing. An important prerequisite in order for customer orientation to become such a competitive advantage is not only to survey adequate customer information, but also to analyze and interpret these data accordingly and derive appropriate clusters and marketing measures from it.

Questions for Discussion

1. Please explain the difficulties concerning data analysis, especially the problems that companies have in drawing adequate consequences and measures from the surveyed data.

2. As a result of its broad data analysis, Tesco receives detailed knowledge about the existing, differentiated customer structure, and the various needs, expectations, and desires that these customers have. What are the direct and indirect consequences of having this knowledge for the company?

3. How would you describe Tesco's international strategy at the time of the case?

Case Study 6

Mikhak Fresh Cut Flowers

Masoud Kavoossi
Howard University, Washington D.C., USA

Mikhak Fresh Cut Flowers is a Moroccan firm, run by cooperatives of local growers, with ambitions to penetrate the global markets. The company's leadership is keen on obtaining and maintaining real time and accurate data on consumer patterns and behavior.

It is believed that more than half of the company's products and services will be mostly or totally personalized in five years, up from 37 percent today. Although companies have long been offering customized merchandise, customization in the fresh cut flowers industry has been based on templates, and does not take individual customer preferences into account. Personalization, by contrast, allows the customer to stamp a product with his or her own applications, preferences, and configurations. Mikhak wants to collaborate and coordinate its marketing internationally. Mikhak is interested in learning how it can use personalization to increase sales and margins enough to transform business models. It is not, however, financially prepared to invest much to make its wishes a reality.

Forty percent of Mikhak's inventory is sold prior to delivery, and 58 percent is sold directly from the backs of trucks to florists who climb onboard to see what they would like on that particular delivery. The remaining 2 percent wilts. The business is somewhat seasonal, with quiet summers and spikes in demand around Mother's Day, and religious holidays in Morocco such as Prophet Muhammad's birthday and Eid festivals.

Having the right product mix is the key to enter the international markets and have a chance at being successful. The company achieved annual revenues of US$3.1 million in 2004, US$3.5 million in 2005, and US$4 million in 2006, with a consistent profit margin of between 11–12 percent each year.

Before the Second World War, cut flowers were grown locally near intended customer markets. Later, improved varieties and better transportation mechanisms allowed growers in southern Europe, Israel, and parts of North Africa and South America to supply northern European and North American markets. What was once a seasonal business was transformed into a year-round industry. Roses became a Valentine's Day fixture, and Dutch firms took on a special role as their standards for everything from bucket sizes to environmental certification were adopted.

The trend of importing flowers rather than growing them in the US began in the mid-1980s when companies realized the benefit of the South and Central American climates. Europeans began outsourcing their flower growing in the early 1990s, mostly to the Middle East and North Africa, where flowers can be grown year-round, and labor is cheaper.

Trade in cut flowers in the US is a US$6 billion dollars a year business, and a US$24 billion wholesale business worldwide. The US imports more than US$400 million worth of fresh cut flowers from South America, out of which US$315 million is imported from Colombia. Roses top the list of imports, followed by carnations (or Mikhak in Farsi), chrysanthemums, and tulips. Seventy-five percent of Americans will celebrate Valentine's Day, while 21 percent plan to ignore it. In our globalized economy, 90 percent of roses sold in the US come from abroad, and most of those come from Latin America. California leads the nation in the domestic production of fresh cut roses. The Census Bureau reports that 21,387 US florists are part of a booming global marketplace. China is also flexing its trade muscles in this area. China has announced that becoming a major rose exporter is a national policy goal, giving meaning to the idea of red roses! And let's not forget the complimentary product of candy that is produced in the US as well as abroad: Americans consume 25.7 pounds of candy per person each year. These figures correspond with Germany as it relates to celebrating of Valentine's Day, and the purchase of roses.

The Netherlands, which accounts for almost 65 percent of the world trade volume in the industry, is by far the leading exporter. The Netherlands position as world standard-bearer in the fresh cut flowers industry should come as no surprise, given the famous 'tulip mania' in the country during the 17th century, which while temporarily ruinous, established the country's reputation in the eyes of consumers worldwide as a provider of a quality product. Behind it, however, follow a number of developing countries, including Colombia, with 19 percent of the global market, and with Ecuador, India, Lebanon, Tanzania, Thailand, Morocco, and Israel accounting for the remaining product. Iran is a large producer, but currently has little exports given its current political situation. Flower centers are emerging in Dubai, in the Persian Gulf, and elsewhere, with many of these new production centers being closer both to producers and to promising new markets. Recently, large discount retailers such as Wal-Mart and Costco have started buying flowers directly from tropical growers. Grower-retailer interaction is emerging very rapidly, as retailers have found that bypassing the intermediaries can save costs.

Cut flowers are Colombia's third most important agricultural export crop, after coffee and bananas. The industry supports some 75,000 jobs directly, and another 50,000 in related industries. In 2000, cut flowers generated US$580 million in export earnings for the country. In value terms, 84 percent of these exports went to the US, and 10 percent went to the EU—a share that has been declining since the mid-1990s, when it was frequently 15 percent or more. Columbia is the number one source of imported fresh cut flowers into the US. As you can see from this analysis, floral trade is currently primarily taking place at regional levels.

In the early 1990s, several European non-profit organizations, including environmental and non-governmental organization groups began campaigning against what they saw as unacceptable labor and environmental conditions in the flower export industries of many African and Latin American countries. As part of this campaign, several public relations campaigns were created in European countries, most intended to raise environmental and social standards in developing countries. However, significant concerns about their possible trade effects were raised by developing countries, which complained about their loss of access to OECD markets. Middle Eastern firms initiated a debate about the need for market information schemes in the context of the Technical Barriers to Trade Agreement. This World Trade Organization agreement tries to ensure that various national regulations, standards, testing, and certification procedures do not create unnecessary obstacles to international trade. Losing European market opportunities were affecting the business performance of Mikhak Fresh Cut Flowers. In response to this, foreign pressure at the national level, coupled with the work of local growers, spurred Middle Eastern flower producers to adopt their own consumer data collection policies and procedures, and to implement other changes in the industry in the region to initiate data collection at the customer level. The pressures of international protective barriers thus led firms such as Mikhak Fresh Cut Flowers to attempt to better understand their customers.

Development of the Measure

In the area of green marketing, customer sensitivity and awareness of the environment is considerable. The environmental and social impacts of flower production can be significant. They include excessive application of agrochemicals and health effects stemming from inadequate protection of workers who handle dangerous chemicals. In some companies, environmental concerns have also included the use of pesticides banned for safety or health reasons in OECD countries. Mikhak is not one of those firms, as it is relatively small in production. It employs 22. mostly seasonal. workers who receive no company benefits.

In 1991, concerned about the plight of worker conditions in developing countries where flowers for the cut flower market were being grown, a group of German human rights and church organizations, including FIAN (Food-First Action and Information Network), and *Brot für die Welt* (Bread for the World, located in Washington DC), formed the Flower Campaign 'to secure environmental protection in flower production and educate consumers on the benefits to them of environmentally friendly flower production methods'.

In 1994, FIAN joined together with the German Flower Wholesale and Import Trade Association to discuss appropriate social and environmental criteria for flower growing. The German Flower and Wholesale Import Trade Association subsequently sat down with representatives of flower exporters in the EU, and formed the Education for Flower Growers and Exporters' Association, to develop a data bank on consumer habits and preferences including their environmental sensitivity in the EU market. The scheme covered 12 social and environmental criteria relating to pesticide and fertilizer use, health and safety measures, and general consumption traits. Some 35 producers in the Middle East, and around the world, signed up to participate in the scheme, including Mikhak. It was not sure if it would lead to greater market share, but the firm's owners felt that they were not in a position to decline participation.

Costs of participation from €3,000 to €10,000, depending on the size of the enterprise, were to be paid by the producers on a one-time basis. Given a given country's Euro exchange rate, it could be a large sum for something with uncertain benefits. FIAN also approached the larger of Morocco's flower exporting associations, with a proposal to establish a separate database called 'Mena Flowers'. The idea was that fresh cut flower companies that wanted to export to the EU would sign on to the agreement in order to be placed on a 'market list'. In so signing, the companies would declare that they would strictly comply with all EU laws and norms concerning consumer protection regulations, agrochemical use, and handling. In exchange, they would get data information on market leads, training, and promotions in the EU.

The companies would have also had to consent to having their information checked by a commission comprised of both EU and Mena member companies that had export markets in the EU. Despite the risk of losing access to the European market, Mikhak decided not to subscribe to the plan, echoing the position of some other enterprises that in so doing would be compromising too much of the cooperatives core customer information, which can be detrimental to the firm's competitive advantage. The enterprises did not feel the market information access would be of great value in terms of market personalization or even customization efforts.

At around the same time, in the Netherlands, the EU commission began to collect data on consumer purchasing patterns including flowers imported from the Middle East producers, notably Morocco, Lebanon, and Iran. The idea meant to assure consumers that the products were considerably less damaging to the environment than those produced using conventional methods. For the cultivation of flowers, only limited and selected use of chemicals and artificial fertilizers were permitted. After initial difficulties, some growers in Morocco, Lebanon, India, and Iran were eventually able to meet the EU requirements and export fresh cut flowers, and receive limited market and retail information.

The focus of the exchange was on providing detailed information and training in the following areas:

- business environments in different EU countries: economic, regulatory, social;
- business knowledge and business skills through workshops on data collection;
- experience of successful entrepreneurs and business in leading market positions;
- trade fair selling flowers from enterprises owned and managed by Mena member enterprises.

Objectives

- To motivate and empower competent businesses in an ever-changing business environment to enhance and develop their own businesses and market research.
- To create a network of producers from different Mena countries as a dynamic and sustainable forum for sharing experience, consumer trends, and new ideas
- To enable knowledge and information to be transferred between participants

- To work together on sustainable solutions to problems faced by small- and medium-sized enterprises (SMEs), focusing on the export business in to the EU.
- To transfer and exchange positive experience of working with entrepreneurs throughout the world.
- To create international networks designed to promote export/import-oriented fresh cut flower businesses.
- To allow for international strategic alliances with EU retail.

This case study demonstrates that private consumer producer schemes, because they are voluntary, can be used effectively to bring about changes in production methods. However, private schemes should not assume that all foreign producers, much less their governments, would be willing to participate in them. By maintaining transparency and encouraging dialogue, however, common ground can often be found where growers, retailers, and consumers can benefit. Obtaining market data remains an important element.

Questions for Discussion

1. What are the strengths and weaknesses of Mikhak's customer data collection strategy? Did Mikhak make the right decision by not participating in the European market plan?

2. What are some examples of common trends in the fresh cut flowers industry for the high-income countries of the EU and the US?

3. Do the numbers add up? Research whether current US import figures from Colombia match the export totals referenced in the case.

4. Have their been any effective institutional arrangements enabling government officials or the private sector firms to stay abreast of emerging standards of international trading partners or within the private sector of specific countries? Or, is the flow of information very fragmented in the industry?

5. What do you see as the primary benefits that would have stemmed from Mikhak's membership in the 'Mena Flowers' agreement? What do you see as the important shortcomings of the agreement?

Resources/References

Colombia Flower Exporter's Association website, http://www.colombianflowers.com, accessed on May 20, 2007.
Flora Culture International website, http://www.floracultureintl.com, accessed on May 20, 2007.

GTZ Organization website, http://www.gtz.de, accessed May 24, 2007.

Pacific Shipper website, 'Pacific Shipper's Cool Cargoes Fall 2006', http://www.pacificshipper.com, accessed May 20, 2007.

'Petal Power', *Economist*, May 12, 2007, Vol., 383, Issue 8528.

Bibliography

Ajami, R., Cool, K., Goddard, G.J., Khambata, D., *International Business: Theory and Practice*, Second Edition, M.E. Sharpe, Armonk, NY, 2006.

Akao, Y., *QFD–Quality Function Development*, Moderne Industrie, Landsberg, 1992.

Avlonitis, G., Panagopoulos, N., Antecedents and consequences of CRM technology acceptance in the sales force, *Industrial Marketing Management Journal*, 34 2005, pp. 355–368.

Backhaus, K., *Multi-variant Analysis Methods: An Application Orientated Introduction*, Springer, Berlin, 2000.

Backhaus, K., Baumeister, C., Customer relations in industrial goods marketing, in: Bruhn and Homburg (eds), *Handbook of Customer Relationship Management*, Springer, Wiesbaden, 2000, pp. 201–225.

Backhaus, K., Erichson, B., Plinke, W., Weiber, R., *Multi-variant Analysis Methods: An Application Orientated Introduction*, Heidelberg, 2003.

Bailom, F., Hinterhuber, H., Matzler, K., Sauerwein, E., The Kano model of customer satisfaction, *Marketing ZFP*, 2, 1996, pp. 117–125.

Baumann, S., *Customer Orientation and Incentive Systems: External and Internal Customer Satisfaction as Assessment Basis of Incentive Systems*, Deutscher Sparkassen Publishers, Stuttgart, 2000.

Belz, C., Tomczak, T., *Customer Clubs as Customer Relationship Instrument – Advice for the Development of Successful Club Concepts*, Thexis, St.Gallen, 1996.

Berger, P., Eechambadi, N., George, M., Lehmann, D., Rizley, R., Venkatesan, R., From customer lifetime value to shareholder value: Theory, empirical evidence, and issues for future research, *Journal of Service Research*, 9(2), 2006, pp. 156–167.

Berger, C., Blauth, R., Boger, D., Kano's methods for understanding customer defined quality, *Centre for Quality Management Journal*, 3(2), 1993, pp. 3–35.

Berke, J., Maintaining regular customers, *WirtschaftsWoche*, 11, 2004, pp. 52–61.

Berke, J., Hennersdorf, A., Ready for Aldi, *Wirtschaftswoche*, 11, 2004, p. 52.

Berson, A., Smith, S., *DATA Commodity Housing, DATA Mining & OLAP*, McGraw-Hill Education, Osborne, 1997.

Berson, A., Smith, S., Thearling, K., *Building DATA Mining Applications for CRM*, McGraw-Hill Professional, Osborne, 2000.

Besterfield, D., Besterfield-Michna, C., Besterfield, G., *Total Quality Management*, Second Edition, Prentice Hall, Upper Saddle River, NJ, 1998.

Bliemel, F., Eggert, A., Customer relationship – The new target strategy?, *Marketing – Journal for Research and Practice*, 1, 1998, pp. 37–44.

Bohling, T., Bowman, D., LaValle, S., Vikas, M., Das, N., Ramani, G., Varadarajan, R., CRM implementation: Effectiveness issues and insights, *Journal of Service Research*, 9(2), November 2006, pp. 184–194.

Bollinger, T., Association rules – Analysis of a DATA mining procedure, *Computer Science Spectrum*, 19, 1996, pp. 257–261.

Brommer, A., Personnel from the PC, *Werben & Verkaufen*, 8, 2001, pp. 84–85.

Bruggemann, A., Determining different forms of job satisfaction, *Arbeit und Leistung*, 28, 1974, pp. 281–284.

Bruhn, M., *Customer Orientation: Components for Excellent Customer Relationship management (CRM)*, DTV-Beck, Munich, 2007.

Buzzell, R., Gale, B., Greif, H., *The PIMS Program: Strategies and Corporate Success*, Gabler, Wiesbaden, 1989.

Christianus, D., *Management of Customer Satisfaction and Customer Loyalty: How to Increase the Profit and Value of the Enterprise*, Expert Publishers, Renningen-Malmsheim, 2002.

Delhaes, D., Public services: No fun with change, *Wirtschaftswoche*, 8, 2001, p. 136.

Diller, H., Customer loyalty as a marketing goal, *Marketing Journal for Research and Practice*, 2, 1996, pp. 81–93.

Donnelly, J., Ivancevich, J., Post purchase reinforcement and back-out behavior, *Journal of Marketing Research*, 7, 1970, pp. 399–400.

Ederer, G., Seiwert, L., Küstenmacher, W., *The Customer is King: the 1 × 1 of Customer Orientation*, Gabel, Offenbach, 2000.

Erlbeck, K., *Customer-oriented Management: Customer Satisfaction and Loyalty*, Germany University. Wiesbaden, 1999.

Fest, A., *Motives of Bank Loyalty of Private Customers*, Sparkasse, 3, 1999, pp. 106–115.

Festinger, L., *A Theory of Cognitive Dissonance*, Stanford University Press, New York, 1957.

Galbraith, J.K., The new industrial state, *Sentry Edition 58*, Houghton Mifflin, Boston, MA, 1967, p. 221.

Galguera, L., Luna, D., Mendez, P., Predictive segmentation in action: Using CHAID to segment loyalty cardholders, *International Journal of Market Research*, 48(4), 2006, pp.459–479.

Gammelin, C., Unrivaled expense, *Die Zeit*, 30/12/2004, p. 28.

Garvin, D., What does product quality really mean? *Sloan Management Review*, Fall/1984a, pp. 25–43.

Garvin, D., Product quality: An important strategic weapon, *Business Horizons*, March-April, 1984b, pp. 40–43.

Göbbel, K., Customer relationship management in practice: The hated customer, *IT Services*, 2, 2001, pp. 27–30.

Gresch, T., Customer orientation through competence models, *Personalwirtschaft*, 1, 1997, pp. 8–11.

Griffin, A., Hauser, J., The voice of the customer, *Marketing Science*, Winter, 1993, pp. 1–27.

Griffin, J., Lowenstein, M., *Customer Win-Back*, Wiley & Sons, San Francisco, 2001.

Grönroos, Ch., *Service Management and Marketing: A Customer Relationship Management Approach*, Wiley, Chichester, 2000.

Günter, B., Helm, S., *Customer Value: Fundamentals – Innovative concepts – Practical Implementation*, Gabler, Wiesbaden, 2006.

Haines, S., McCoy, K., *Sustaining High Performance. The Strategic Transformation Ton of a Customer-Focused Learning Organization*, Delray Beach, St Lucie Press, Florida, 1995.

Handlbauer, G., Core competencies in international enterprises, in: Hinterhuber (ed.), *The Challenges of Mastering the Future, Brochure*, Frankfurt, 1995, pp. 263–284.

Haseborg, F., Mäßen, A., The phenomenon of variety seeking behavior: Modeling, empirical findings and political marketing implications, *Yearbook of Sales and Consumer Research*, 2, 1997, pp. 164–187.

Hauser, J., Clausing, D., When the voice of the customer should expand into production, in: Simon and Homburg (eds), *Customer Satisfaction*, Dr. Th. Gabler, Wiesbaden, 1998, pp. 59–79.

Helson, H., *Adaptation-Level Theory*, Gabler, New York, 1964, p. 62.

Henry, A., Ruess, A., Salz, J., Like the key to the castle, *Wirtschaftswoche*, 12, 2003, p. 62.

Herrmann A., Huber F., Braunstein, C., Customer satisfaction does not always guarantee more profit, *Harvard Business Manager*, 1, 2000, pp. 45–55.

Herrmann, A., Johnson, M., Customer satisfaction as determination factor of customer relations, *Magazine for Operations Research*, 6, 1999, p. 579.

Hinterhuber, H., Aichner, H., Lobenwein, W., *Enterprise Value and Lean Management*, Manz'sche, Vienna, 1994.

Hippner, H., Wilde, K., *IT Systems in CRM: Structure and Potential*, Gabler, Wiesbaden, 2004.

Hirschman, A.O., *Exit, Voice, and Loyalty: Responses to Decline in Firms, Organizations, and States*, Harvard University Press, Boston, MA, 1972.

Hofstede, G., *Culture and Organizations: Software of the Mind*, McGraw-Hill, New York, NY, 1991.

Holland, H., Heeg, S., *Successful Strategies for Customer Retention*, Gabler, Wiesbaden, 1998.

Homburg, C., Switch-point turn around, *Manager Magazine*, January, 1996, pp. 144–152.

Homburg. C., *Customer Satisfaction: Concepts – Methods – Experiences*, Gabler, Wiesbaden, 2003.

Homburg, C., Bruhn, M., Customer relationship management – An introduction to the theoretical and practical way of looking at a problem, in: Bruhn and Homburg (eds), *Handbook of Customer Relationship Management*, Gabler, Wiesbaden, 2000, pp. 3–36.

Homburg, C., Fürst, A., Complaint management excellence, in: Homburg (ed.), *Perspectives of Market-Focused Management*, University of Mannheim Institute, Wiesbaden, 2004, pp. 329–370.

Homburg, C., Jensen, O. Customer-oriented payment systems: Requirements, distribution, determinants, *Magazine for Marketing and Management*, 1, 2000, pp. 55–74.

Homburg, C., Rudolph, B., Theoretical perspectives of customer satisfaction, in: Simon and Homburg (eds), *Customer Satisfaction*, Wiesbaden, 1998. pp. 33–55.

Homburg, C., Schäfer, H., *Customer Recovery, Paper 39*, Institute for Market-Focused Management, University of Mannheim, 1999.

Homburg, C., Sieben, F., Stock, R., Measured variables of successfully winning back customers, *Marketing – Magazine for Research and Practice*, 1, 2004, pp. 25–41.

Homburg, C., Werner, H., *Customer Orientation with System: With Customer-Orientation-Management to Profitable Growth*, Campus Fachbuch, Frankfurt, 1998.

Hoyer, W., Ridgway, N., Variety seeking as an explanation for exploratory purchase behavior, in: Kinnear (ed.), *Advances in Consumer Research*, 1983, pp. 114–119.

Iyengar, S., Lepper, M., When choice is demotivating: CAN one desire too much of a good thing, *Journal of Personality and Social Psychology*, 6, 2000, pp. 995–1006.

Jensen, O., Customer-oriented payment systems, in: Homburg (ed.), *Perspectives of the Market-Focused Management*, University of Mannheim, Wiesbaden, 2004, pp. 393–407.

Kale, S., CRM failure and the seven deadly sins, *Marketing Management*, September/October, 2004, pp. 42–46.

Kaplan, R., Norton, D. Klein, B., *Balanced Scorecard: Strategies Successfully Translated*, Schaffer-Poeschel, Stuttgart, 1997.

Kierkegaard, S.A., Oden, T., *The Parables of Kierkegaard*, Princeton University Press, New York, 1989, p. 38.

Klein, B., *QFD – Quality Function Deployment*, Expert Publishers, Renningen-Malmsheim, 1999.

Köhler, R., Customer-oriented account system as a requirement of customer relationship management, in: Bruhn and Homburg (eds), *Handbook of Customer Relationship Management*, DTV-Beck, Wiesbaden, 2000, pp. 415–444.

Koppelmann, U., Variety seeking: How you profit from the curious client, *Absatzwirtschaft*, 1, 2002, pp. 44–47.

Kowalski, M., Kroker, M., Lightyears ahead, *Focus*, 43, 2000, p. 338.

Krafft, M., *Customer Connection and Customer Value*, Physica Publishers, Heidelberg, 2007.

Krafft, M., Marzian, S., Customer value on track, *Marketing*, 6, 1997, pp. 104–107.

Krahl, D., Windheuser, U., Zick, F., *DATA Mining: Employment in Practice*, Addison Wesley Publishers, Bonn, 1998.

Kroker, M., With high-complex miracle weapons in competition engagement, *IT Services*, 3, 2000, pp. 18–21.

Kurz, A., New accomplishments of data analysis using novel knowledge discovery and DATA mining methods, in: Martin (ed.), *DATA Commodity Housing – DATA Mining – OLAP*, McGraw-Hill Education, Bonn, 1998, pp. 249–281.

Liihe, M. von der., DATA mining and marketing intelligence, in: Martin (ed.), *DATA Commodity Housing – DATA Mining – OLAP*, Bonn, 1998, pp. 283–299.

McAlister, L., Pessemier, E. Meffert, H., Variety seeking behavior: An interdisciplinary review, *Journal of Consumer Research*, 9, 1982, pp. 311–322.

Meffert, H., *Marketing: Basics of Market-Focused Corporate Management; Concepts, Instruments, Practical Examples*, Gabler, Wiesbaden, 2000.

Meyer, A., Dornach, F., Müller, W. *(eds)*, *The German Customer Barometer – Quality and Satisfaction, German Marketing Consortium, Inc. and the German Federal Post Office Postal Service*, Gabler, Berlin, 1998.

Müller-Stewens, G., Lechner, C., *Strategic Management: How Strategic Initiatives Lead to Change*, Schaffer-Poeschel, Stuttgart, 2005.

Nakhaeizadeh, G., Applied customer satisfaction research, *Market Study and Management*, 4, 1996, pp. 149–159.

Niebisch, P., Betz, B., *DATA Mining: Theoretical Aspects and Applications*, Physica Publishers, Heidelberg, 1998.

Niemand, S., *Attitudes of Consumers to Personnel Service in Different Commerce and Service Branches. Results of an Investigation on Behalf of the News Magazine FOCUS*, Gabler, Starnberg, 1996.

Nieschlag, R., Dichtl, E., Hörschgen, H., *Target Costing for Industrial Services*, Duncker & Humblot, Munich, 1996.

Nieschlag, R., Dichtl, E., Hörschgen, H., *Marketing*, Berlin, 1994.

Nieschlag, R., Dichtl, E., Hörschgen, H, *Marketing*, Berlin, 2002.

Oehler, A., Support by relationship management, *Die Bank*, 3,1995, pp. 137–142.

Osarenkhoe, A., Bennani, A., An exploratory study of implementation of customer relationship management strategy, *Business Process Management Journal*, 13, (1), 2007, pp. 139–164.

Otte, R., Otte V., Kaiser,V., *DATA Mining for the Industrial Practice*, Hanser Fachbuch Publishers, Munich, 2004.

Peter, S., Customer connection as a marketing goal, *Absatzwirtschaft*, 7, 1998, pp. 74–80.

Petouhoff, N., The scientific reason for CRM failure, *Customer Relationship Management*, March, April, 2006, p. 48.

Plinke, W., Söllner, A., Customer connection and dependency relationships, in: Bruhn and Homburg (eds), *Handbook of Customer Relationship Management*, DTV-Beck, Wiesbaden, 2000, pp. 55–79.

Raab, G., *Map-Supported Payment Systems and Consumer Behavior*, Duncker & Humblot, Berlin, 1998.

Raab, G., Neuner, M., *Development of a Behavioral Based Simulation Game for Assessing Entrepreneurial Potentials*, Paper presented at the 8th. Annual Interdisciplinary Entrepreneurship Conference, Stuttgart (Germany), 2004.

Raab, G., Unger, A., Unger, F., *Methods of Marketing Research*, Gabler, Wiesbaden, 2004.

Raab, G., Unger, F., *Market Psychology*, Gabler, Wiesbaden, 2005.

Ramaseshan, B., Bejou, D., Jain, S., Mason, C., Pancras, J., Issues and perspectives in global customer relationship management, *Journal of Service Research*, 9, (2), November 2006, pp. 195–207.

Rapp, R., *Customer Satisfaction Through Service Quality: Conceptualization – Measurement – Conversion*, Germany University Publishers, Wiesbaden, 1995.

Rapp, R., *Customer Relationship Management*, Campus Publishers, Frankfurt, 2000.

Reichheld, F., Sasser, W., Zero defections: Quality comes to services, *Harvard Business Review*, 1990, pp. 105–111.

Reinartz, W., Kumar, V., The mismanagement of customer loyalty, *Harvard Business Review*, 2002, pp. 86–94.

Rigby, R., Reichheld, F., Schefter, P., CRM – how you avoid the four largest mistakes, *Harvard Business Manager*, 4, 2002, pp. 55–63.

Rust, R., Zahorik, A., Keiningham, T., *Service Marketing*, Longman, Auckland, New Zealand, 1996.

Scharnbacher, K., Kiefer, G., *Customer Satisfaction: Analysis, Measurability and Certification*, Munich, Vienna, 1998.

Scharrer, J., Bitter lesson, *Capital*, 11, 2000, p. 32.

Schaudwet, C., Wager of the strategists, *Wirtschaftswoche*, 35, 2004, pp. 52–54.

Schinzer, H., Bange, C., Mertens, H., *DATA Warehouse and DATA Mining: Market-Leading Products in Comparison*, Vahlen, Munich, 1999.

Schmid, R., Bach, V., Österle, H., With customer relationship management to the process portal, in: Bach and Oesterle (eds), *Customer Relationship Management*, Spinger, Berlin, 2000, pp. 3–55.

Schulz, B., *Customer Potential Analysis in the Client Base of Firms*, Brochure, Frankfurt, 1995.

Sherif, M., Hovland, C., *Social Judgements: Assimilation and Contrast Effects in Communication and Attitude CHANGE*, Greenwood Press, New Haven, Connecticut, 1961.

Simon, H., Homburg, C., Customer satisfaction as strategic success factor – introductory considerations, in: Simon and Homburg (eds), *Customer Satisfaction*, Dr. Th. Gabler, Wiesbaden, 1998, pp. 18–31.

Sommerlatte, T., Wedekind, E., Performance processes and organizational structure, in: Little (ed.), *Management of the High-Performance Organization*, Dr. Th. Gabler, Wiesbaden, 1990, pp. 25–41.

Stauss, B., Friege, C., Regaining service customers: Costs and benefits of regain management, *Journal of Service Research*, 1(4), May 1, 1999, pp. 347–361.

Thomas, J., Blattberg, R., Fox, E., Recapturing lost customers, *Journal of Marketing Research (JMR)*, 41, (1), Feb 2004, pp. 31–45.

Thomas, J., Reinartz, W., Kumar, V., Getting the most out of all your customers, *Harvard Business Review*, 2004, pp. 116–123.

Töpfer, A., Customer as a king, *Wirtschaftswoche*, 43, 1996, pp. 86–110.

Töpfer, A., Mann, A., Customer satisfaction as the measuring stick for success, in: Toepfer (ed.), *Measuring and Increasing Customer Satisfaction*, Neuwied, Kriftel. Berlin,1999, pp. 59–110.

Weber, J., Lissautzki, M., *Customer Value Controlling*, Wiley-VCH, Koblenz, 2004.

Wilson, J., *Mouth-to-Mouth Marketing*, Modern Industrie, Landsberg, 1991.

Wottawa, H., Gluminski, I., *Psychological Theories for Enterprise*, Hogrefe Publishers Goettingen, 1995, p.164.

Wunderer, R., Jaritz, A., *Business Personnel Controlling: Evaluation of Value Added in Personnel Management*, Luchterhand (Hermann), Koln, 2006.

Zezelj, G., The CLV management concept, in: Hofmann and Mertiens (eds), *Customer Lifetime Value Management*, Dr. Th. Gabler, Wiesbaden, 2000, pp. 9–29.

Internet

www.agv.de
www.experian.de
www.servicebarometer.de/kundenmonitor/mitarbeiterorientierung
www.vw-club.de
www.bbdo.de

Index

About the Authors

Gerhard Raab is Prof. Dr. oec; Master of business and psychology; pursued studies in economics and psychology at the universities of Mainz and Hagen; after studying, Dr. Raab worked as research associate and was promoted to Doctor of Economics at the University of Hohenheim; subsequently was strategy advisor and project leader in the management board of the DG BANK Deutsche Genossenschafsbank AG (German Mutual Savings Bank) in Frankfurt am Main, from 1992-1997; since 1997 Professor of marketing and company management at the Fachhochschule (College of Higher Education) Ludwigshafen--Hochschule für Wirtschaft (Institute of Economics). Dr. Raab has authored or co-authored many books on Customer Relationship Management in German, and is the Executive Director of the Transatlantic Institute, Ludwigshafen University of Applied Sciences, Germany. Since 2001, Dr. Raab has been the Guest Professor for Customer Relationship Management at the University of North Carolina at Greensboro.

Riad A. Ajami is currently professor of International Management and Global Strategy at the Raj Soin College of Business at Wright State University. Prior to joining Raj Soin College of Business, Professor Ajami held the position of Charles A. Hayes Distinguished Professor of Business and Director, Center for Global Business Education and Research at the University of North Carolina, Greensboro (UNCG). Prior to joining UNCG Professor Ajami held the position of Benjamin Forman Chair Professor of International Business and Director, Center for International Business and Economic Growth at the Rochester Institute of Technology. Professor Ajami previously held the position of Professor of International Business, at the Fisher College of Business at Ohio State University. He has had visiting appointments as the Dr. M. Lee Pearce Distinguished Professor of International Business and Economic Cooperation, School of International Studies at the University of Miami; the School of Business Administration at the University of California, Berkeley; the Wharton School, University of Pennsylvania; and the Harvard Center for International Affairs at Harvard University, Hautes Etudes Commercials – HEC (Grande Ecole of Management), France; and is a distinguished faculty affiliate at Audencia (School of Management), France. Dr. Ajami received his Ph.D. from Pennsylvania State University in International Business, Strategic Management and Oil Economics. Currently, Dr. Ajami is the Editor-in-Chief of the *Journal of Asia-Pacific Business* and Editor-in-Chief of the *Haworth International Business Press Series in Asia-Pacific Business*. Dr. Ajami is also an Editorial Board Member of *Competitiveness Review, Journal of Global Marketing, Journal of Transnational Management Development, Journal of Business and Industrial Marketing, International Business: Annual Editions, Global Finance Journal* (1990-1996)*, Multinational Financial Management* (1988-1993). Dr. Ajami is the co-author of *The Global Enterprise:*

Entrepreneurship and Value Creation (2007, The Haworth Press). He has also co-authored *International Business: Theory and Applications*, (Prentice Hall) first edition (M. E. Sharpe) second edition 2006. He is also a frequent contributor to a number of books on the subject of International Business. He has had articles published on International Business in the *Wall Street Journal, Journal of International Business Studies, Management International Review, Strategic Management Journal, International Journal of Management, Journal of Global Marketing, International Journal of Commerce and Management, International Journal of Technology Management, Journal of Multinational Financial Management, Multinational Business Review, Business and Society Review*, and *Cybernetica*. Professor Ajami has appeared on national television and radio, including, among others, Nightline, the Lehrer News Hour, NBC News, CNN, National Public Radio and CBS Radio.

Vidyaranya B. Gargeya is Professor of Operations Management and Director of the MBA Program at The University of North Carolina at Greensboro. Dr. Gargeya currently teaches in graduate and executive programs. He holds a bachelor's degree in Chemical Engineering from Andhra University, Visakhapatnam (India), a Post Graduate Diploma in Management from the Indian Institute of Management, Bangalore, and a Ph.D. in Business Administration from Georgia State University. Dr. Gargeya has received, for his contributions to teaching, numerous awards including the UNCG Alumni Teaching Excellence Award (2006), Wick Skinner Award for Teaching Innovation from the Production and Operations Management Society (2003), Bryan School of Business and Economics Tenured Faculty Teaching Excellence Award (2007), Bryan School of Business and Economics Senior Faculty Teaching Excellence Award (2002), and the Bryan School of Business and Economics Teaching Excellence Award (1997). Vidyaranya Gargeya has published more than 20 journal articles, and has presented more than 50 papers at national and international conferences. Dr. Gargeya served on the Board of Examiners of the Malcolm Baldrige National Quality Award (in 2006) and he has consulted with several Fortune 500 companies.

G. Jason Goddard is Vice President at Wachovia Bank, where he has been a commercial lender for over 10 years. Mr. Goddard is currently real estate risk advisor for income producing investment real estate loans in the business and community banking segments, and works in Winston-Salem. All of Mr. Goddard's financial services industry experience has involved direct customer relationship management experience, since providing financial expertise is of paramount importance for the business and community banking segments, and is a key to winning profitable, long-term relationships for Wachovia Bank. He obtained his MBA from the Bryan School at the University of North Carolina at Greensboro. Mr. Goddard is currently instructor at the Bryan School, and is the Assistant Editor of the *Journal of Asia-Pacific Business,* where he has authored numerous articles. Mr. Goddard teaches the investment real estate course at UNCG in the Finance and Accounting Department. He also teaches an introductory undergraduate course in international business at UNCG, and has co-taught the subject in the MBA program at the Bryan School. Mr. Goddard has also taught Customer Relationship Management in the MBA program at UNC-G. Mr. Goddard is co-author of *International Business: Theory and Practice, Second Edition,* which was issued by M.E. Sharpe Publishers in September 2006.

For Product Safety Concerns and Information please contact our
EU representative GPSR@taylorandfrancis.com Taylor & Francis
Verlag GmbH, Kaufingerstraße 24, 80331 München, Germany